THE ROAD TO BELLAPAIS
THE TURKISH CYPRIOT EXODUS
TO NORTHERN CYPRUS

BY
PIERRE OBERLING

SOCIAL SCIENCE MONOGRAPHS, BOULDER
DISTRIBUTED BY COLUMBIA UNIVERSITY PRESS
NEW YORK

1982

EAST EUROPEAN MONOGRAPHS, NO. CXXV

ATLANTIC STUDIES
Brooklyn College Studies on Society in Change, No. 25
Editor-in-Chief Béla K. Király

Dr. Pierre Oberling is Professor of History
at Hunter College CUNY

To my wife Gerry, with love

TABLE OF CONTENTS

ACKNOWLEDGEMENTS

I would like to thank my many friends and colleagues who have helped me in the writing of this work. I am especially indebted to Professor JoAnn McNamara and Dr. Fanny Davis, who read the manuscript and offered valuable suggestions for improving it. I also wish to express my gratitude to the government and people of the Turkish Federated State of Cyprus for their kindness and hospitality. Finally, I would like to include a word of personal thanks to Dr. Lâtife Birgen, the Director of the Ministry of Foreign Affairs of the Turkish Federated State of Cyprus, who greatly facilitated my research while I was in Cyprus, and to His Excellency Nail Atalay, the Representative of the Turkish Federated State of Cyprus at the United Nations, who patiently answered my many questions and was instrumental in furnishing the documents which I needed for my research. Their enthusiasm for getting at the truth behind complex socio-political problems was a great catalyst and constantly renewed my interest in the subject of this study.

CYPRUS TODAY

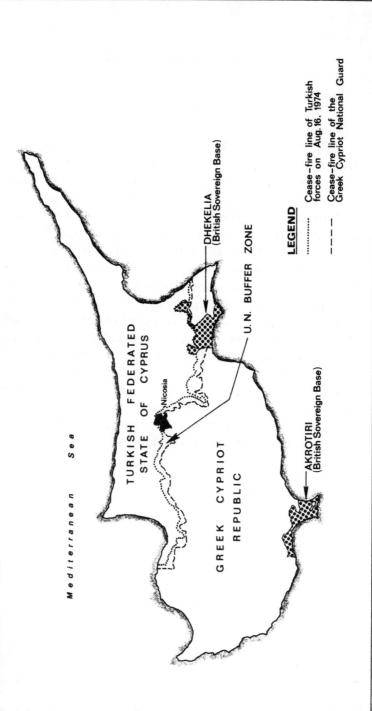

Mediterranean Sea

TURKISH FEDERATED STATE OF CYPRUS

Nicosia

GREEK CYPRIOT REPUBLIC

DHEKELIA
(British Sovereign Base)

U. N. BUFFER ZONE

AKROTIRI
(British Sovereign Base)

LEGEND

.... Cease-fire line of Turkish forces on Aug. 16, 1974

‒ ‒ ‒ Cease-fire line of the Greek Cypriot National Guard

i.e. omann

INTRODUCTION

There were 104 refugees—men, women and children. They were fleeing their homes in the foothills of the Troodos mountains. They had to travel light, for they had rough climbing to do and they had to elude Greek Cypriot patrols which were trying to block the Turkish Cypriot exodus to the north. All they could carry was a small bundle of clothing and a few personal effects. Their guide was an aged but sturdy shepherd by the name of Yakub Cemal. He knew the Troodos better than any other Turkish Cypriot and had already led more than 500 other refugees to safety in the Turkish zone.

The refugees were hurriedly gathered like a flock of stray sheep by Yakub Cemal. It was vital not to alert the surrounding Greek Cypriot population, for the merest suspicion that an escape was in progress would unleash the full fury of the Greek Cypriot police against the helpless Turkish Cypriot villagers of the area. Bundles were picked up and front doors locked—an instinctive but useless gesture because the refugees knew that they would never return.

All day long the column climbed up the lower slopes of the Troodos range. By midnight the refugees could already see the lights of Kykko monastery, shining like a beacon across the almost Siberian stillness. Perched on a craggy height, Kykko is the most important Greek Orthodox sanctuary in Cyprus, and for many years it had symbolized what the Turkish Cypriot villagers most dreaded: the deeply entrenched bigotry of many of their Greek Cypriot neighbors. The sanctuary contains a famous icon, one of the three attributed to St. Luke. It has a reputation for bringing rain. That cold night, as the refugees were hastening along a near-by mountain path, they could be thankful that the icon was not working its magic.

Because the night was unusually dark, Yakub Cemal decided to reconnoiter ahead. He asked his assistant, a young shepherd who had accompanied him on previous missions of this sort, to watch over the group while he was away. Finding that no Greek Cypriot patrol was within sight, the old shepherd soon returned and the human centipede resumed its northward march. After an hour or so had passed, it seemed to Yakub Cemal that the refugee column was shorter than before. He counted the refugees and, to his horror, realized that 38 of them were missing. He ordered his assistant to move on with the advance party. Meanwhile, he hurried back to the spot where the expedition had halted earlier that night. As he reached it, he stumbled upon a middle-aged woman who was sitting on the path. He discovered that, unaware that the go-ahead signal had been given, the woman had simply remained where she was, and that those in back of her, seeing her quietly resting on the path, had come to the conclusion that the column had stopped for the night. Yakub Cemal told the stragglers to follow him and, together, they walked briskly, hoping to catch up with the rest of the party before light. But, unbeknownst to him, a twelve-year-old boy, who had fallen asleep on the path, had been left behind. He was soon apprehended by a Greek Cypriot patrol, taken to Kykko monastery and tortured to reveal the location of the column.

When Yakub Cemal and the stragglers finally caught up with the advance party, they learned that during the night it had suffered a casualty. A middle-aged man had slipped and fallen into a ravine. When picked up, he was found to have suffered extensive injuries. For hours the wounded man was carried by various relatives and friends. But by morning it was obvious that he was too seriously wounded to be carried further. So he was left in an orchard. His wife wanted to stay with him, but he refused, ordering her to save her honor by accompanying the rest of the expedition. He too was later captured and beaten by the Greek Cypriot police.

Fully aware now that the secrecy of the expedition had been compromised, Yakub Cemal decided to forge ahead, in spite of the danger of being spotted during the day and of the fact that the refugees had had no sleep to speak of the beginning of the journey. All day long, the column made rapid progress by walking along a stream. However, as night fell, it had to climb high up on a mountain slope to avoid Greek Cypriot patrols.

At about midnight the expedition neared a dirt road. Yakub Cemal ran ahead to see if it was safe to cross it. But, just as he reached the road, a Land-Rover approached. He dove headlong into a ditch. He was sure that he had been seen, for after he had been in utter darkness for several hours the car's headlights had seemed bright enough to illuminate the whole countryside. As if to confirm his worst fears, the Land-Rover stopped and three men got out holding flashlights. As the men advanced towards him along the road, he lay motionless in the ditch. The men—he could see now that they were heavily armed Greek Cypriot policemen— passed within a few feet of him. Then, unexpectedly, they returned to the Land-Rover, fired at random into the surrounding brush and sped away.

The expedition moved on. It followed the crest of an elongated hill. Yakub Cemal could see the lights of the villages of Khakistra and Kambos in the distance. The expedition then slipped past a Greek Cypriot position. A little while later Yakub Cemal, having discovered a convenient hiding place, ordered the expedition to settle down for a few hours of much-needed sleep.

Before dawn on the next day, the refugees set out once more. They followed a winding stream, passing by several Greek Cypriot posts. Suddenly, a large number of soldiers barred their way. Yakub Cemal and the Turkish Cypriot refugees were certain that their luck had at last run out and that they were about to be captured. But when the soldiers spoke to them in Turkish, they realized that they had reached the Turkish zone and that they were safe.

What was the meaning of this exodus? Why were Turkish Cypriot villagers fleeing their ancestral lands, leaving behind them everything that was dear to them—their homes, their fields, their orchards and their flocks? The purpose of this book is to provide an answer to these questions and to place the traumatic events of the years 1974 and 1975 in their historical context.

CHAPTER I
ORIGIN OF THE TURKS OF CYPRUS

Although the Turks originated in Central Asia, they are by no means newcomers in the Middle East. As early as the eighth century Turkish mercenaries were hired by the Arab 'Abbasid Caliphate (capital Baghdad) to form a Praetorian Guard. Because these fighting men were both able and courageous, the demand for them rapidly increased. Soon the Caliphate was swarming with Turkish soldiers, officers and administrators. In the eleventh century several hundred thousand Turkish tribesmen poured into the Middle East from their ancestral grazing lands in Turkestan and Transoxiana. They took over the Caliphate and established their own dynasty—the Seljuqs. As the Greek Orthodox Byzantine Empire declined, its strength sapped by internal dissension and the depredations of the crusaders, the Muslim Seljuq Empire and its Turkish successor states swallowed ever larger chunks of Asia Minor (today Anatolia, the Asian part of Turkey). The Mongol invasions of the thirteenth century only momentarily impeded this process. By that time, the Byzantine Empire had become but "a slender, dislocated, miserable body upon which rested an enormous head, Constantinople",[1] and the Turkish states which survived the Mongol cataclysm continued to gnaw at its eastern boundaries. In 1326, the Ottoman Empire, the most dynamic of these states, captured Bursa, the last major Byzantine urban center on the Asiatic continent. In 1453, the Ottoman sultan Mehmet the Conqueror seized Constantinople (which

---

1. William L. Langer and Robert P. Blake, "The Rise of the Ottoman Turks and its Historical Background", *American Historical Review*, Vol. XXVII (April 1932), p. 472.

under the name of İstanbul became the new Ottoman capital), thus completing the conquest of the Byzantine Empire. In 1571, the Ottomans conquered Cyprus and the first Turkish settlers embarked for the island. Therefore, the Turks of Cyprus have inhabited the island for over four hundred years, having reached their new home well before the Pilgrims landed at Plymouth, and even before the Jamestown Colony was founded. At the time of their arrival, Cyprus' population, which numbered between 100,000 and 200,000,[2] was almost wholly Greek in religion and in language, although there were small Latin, Maronite, Coptic, Jacobite and Armenian colonies as well.

The French Lusignan knights (1192-1489) and the Venetians (1489-1571) had preceded the Ottomans as rulers of Cyprus. During this period of Latin domination the Cypriots had been reduced to a state of complete serfdom. Even the Orthodox bishoprics had been shorn of their lands, which had been allocated to the Roman Catholic sees. A series of oppressive acts directed against the autocephalous (self-ruling) Orthodox Church of Cyprus had culminated in the *Bulla Cypria* of Pope Alexander IV, in 1260, which had made the Latin archbishop the supreme ecclesiastical authority over both the Latin and the Orthodox components of the population, empowered the Latin clergy to get hold of the tithes, abolished the Orthodox Archbishopric, and forced the few remaining Orthodox bishops, who had been sent to out-of-the-way villages, to take an oath of obedience to the Latin bishops who had replaced them.[3] During the Venetian period, the poverty of the Cypriots who, in the words of a sixteenth century traveller, were treated "worse than slaves",[4] was so extreme that many fled to Rhodes and

---

2. Sir George Hill, *A History of Cyprus* (Cambridge, 1952), Vol. III, p. 787. This four-volume work is the most detailed and scholarly study of the island's history.

3. *Ibid.*, pp. 1059-1060.

4. Stephan Gerlach, *Tagebuch* (Frankfurt am Main, 1674), p.123.

various parts of the Ottoman Empire.

In February 1570, as he was preparing to go to war with Venice for the purpose of annexing Cyprus, Sultan Selim II sent a firman (edict) to the governor of Mersin (the seaport from which the invasion force was to embark) ordering him "to do his utmost to win the hearts of the masses" on Venetian-held Cyprus and to carry out the old Ottoman policy of *istimâlet*, or leniency, towards the Cypriots in the course of the conquest to come.[5] On May 6, 1572, after he had routed the Venetians, he dispatched a similar firman to the new governor-general of Cyprus and his chief aides urging them to bestow on the Cypriots, "who are a trust from God to us, as much protection and mercy as you can, abstaining from such actions as may lead to their dispersion", and stressing that it was his desire "to ensure that everybody may attend to his daily work and concerns with a mind free from discomfort and anxiety, and that the island may be restored to its former flourishing condition".[6]

As the Turks established their suzerainty over Cyprus, they confiscated most of the estates belonging to the Cypriots' erstwhile Latin overlords, although a few of the latter were able to keep some of their lands by paying a ransom, and a handful of them were even allowed to enroll in the Ottoman cavalry.[7] As for the Greek population, it greeted the incoming Turks as liberators and was treated with consideration in return. The Ottomans abolished serfdom and gave the Cypriots permission to acquire houses and land. They recognized the supremacy of the Orthodox community over all other Christian denominations and restored the Orthodox archbishopric. Above all, the Cypriots were integrated into that remarkable institution known as the Millet System, which for centuries provided members

---

5. Halil İnalcık, *Ottoman Policy and Administration in Cyprus After the Conquest* (Ankara, 1969), p. 5.

6. *Ibid.*, p. 7.

7. Hill, *op. cit.*, Vol. IV, p. 27.

of religious minorities within the Ottoman Empire with more freedom than was enjoyed by such groups anywhere in Europe.[8]

But Cyprus was too sparsely inhabited to be an economic asset to the Ottoman Empire. One of the cardinal principles of Ottoman rule was that inasmuch as the income of the state depended upon the prosperity of the country, every province had to be rendered as productive as possible. Accordingly, when the productive capacities of a given province were found to be wanting, additional farmers or

---

8. Sir Harry Luke, *Cyprus Under the Turks, 1571-1878* (London, 1921), pp. 15-16. The Ottoman population was divided into *millets* (nations) on the basis of religious affiliation. Thus, all Muslims belonged to the Muslim *millet*, all Jews to the Jewish *millet*, etc. Each *millet* formed a semi-autonomous unit within the Empire. It was in charge of its own clerical discipline, it managed its own cemeteries, schools and churches, and it had jurisdiction in cases involving marriage, dowries, divorce, alimony and civil rights. (For additional information on the Millet System, see Sir Harry Luke, *The Old Turkey and the New*, London, 1955, pp. 66-101). Refugees from the tyranny of other governments could readily be absorbed into their corresponding *millets* within the Ottoman Empire. Thus, when the Jews were expelled from Spain in 1492, Sultan Beyazit II (who is reported to have said of King Ferdinand, "Can you call such a king wise and intelligent? He is impoverishing his country and enriching my kingdom!") welcomed them into his realm (see Yaacov Geller and Haim Z'ew Hirschberg, "Ottoman Empire", *Encylopaedia Judaica*, Vol. XVI, p. 1533). Interestingly, the prime exponents of the annexation of Cyprus at the Ottoman Court in 1570 were Selim II's Jewish financier and adviser, Don Joseph, who hoped to transform the island into a homeland for his persecuted coreligionists in Europe, and Nur Banu Sultan, the Jewish-born mother of the Sultan's eldest son and successor-to-be, Prince Murat, the future Murat III (Stanford J. Shaw, *History of the Ottoman Empire and Modern Turkey*, Cambridge, 1976, Vol. I, p. 178). The idea of using Cyprus as a homeland for the Jews of the world was taken up again by the Zionist leader, David Trietsch, in 1899 (Hyman E. Goldin, *Universal History of Israel*, New York, 1935, Vol. IV, p. 331). Ironically, after World War II, detention camps were established by the British on Cyprus to accommodate illicit Jewish immigrants to Palestine, and today the Greek Cypriot part of the island is used as a training ground for PLO terrorists.

workers were recruited from other provinces by means of a procedure called *sürgün*, or population transplant. Lala Mustafa Paşa, the commander of the Ottoman army which had conquered Cyprus, was instructed to allow those among his men who wanted to settle down on the island to do so. Apparently some 20,000 of them chose to remain and were given appropriate grants of land.[9] However, these settlers did not prove numerous enough to make the island prosper. Therefore, in 1572, Sinan Paşa, the governor-general of Cyprus, wrote a letter to Selim II in which he requested that more settlers be sent. In answer, the Sultan, on September 21, 1572, issued a firman to the *kadı*s (judges) of Anatolia (at that time the region to the west of the Kızıl Irmak river), Rum (at that time the region to the east of the Kızıl Irmak), Karaman (the region around Konya) and Dulgadir (the region around Maraş and the headwaters of the Euphrates river). In this edict, he ordered the deportation to Cyprus of thousands of persons and their families. Among those chosen were:

1) Peasants who, because of poor land, could not make a decent living.
2) Sons of peasants whose names had not yet been inscribed on the provincial tax registers.
3) Sharecroppers.
4) Tenant farmers.
5) Quarrelsome individuals who ceaselessly indulged in litigation concerning summer pastures, vineyards, and other kinds of property.
6) Vagrants who had moved to the cities and towns after abandoning their farmlands without official authorization.
7) Craftsmen and artisans in cities and towns (such as shoemakers, bootmakers, tailors, skullcap makers, damask weavers, mohair weavers, wool carders, silk weavers, cooks, sellers of cooked sheeps' heads, candlemakers, saddlemakers, blacksmiths, grocers, tanners, carpenters, masons, stone cutters, goldsmiths and coppersmiths).

---

9. Luke, *Cyprus Under the Turks*, p. 22.

6 THE ROAD TO BELLAPAIS

These were to be deported on the basis of one out of every
ten households and they were to be brought to their destination with their immediate families, plow teams, livestock
and all necessary equipment before the onset of winter. The
properties of the deportees were to be sold at a fair price
by the *kadıs*, who were made responsible for handing over
the proceeds of the sales to the appropriate parties and for
seeing to it that the deportees were not robbed while on
their way to Cyprus. The *kadıs* were also ordered to issue a
firm warning to the officials who were appointed to supervise the migration not to commit any unlawful seizures of
the deportees' chattels or to extort any money from them.
By the time the deportees were to reach Cyprus the necessary arrangements were to have been made to receive them.
Finally, the deportees were to be given a dispensation of
two years from paying any taxes.[10]

Following the arrival of these settlers, further transfers
of population took place. When deposits of saltpeter were
discovered in Cyprus, workers were at once despatched from
Anatolia to refine it so that gunpowder could be produced
locally.[11] During the succeeding centuries, unruly tribesmen
or individuals who had broken social taboos were also on
occasion banished to Cyprus.[12] It is interesting to note that
even in the latter cases great care was taken in the way the
newcomers were to be settled on the island. For instance, a
firman of 1714 specified that some refractory nomads who
were to be exiled to Cyprus were to be resettled in unin-

10. Ömer Lutfi Barkan, "Osmanli Imparatorluğunda bir iskân ve
kolonizasyon metodu olarak sürgünler", Part I, *İktisat Fakültesi
mecmuasi*, Vol. XI, pp. 550-553.

11. Ahmet Refik, *Osmanlı devrinde Türkiye medenleri* (İstanbul,
1931), documents no. 20, 28 and 30 of 1572-1574.

12. Barkan, *op. cit.*, pp. 556-558; Ahmet Refik, *Anadolu'da Türk
aşiretleri* (İstanbul, 1930), pp. 13, 15-16, 26-27, 140-145, 148-153,
190-191.

habited areas, so that they would not constitute a threat to their neighbors.[13]

As a result of these population transfers, Turks from a wide variety of professional backgrounds made their way to the island. In this respect, the process of colonization carried out by the Turks in Cyprus was similar to that of the British in North America. But an important difference was that the Turks made a wholehearted effort to integrate the local inhabitants into the economic and political life of the Ottoman Empire (while allowing them to retain their own social institutions and cultural identity), whereas in the New World the Indians were simply pushed aside as impediments to the fulfillment of white man's dreams. It should also be pointed out that the *sürgün* system, though largely compulsory, was far more humane than the British system of forcibly shipping over young men and women to America as indentured servants.

Finally, it is worth noting that the Ottoman government never attempted to establish a Turkish majority on Cyprus.[14] Nor did it seek to set up an economically dominant upper class, as did the English in Ireland at the time of Cromwell.[15]

---

13. Ahmet Refik, *Anadolu'da Türk aşiretleri*, p. 150.

14. When Cyprus became an independent country in 1960, there were 442,521 Greeks, 104,350 Turks, 3,628 Armenians, 2,708 Maronites, 502 Gypsies and 2,951 persons of various other ethnic origins on the island. The Turks, therefore, comprised only 18.07 per cent of the total population, and these were scattered in small and potentially vulnerable enclaves throughout the island.

15. Under Turkish rule, Greek Cypriots controlled the island's principal business enterprises, especially those concerned with manufacturing and import-export trade.

CHAPTER II
THE BIRTH OF AN IDEA

In the eighteenth and early nineteenth centuries, Greek merchants and shipping tycoons in the Ottoman Empire and in the major commercial centers of Europe were influenced by the secular ideas of the Enlightenment, as well as by the then fashionable Philhellenic literary movement. They acquired a historical consciousness and a growing pride in the achievements of the ancient Greeks. Then, riding the crest of the tidal wave of nationalism which swept Europe after the Napoleonic wars, they began to agitate for Greek independence.[1] Nationalism rapidly caught on in the Greek provinces of the Ottoman Empire, and soon Greeks of all classes rose against their Turkish overlords. But the liberal nationalism preached by Westernized Greeks, which corresponded to the social, economic and political realities of Western Europe, underwent a complete metamorphosis as more and more non-Westernized Greeks joined the struggle and adapted it to conditions in Greece. There, the largely agrarian inhabitants were still tradition-minded. They retained the old *millet* mentality (the habit of classifying all human beings according to religion), and if they were receptive to nationalism it was because through the long centuries of Ottoman rule it was the local priests who had kept alive their sense of cultural identity. Therefore, the Greece that most Greeks hoped to bring back to life was not the Hellas of Pericles (so dear to the Westernized Greeks) but Orthodox Byzantium. As Professor Dennis Skiotis, of Harvard University, has recently written in a perceptive article:

---

1. For more information on the secular origin of modern Greek nationalism, see Stephen G. Xydis, "Modern Greek Nationalism", in Peter F. Sugar and Ivo J. Lederer, eds., *Nationalism in Eastern Europe* (Seattle, 1971), pp. 207-258.

This millenarian expectation that a day would surely dawn when God would lift the infidel yoke from his chosen people and would restore to them the Christian Roman Empire [Byzantium] in all its majesty and splendor is of fundamental importance in understanding how the Greeks perceived their historical identity and destiny. The cataclysmic transformation they awaited was encapsulated in a single term: To Romaiko—the Romaic (Restoration). 'Before the Revolution', observed a western educated intellectual, 'the common people of Greece were ignorant of the sacred word *eleutheria* (liberty). And whenever they wanted to talk about their future liberation, they would always say: when we achieve to *Romaïko*, or, when *to Romaïko* will happen'.[2]

Even Rhigas Pheraios, for all his European veneer, showed that deep in his soul he held a similar vision when he wrote his famous war song, *Thourios*, in which he urged his fellow-Greeks to put all of Turkey to the torch, "from Bosnia to Arabia".[3]

Under these circumstances, it was inevitable that the Greek War of Independence would turn into a religious crusade. In the words of Professor Skiotis, "With savage jubilance, [the Greeks] sang the words 'Let no Turk remain in the Morea, nor in the whole world'. The Greeks were determined to achieve to *Romaïko* in the only way they knew how: through a war of religious extermination".[4]

To a people with such high expectations, the period following the Treaty of Adrianople of 1829 (which gave to the new Greek state only the Pelopponesus, Attica, a slice of territory north of Athens and the Cyclades) must have been intensely depressing. The Greeks had fought to gain an empire; instead they had had to settle for a small and wretchedly poor country which was so weak it had to remain a permanent ward of England, France and Russia just to survive. Even more humiliating was the fact that because

---

2. "The 'Past' in Medieval and Modern Greek Culture", in Speros Vryonis, ed., *Byzantina kai Metabyzantina*, Vol. I (Malibu, Calif., 1978), p. 158.

3. *Ibid.*, p. 159.

4. *Ibid.*, p. 161.

of their inability to form a stable government they had had
to recruit a foreign prince (Otto of Bavaria) to rule their
country—a ruler who, in turn, had thought so little of his
new subjects that he had brought along with him his own
administrators. Finally, as if to add insult to injury, doubts
were being cast about the Greeks' ethnic origin: in 1830
the prominent German historian, Jakob P. Fallmerayer,
had published a treatise in which he had made the disturb-
ing assertion that during the Middle Ages Slavic tribes had
poured into Greece and had annihilated the entire Greek
population.[5] As the morale of the young nation sank ever
lower, some of its leaders began to think that it was time
to rekindle patriotic fervor. They decided to do this by
raising the deepfelt desire to achieve *to Romaïko* to the
status of a national ideology. This was the famous *Megali
Idea*, or Great Idea, which was to figure so prominently in
shaping the modern Greek nation.

The essence of the *Megali Idea* can be found in a speech
delivered by one of its most ardent advocates, Premier John
Kolettis, in January 1844, an excerpt of which follows:

> The kingdom of Greece is not Greece; it is only a part, the
> smallest and poorest, of Greece. A Greek is not only he who
> lives in the kingdom but also he who lives in Yannina, or Thes-
> saloniki, or Serres, or Adrianople, or Constantinople, or Trebi-
> zond, or Crete, or Samos, or in whatever country is historically
> Greek, or whoever is of the Greek race. . . . The Heroes of the
> independence do not belong solely to the kingdom, to the
> small Kingdom of Greece. They belong to all the provinces of
> the Greek world from the Haimos to the Tainaron, from Trebi-
> zond to Cilicia. . . . There are two great centers of Hellenism:
> Athens and Constantinople. Athens is only the capital of the
> kingdom. Constantinople is the great capital, the City, the joy
> and hope of all Hellenes.[6]

In other words, the *Megali Idea* aimed at nothing less than
the recreation of the Byzantine Empire at its apogee. It
was, of course, an unrealistic goal. In order to achieve it,
Greece would have had to conquer the Ottoman Empire,

---

5. *Geschichte der Halbinsel Morea* (Stuttgart and Tübingen,
1830).

6. Quoted in Xydis, *op. cit.*, p. 237.

which was both stronger and more populous than the new Hellenic kingdom. It would also have had to overcome British opposition, for one of the principal objectives of England's foreign policy during the nineteenth century was to prevent Russian access to the Mediterranean by shoring up the Ottoman Empire. Finally, it would have had to compete with Balkan nationalities, such as the Serbs, the Rumanians and the Bulgarians, which were beginning to entertain their own dreams of grandeur and to stake their claims to various parts of the Ottoman Empire. Like the *élan vital* of the French Third Republic, or Victor Hugo's "idea with a sword", the *Megali Idea* involved considerable wishful thinking and more than a little hubris. It was also a potentially dangerous idea: mixing nationalism with the heady wine of religious fanaticism can lead to extremes of savagery and even collective suicide. During World War II, just such a combination of ideologies inspired the Ustachis to murder some 600,000 Serbs in their short-lived "Independent Croatian State".[7] Like many other nationalists in Central and Eastern Europe, the champions of the *Megali Idea* displayed a tendency to create "out of myths of the past and the dreams of the future, an ideal fatherland, closely linked with the past, devoid of any immediate connection with the present, and expected to become sometime a political reality".[8]

King Otto (who ruled between 1832 and 1862) boosted his waning popularity by eagerly endorsing the new ideology, and Greece—now regarded by its leaders as a mere beachhead in the Land of Promise—became the launching site of a determined campaign of subversion against the Ottoman Empire. The late Professor Xydis aptly described

7. See Manes Sperber, "Mort d'un contemporain: Ante Pavelic", *Preuves*, March 1960, p. 61. The Ustachis were Croatian fascists who collaborated with the Axis powers.

8. Hans Kohn, *The Idea of Nationalism: A Study in its Origins and Background* (2nd ed.; New York, 1961), p. 330.

the Greek leaders of that time as "Trotskyites, in the ethno-centric not the classicentric sense" who "favored permanent revolution in the territories of the Ottoman Empire".[9] In 1841, and again in 1858, the Greeks on the island of Crete rose against their Turkish overlords. When he was chosen as Greece's second ruler, in 1863, King George I assumed the title of King of the Hellenes rather than that of King of Greece to suit his subjects' soaring national aspirations. A third revolt erupted in Crete in 1866. Meanwhile, the Greek government was also fomenting unrest in Turkish-controlled Epirus and Thessaly. As the Turkish armies were locked in combat with Russian forces invading the Balkans during the Russo-Turkish War of 1877-78, a Greek army marched into Thessaly. As a result of this military campaign, the Greeks were awarded Thessaly and part of Epirus (Arta) at the Constantinople Conference of 1881. Greece was so encouraged by this military and diplomatic triumph that, in 1897, though totally unprepared for a major conflict, it declared war on Turkey. A Greek force made a successful landing in Crete, but Crown Prince Constantine was decisively defeated in Thessaly, and only the timely intervention of the Powers saved his army from complete annihilation. As the prominent Greek historian, D. George Kousoulas, points out, "The Great Idea had by now been taken over by romantic enthusiasts who were unable or unwilling to understand that a country's foreign policy must be consistent with her capabilities and with the prevailing international conditions".[10] But Greek aggression was nonetheless rewarded, for when the fighting stopped the Powers forced the Ottoman Empire to allow the creation of an autonomous Crete under a Christian prince (who turned out to be none other than Prince George, the Greek king's second son). In 1912, at a time when the Turks were fighting an exhausting war against the Italians in Tripolitania, Greece

9. *Op. cit.*, p. 240.
10. *Modern Greece: Profile of a Nation* (New York, 1974), p. 83.

allied itself with Serbia, Bulgaria, and even tiny Montenegro, and again attacked the Ottoman Empire. This time, the Greeks acquired most of Epirus, as well as large portions of Macedonia (which included the important city of Salonica). Finally, they were able to annex Crete, which had for so long eluded their grasp. By then, the Greeks had convinced themselves that they were a chosen people to whom the world owed homage. According to the insightful journalist-historian, David Holden,

> they were encouraged in this belief by many of their foreign friends and patrons who, either out of cynical political calculation or sentimental and misinformed philhellenism, offered all too many words and gestures of admiration and support. The result was to convince the Greeks that in any serious conflict with their neighbours they would always enjoy a moral advantage, so that in a constant spiral of Greek ambition, factional dispute and foreign patronage the pursuit of a legitimate national purpose was transformed into a *folie de grandeur*—the tragically anachronistic vision of a new Greek Empire that would rise, like the phoenix, from the ashes of Ottoman defeat.[11]

During this period of expansion, the Greeks also coveted Cyprus, wishing to achieve *enosis* (union) with that island. When the Ottoman government ceded the administration of Cyprus to Great Britain in 1878 as a reward for British support at the Congress of Berlin, many Greeks expected that the British would shortly hand over the island to Greece, as they had so obligingly done in the case of the Ionian islands. What they failed to take into account was that Cyprus was still nominally under Ottoman suzerainty, that it contained a substantial Turkish population and that it was needed by England for strategic reasons (to protect the approaches to the Suez Canal and to act as a base of operations against a possible Russian incursion into Armenia). In an address of welcome to Sir Garnet Wolseley, the first British High Commissioner, on July 23, 1878, Kyprianos, the Bishop of Kition, reflected both this optimism and its

---

11. *Greece Without Columns: The Making of Modern Greece* (New York, 1972), pp. 123-124.

accompanying myopia: "We accept the change of government inasmuch as we trust that Great Britain will help Cyprus, as it did the Ionian Islands, to be united with Mother Greece, with which it is naturally connected."[12]

As it became apparent that the British had no intention of accommodating their nationalist strivings by withdrawing from the island, mainland Greeks and the Greek Cypriot advocates of *enosis* launched a campaign to push the British out of Cyprus by means of Greek Cypriot popular pressure. The chief Greek promoters of this policy before World War I were:

1) *Greek Diplomats*: The highest ranking Greek official in Cyprus under the British was the Greek consul at Nicosia. The individuals occupying that post tended to be militant nationalists, whose behavior was calculated to embarrass the British and to further arouse the Greek Cypriot population against the British administration. A typical case was that of Consul Philemon: on Greek Independence Day, in 1895, he "appeared at Limassol in uniform, and allowed himself to be publicly fêted as the representative of 'our King'"; during the Greco-Turkish War of 1897, he openly recruited Greek Cypriot volunteers for the Greek Army; at an athletic event in 1899, in which he figured prominently, Greek flags were displayed , the Greek National Anthem was played and speeches were made calling for the union of Cyprus with Greece; after a church service on the same day, in the course of which prayers had been offered for the King of Greece, the Royal Family and Hellenism, he called for cheers for Hellenism; and he subsequently sent a telegram to King George I in which he conveyed the good wishes of the Hellenic population of Cyprus.[13]

---

12. Hill, *op. cit.*, Vol. IV, p. 297.

13. Hill, *op. cit.*, Vol. IV, pp. 501-502; also letter from the Marquess of Salisbury, dated September 12, 1899, in British Colonial Office, CO 883/6, 1902.

2) *Greek Teachers*: Because Cyprus was still under nominal Ottoman suzerainty, the British were reluctant to give the impression that they were trying to anglicize the population. Therefore, they allowed each community on the island to select its own teachers and permitted the mainland Greek Ministry of Education to staff Greek Cypriot secondary schools. This enabled the Greek government to convert the schools into indoctrination centers for Greek nationalism, and most of the Greek teachers sent to Cyprus were, in the words of Sir Harry Luke, "apostles of Greek nationalism in an extreme form."[14] The report of a British inspector of schools, in 1901, states:

> At nearly every school the Greek 'flag, or its blue and white striped staff, is found, either in position outside or standing in a corner of the room, waiting for the next festival or holiday, on which occasions its use is universal.

> I find the walls of every Greek-Christian schoolroom, except in some of the remotest villages, adorned with chromolithographs of the Greek Royal Family, politicians, heroes of the War, a battle piece, and especially an allegorical picture, 'The Resurrection of Crete'.

> On examining the schools I find that the only history that is taught is modern Greek history, and almost the only geography, certainly the only geography over which any trouble is taken, is that of Greece. However bad other maps are, there is sure to be a large map of Greece.[15]

> The reading books in use above the lowest classes, usually contain, as might be expected from their origin, selections in glorification of the Hellenic people; and, in the fourth class and upwards, modern Greek renderings of the Odyssey and Anabasis are in constant use, one may say to the exclusion of all others.[16]

---

14. Sir Harry Luke, *Cyprus: A Portrait and an Appreciation* (London, 1957), p. 173. The author served for many years in Cyprus, first as Private Secretary to the High Commissioner and, later, as Commissioner of Famagousta.

15. The maps showed Cyprus as part of "Unredeemed Greece" (Hill, *op. cit.*, Vol. IV, p. 492).

16. CO 883/6, 1902. Writing in 1918, a British authority observed that "Greek schoolmasters present florid addresses to the High Commissioner when he visits their villages, in which union with Greece is represented. . . as the predominant ideal filling the breasts of all the villagers, and the school children are marshalled in an imposing phalanx, and taught to shout in unison 'Zeto Enosis' (Long live Union), as the High Commissioner approaches" (C. W. J. Orr, *Cyprus Under British Rule*, London, 1918, pp. 131-132.

3) *Greek Patriotic Organizations*: Sir George Hill writes that when the British occupied Cyprus "patriotic committees" were set up in Greece "to encourage emigration of Greeks to Cyprus for the promotion of the cause of Union".[17] In 1898, the Patriotic Cypriotic League was founded in Athens by a certain George Phrankoudes "with the object of effecting in Cyprus the same revolution as had taken place in Crete".[18] In a 1902 report to the Colonial Secretary, Sir W. F. Haynes-Smith, the British High Commissioner in Cyprus, asserted that the movement for *enosis* "is engineered from abroad by past masters in the art of intrigue, who have established a very complete organization of so-called 'Patriotic Clubs' throughout the island, and who have the command of money".[19]

4) *The Greek Kings George I and Constantine I*: Because Greece still depended upon England for protection, the Greek rulers were reluctant to encourage openly the activities of Greek revolutionaries in Cyprus. But they did so indirectly by decorating or receiving Greek Cypriots who were known for their wholehearted support of *enosis*. For example, in the early 1900's, George I decorated the prominent enosist Andreas Themistokleos, the director of the Limassol Gymnasium, who for twenty years had agitated against the British administration and who in a speech to Cypriot youths in 1903 underscored the value of target practice.[20]

5) *The Athenian Press*: The Athenian press became one of the chief disseminators of Greek nationalistic propaganda in Cyprus.

In their effort to promote enosist sentiments among the Greek Cypriots, the Greeks had the powerful backing of the Greek Cypriot clergy. Indeed, the Greek Cypriot clergy advocated *enosis* with such vigor that it was said, with some

---

17. Hill, *op. cit.*, Vol. IV, p. 496.
18. *Ibid.*, p. 504.
19. CO 883/6, 1902.
20. Hill, *op. cit.*, Vol. IV, p. 511.

justification, that its aim was for Cyprus to absorb mainland Greece, and not vice versa. Having received its status as an autocephalous church at the Council of Ephesus, in 431 A.D., the Church of Cyprus was functionally independent of the Turkish-dominated Orthodox Patriarchate in İstanbul. In addition, because of its age, it possessed unquestionable seniority over the autocephalous church which the mainland Greeks had established in 1850. *Enosis* could only increase its influence in mainland Greece. But the Greek Cypriot clergy was also dissatisfied with British rule. Under the Turkish administration, the Church had become the biggest landowner in Cyprus. It had also attained great political power. Its archbishop had enjoyed the titles of *ethnarch*, or community leader, and *kocabaşı*, or official spokesman for the Greek Cypriot people, with the right of presenting petitions and complaints directly to the Turkish government in İstanbul. By the beginning of the nineteenth century, the archbishop had become so powerful that the British diplomat, William Turner, who visited Cyprus in 1815, was prompted to write: "Cyprus, though nominally under the authority of a Bey appointed by the Qapudan Pasha,[21] is in fact governed by the Greek Archbishop and his subordinate clergy."[22] But these political prerogatives (which had been much abused for personal gain[23]) had subsequently evaporated under the reformist sultans of the nineteenth century and, later, under the British administration. The archbishops had to fight for political survival. In the words of the Greek Cypriot historian, Zenon Stavrinides:

---

21. The Ottoman minister of the navy.

22. Quoted in Claude Delaval Cobham, *Excerpta Cypria* (Cambridge, 1908), p. 447.

23. In 1806, the French Consul, M. Regnault, had observed that the government of the bishops had become as hateful as that of the most odious of the pashas (Hill, *op. cit.*, Vol. IV, p. 112).

Under a modernizing, secular British regime, the Church had to make sure that its leadership and spiritual authority was not diminished. It continually reminded its flock that they were members of the Greek Orthodox faith, and thus brothers of the mainland liberated Greeks. There was a spiritual union between all Greeks—which the Greek Orthodox Church was but an expression of—and Greek Cypriots would, in justice, have to become united politically too, with their redeemed brothers.[24]

The most fervently nationalistic of the Greek Cypriot religious leaders during the early years of the British occupation was Archbishop Cyril II (1909-1916). He turned his campaign for the archbishopric into a campaign for *enosis*, and he excoriated all those among his compatriots who cooperated with the British authorities.[25]

Greek Cypriot politicians were also early converts to *enosis*. They were frustrated by their lack of power under British rule and, like most Cypriots, they deeply resented British tax policy. Particularly loathed was the Tribute, which the British paid to the Sultan of Turkey as a kind of yearly rental fee for the island. This amount, which was drawn from the revenues of Cyprus, was so great that it strained the slender economic resources of the island. Greek Cypriot politicians expressed their anger through the Greek-language press and through the Legislative Council, established by the British in 1882. Upon the coronation of King Edward VII, in 1902, the nine Greek Cypriot members of that body sent a telegram to the new monarch expressing their wish that *enosis* become a reality.[26] On several occasions, they tried to ram through the Legislative Council motions giving voice to the same sentiments.[27] Finally, in 1912, they resigned *en masse* and proposed the formation of a "Central Committee" to organize the struggle against continued British occupation of Cyprus.[28]

---

24. *The Cyprus Conflict: National Identity and Statehood* (Nicosia, n.d.), p. 20.

25. Hill, *op. cit.*, Vol. IV, pp. 508-509;

26. *Ibid.*, p. 511.

27. *Ibid.*, pp. 512-513.

28. *Ibid.*, p. 518.

But the ire of the enosists was not solely directed at the British. The Turks, as the nominal owners of Cyprus until 1914, received their share of invective. So did the Turkish Cypriots, for the enosists' goal was not only to oust the British and attach Cyprus to Greece but also to Hellenize the entire population of the island, and the Turkish Cypriot community, which stubbornly clung to its Muslim faith, its Turkish language and its traditional way of life constituted a barrier to the fulfillment of that aim. The British inspector of schools whose report is quoted above found that many of the songs used in Greek Cypriot schools were strongly anti-Turkish. He wrote:

> A song-book is prescribed in the 'Programme', out of which it is directed that a certain number of songs shall be taught. It consists to a large extent of matter intended to inflame Greek patriotism, war songs (against the Turks), Kleptic outlawry ballads, or those of a Religio-patriotic sentiment, of course all referring to Greece. In practice, whenever I ask to hear the children sing, it is a war song, 'Forward, follow the drum that leads us against the Turks', or often the Greek Anthem is produced.[29]

An article which appeared in the Greek Cypriot newspaper *Kypriakos Phylax*, on April 7, 1911, was so virulently anti-Turkish that the British authorities felt compelled to fine the editor.[30]

One of the results of this campaign of hate was a growing tendency on the part of Greek Cypriots to bait their Turkish Cypriot neighbors. A typical case of harassment is described by B. Travers, the Commissioner of Famagousta, in a report to the Chief Secretary of Cyprus, dated May 4, 1895:

> A few disorderly characters (Greeks) have endeavoured to create a disturbance at Vatili, but owing to the sensible behaviour of the Moslem portion of the inhabitants. . . nothing has occurred. It appears the same method was carried out both at Vitsada and Vatili, that is, a few Greeks march about in the middle of the night armed and warn others to do the same for their common

---

29. CO 883/6, 1902.
30. Hill, *op. cit.*, Vol. IV, p. 518.

safety. At Vitsada a gun was fired, and whilst the Greeks complained to me in writing that they had been fired at, I am satisfied they themselves were guilty of the act, and committed it for the purpose of supporting a charge against the Turks.[31]

In another incident, a few years later, Greek Cypriots entered the Lala Mustafa Mosque in Famagousta (which in the sixteenth century had been a Catholic cathedral), and delivered nationalist speeches, expressing the hope that someday the building would once more become a place of Christian worship.[32]

In May 1912, Greek Cypriots in Limassol, by insulting the Turkish Cypriots and jeering at them because of the Ottoman Empire's loss of Tripoli during the Italo-Turkish War, provoked a major inter-communal riot in the course of which five persons were killed and 134 were wounded.[33]

But how much success the Greek propaganda campaign had in promoting *enosis* in those early days of British rule is debatable. Sir Harry Luke was probably right when he wrote:

Even twenty-nine years after the Occupation [1907], when I first began to know the island, I would say that the feelings of the great majority of them for Hellas, particularly in the villages, were based primarily on a cultural, social, sentimental, emotional urge of kinship born of a common language, a common faith (though not of a common ecclesiastical authority) and, above all, of common customs and a common way of life, which include (an important item) the same habits in eating and drinking. They were based far less, except in the minds of some of the lawyer-politicians, on a conscious wish to become the inhabitants of a new *nomos* (province) of the Greek State, accepting the officials, laws, taxation, conscription and other circumstances and obligations of that political entity.[34]

---

31. CO 8544, May 1895.

32. Hill, *op. cit.*, Vol. IV, p. 515n.

33. *Ibid.*, pp. 518-519.

34. *Cyprus: A Portrait and an Appreciation*, p. 172.

CHAPTER III
THE HIGH TIDE OF GREEK NATIONALISM

The period immediately following World War I represented the high-water mark of the *Megali Idea* as a national ideal. Greece was one of the victorious Entente powers, whereas the Ottoman Empire, the principal barrier to the fulfillment of the *Megali Idea*, had disintegrated. Consequently, the expectations of Greek nationalists rose to unprecedented heights. A leading Athenian daily, *Eleftheron Vema*, reflecting the prevailing optimism, stated that "Any Greek who thinks Greece is not going to receive Thrace and Asia Minor must be mad".[1] Even such a normally reasonable statesman as Premier Eleftherios Venizelos promised his countrymen a "Greece of two continents and five seas".[2]

The Treaty of Sèvres of August 1920, which Venizelos negotiated on behalf of his country, awarded Greece the whole of Thrace all the way to the outskirts of İstanbul, all of the Aegean islands, including Imbros and Tenedos, but excluding the Dodecanese (the fate of which was to be determined by means of a separate convention with Italy), and the İzmir (Smyrna) region (the latter for an initial period of five years, after which a local assembly was to have the option of choosing between Greek and Turkish sovereignty). By having extended their territories to within sight of İstanbul and by having gained a substantial foothold on Asia Minor, the Greeks had taken a giant step towards realizing the national dream. Equally auspicious was the fact that at no time in its brief history had modern Greece appeared so well-off politically: the country was ruled by an energetic

---

1. Public Record Office, FO 3147/199026, Lord Granville to A.J. Balfour, Athens Despatch No. 272.

2. Kousoulas, *op. cit.*, p. 117.

[23]

young monarch with the promising name of Alexander, its government was led by a man of genius, Venizelos (who had the enthusiastic backing of the British prime minister, David Lloyd George), and its new boundaries were made secure by the proximity of British troops occupying İstanbul, Italian troops occupying Antalya and French troops occupying Cilicia. The only threat (and it seemed insignificant at the time) was from the insurgent regime of Mustafa Kemal Paşa, later called Atatürk, an Ottoman general and World War I hero who was trying to establish the rudiments of a new Turkish state in the Anatolian hinterland. But a small Greek force despatched by Venizelos into central Anatolia was expected to deal a fatal blow to the rebellious Turkish general before he could become more than a passing nuisance.

Suddenly, however, the dream evaporated as a fatal combination of bad luck, political irresponsibility and egregious overconfidence combined to bring about disaster. In October 1920, Alexander died;[3] in November, Venizelos was badly defeated in a national election; and, in December, a plebiscite returned the crown to Alexander's father, Constantine I, who had been forced to abdicate in 1917 and was anathema to the British for his alleged pro-German sympathies during World War I. Then, in early 1921, the new Greek premier, Dimitrios Gounaris, throwing caution to the wind, launched a major offensive against Mustafa Kemal's forces. Although the Greek treasury did not have the resources necessary to fund a large-scale military undertaking and although it was by then abundantly clear that Mustafa Kemal had won the hearts of the Anatolian masses, the Greeks clung tenaciously to the belief that victory was within easy grasp and that the Kemalist rebellion had offered Greece a golden opportunity for further conquest. Indeed,

3. He died of the bite of a pet monkey. Because of the disasters brought about by his successor, Winston Churchill was to write that "a quarter of a million persons died of this monkey's bite" (*The World Crisis: The Aftermath*, London, 1929, p. 386).

so confident were the Greeks of impending victory that the Athenian press hailed Constantine as destined to be crowned emperor in St. Sophia which, until the fall of Constantinople in 1453, had been the principal Greek Orthodox place of worship in the Byzantine capital. Committing some 150,000 men to his Anatolian theatre of operations, the Greek commander-in-chief, General Anastasios Papoulas, at first made impressive progress in spite of temporary reverses in the two battles of İnönü (January and March-April 1921). In June 1921, Constantine and Gounaris set up their headquarters in İzmir "in readiness for a triumphal entry into Ankara",[4] Mustafa Kemal's main base of operations. In July, the Greek Army captured Eskişehir; on August 7, General Papoulas issued orders for an all-out assault on Ankara. But Mustafa Kemal's retreat, like that of Marshal Kutuzov during Napoleon's invasion of Russia, was calculated to exhaust his enemy and to stretch his lines of communication to the breaking point. As the tired and hungry Greek troops reached the Sakarya river, a mere sixty miles from Ankara, they found Mustafa Kemal's forces solidly entrenched in the chain of rocky hills immediately byond it. There, the Greek advance was checked in the course of a violent, three-week-long battle (August 23-September 13). Following this reverse the Greek Army, its morale shattered, started its lengthy, painful retreat to the sea. The tragedy of defeat was compounded by an unfortunate change in the Greek high command. The dull but battle-tried General Papoulas was replaced by the mentally unbalanced General George Khatzianestis, who had not seen active service since 1916 and who now commanded his troops from the safety and comfort of a luxurious yacht anchored in the harbor at Izmir.[5]

---

4. C. M. Woodhouse, *A Short History of Modern Greece* (New York, 1968), p. 206.

5. It is alleged that he suffered from the delusion that his legs were made of glass, a condition which a British military historian aptly described as being "a serious handicap for a commander" (Cyril Falls, *A Hundred Years of War*, New York, 1953, p. 267).

Meanwhile, the leaders of Great Britain, France and Italy were at a loss as to what to do. They were all equally astounded by Mustafa Kemal's meteoric rise from outlaw to national leader, and none of them could seriously entertain any hope of getting his own nation involved in a major international conflict so soon after the end of World War I. Therefore, Greece could not count on receiving military assistance from any of its former allies in its time of need—not even Great Britain, which had originally encouraged it in its effort to crush Mustafa Kemal. This meant that the Treaty of Sèvres was now a dead letter. It was, indeed, never even ratified. And, to make matters worse, the French, wishing to protect their interests in Syria, concluded an agreement with Mustafa Kemal in October 1921, according to which they ceded Cilicia to his revolutionary government, along with all the war materiel and supplies stored there. Thereupon, the Italians had no choice but to withdraw, in their turn, from Antalya.

Mustafa Kemal's forces captured İzmir, the last bastion of Greek strength in Asia Minor, on September 9. They then headed for İstanbul and Eastern Thrace. Lloyd George, feeling that Great Britain's vital interests were at stake, sent troops to Canakkale, on the Asiatic side of the Dardanelles, to intercept them. But the British public and Parliament, fearing a second Gallipoli disaster, failed to give Lloyd George the backing he needed. Under threat of attack by Mustafa Kemal's forces, the British agreed to an armistice—the so-called Mudros Armistice of October 11— which awarded the Ottoman capital, as well as the Straits and Eastern Thrace as far as the Maritsa river, to Mustafa Kemal's government. The final rout of the Greek armies in Anatolia and the crumbling of British resistance to Mustafa Kemal had far-ranging consequences. In England, Lloyd George resigned eight days after the Armistice. In Turkey, the sultan fled, paving the way for the establishment of the First Turkish Republic. In Greece, the defeat precipitated a military coup d'état. King Constantine abdicated, hundreds of his followers were imprisoned, and three ex-premiers (including Gounaris), two ex-ministers and General Khatzianestis were tried by a revolutionary court and shot. The Treaty of Lausanne, which followed the cessation of hostilities, formally restored İzmir, Eastern Thrace and the islands of Imbros and Tenedos to Turkish rule. It also provided for an exchange of population between Greece and Turkey, except for the Greeks of İstanbul (who numbered 108,725 and remained under Turkish rule) and the Turks of Western Thrace (who numbered 90,899 and remained under Greek rule).[6] As a result, about 1.3 million Greeks were moved to Greece and about half a million Turks were transferred to Turkey.[7] Greek Nationalists severely criticized Venizelos, who had been the chief Greek negotiator, for having agreed to an exchange of population for, in the words of Xydis, it "removed from the *Megali Idea* most of its solid irredentist core".[8] There is no doubt that the *Megali Idea* was temporarily discredited in Greece after the debacle of 1922. Venizelos did his best to discourage its resurgence when he once more became premier in 1928, signing, in December 1930, a treaty of peace with Turkey which reaffirmed the status quo in the eastern Mediterranean. However, to claim, as did the distinguished Greek diplomat, Panayotis Pipinelis, in the prestigious journal *Foreign Affairs*, that "the Treaty of Lausanne did not represent just another truce in the long struggle against the Turks" but "meant a *final arrangement*, implying the wholehearted acceptance of the new status quo and the willingness to abandon forever all aspirations to revive the Byzan-

---

6. K. G. Andreades, *The Muslim Minority in Western Thrace* (Thessaloniki, 1956), p. 3.

7. Shaw, *op. cit.*, Vol. II, p. 368. But Harry J. Psomiades points out that since 1912 some four million Muslims had left Greece or areas occupied by Greece (*The Eastern Question: The Last Phase*, Thessaloniki, 1968, p. 68).

8. *Op. cit.*, p. 243.

tine Empire",[9] is absurd. In the late 1930's the *Megali Idea*
reappeared in the form of the Myth of the Third Greek
Civilization, preached by the dictator John Metaxas. Although by the end of World War II the *Megali Idea* had lost
its status as the official state ideology of Greece, the dream
of a Byzantine revival lived on. The Greek political literature of the past thirty-five years contains many works which
still advocate fulfillment of the *Megali Idea*. For example,
Perikles I. Argyropoulos, in his *Ai axioseis tes Ellados*
(*The Best of Greece*, Athens, 1945), advised his fellow
Greeks to choose a strong leader who will satisfy the territorial claims of the nation, thereby acquiring vitally-needed
"living space", and Nikolaos P. Nikolaides, in his *To erga-
tikon zetema en Elladia* (*The Labor Question in Greece*,
Rhodes, 1949), maintained that Greece's labor problems
could not be solved until redeemed Greek territory was restored. When the author was a teacher in Athens during
the 1962-1963 academic year, he discovered that most of
his students still looked upon İstanbul as the real capital of
their country and entertained the notion—naive, perhaps,
but nonetheless firmly fixed—that some day the great metro-
polis would miraculously shed its Turkish coat and be revealed again in all its primeval Byzantine splendor. This
feeling is echoed in the textbooks used today by Greek
schoolchildren of all ages. In a typical elementary school
textbook, one finds a story entitled "O Ekdikitis" ("The
Avenger"), by Andreas Karkavitsas, which envisions a time
when "Our Polis [Istanbul] will once more become the
pearl of the world, just like before Venetian and Turkish
feet trod on it".[10]

It is especially the case of Cyprus which shows us that
the *Megali Idea* did not perish on the battlefields of Western
Anatolia. Numerous Greek politicians and military leaders

9. "The Greco-Turkish Feud Revived", *Foreign Affairs*, Vol.
XXXVII, No. 2 (January 1959), p. 307.

10. *Anagnostiko: St. Dimotikou* (Athens, 1979), p. 55.

have made the connection between *enosis* and Greek imperialism in their public utterances. For example, Premier
George Papandreou, in a speech delivered at Salonica on
October 27, 1964, declared: "Cyprus must become the
springboard for the dreams of Alexander the Great in the
Orient",[11] and a prominent Greek officer, addressing Greek
commando units in Cyprus on May 29, 1970, reminded
them that

> The principal target for the Hellenes should be a single one; we
> must recapture İstanbul, because it is a vital place for us. Greece
> has been accustomed to accomplish great deeds, she has to
> place her feet on both shores of the Aegean and reach the
> Danube.[12]

The British formally annexed Cyprus on November 5,
1914, when war was declared between England and Turkey.
Because of this, Cyprus was not affected by the exchange
of population agreement in the Treaty of Lausanne. The
fact that a large Greek population remained on the island
seems to have greatly increased its desirability in the eyes
of mainland Greeks. Thus, although the Greek government,
in both the Treaty of Sèvres (Articles 115-117) and the
Treaty of Lausanne (Articles 16, 20 and 21), recognized
British suzerainty in Cyprus, and Premier Venizelos advocated a policy of restraint as far as Cyprus was concerned,[13]
mainland Greeks continued to agitate for *enosis*. Greek con-
suls on the island, in particular, remained active as *agents
provocateurs*, doing their best to undermine the British
colonial administration. One of them, Alexander Kyrou,
worked with such "lack of discretion" that, in October
1931, his accreditation was revoked by the British authorities.[14] The Greek press also retained its enosist fervor. In

11. Quoted in Osman Örek, *The Question of Cyprus* (Nicosia,
1971), p. 3.
12. Document No. 13 in *Cyprus Question and Greek Extermination Plans* (Nicosia, 1977), p. 12.
13. Venizelos argued that "no noble gesture from Great Britain
could be expected so long as it could be interpreted as yielding to
pressure" (Quoted in Hill, *op. cit.*, Vol. IV, p. 551.)
14. *Ibid.*, p. 547.

1928 alone, the British administration felt it necessary to prohibit the sale of five newspapers from mainland Greece for
encouraging sedition.[15] During the riots of 1931 in Cyprus
(see below), a secret committee was organized in Piraeus
for the purpose of sending volunteers to fight alongside
the Greek Cypriot insurgents.[16] Later, a Central Committee for Cyprus was set up in Athens by the ex-president of
Greece, Admiral Paul Koundouriotis.[17] Still later, a Society
of Friends of Cyprus and a Cyprus National Bureau were
formed.[18] The sole purpose of all these organizations was
to stir up opposition to British rule in Cyprus.

But the British, through sheer clumsiness, neglect, *pukka
sahib* offensiveness, misguided good will and political shortsightedness also stoked the furnace of discontent in Cyprus
and unwittingly encouraged enosist sentiment among the
Greek Cypriot population.

The British government debated much too long the future
status of the island. In 1915, the British briefly offered the
island to Greece as an inducement for that nation to join
the Entente powers, but by the time Greece declared war
on the Central Powers in 1917 the offer had been withdrawn. After World War I, many prominent British politicians openly spoke in favor of ceding the island to Greece,
giving the partisans of *enosis* the impression that they were
within sight of their goal. Thus when, on May 1, 1925, Cyprus was simply declared a crown colony, the enosists were
bitterly disappointed. Even the moderates, who had hoped
for some form of autonomy within the British Empire, were
crestfallen.

The British also failed to give Cypriots a meaningful role
in formulating government policy. When England first occupied Cyprus, it grandly bestowed upon its inhabitants a

15. *Ibid*., p. 543.
16. *Ibid*., p. 549.
17. *Ibid*., p. 552.
18. *Ibid*., p. 553.

Constitution and a Legislative Council. But the latter (which was set up in 1882) was a misnomer, for it turned out to be a mere consultative assembly.[19] The High Commissioner retained all executive and legislative powers. Originally, the Legislative Council consisted of eighteen members, six of whom were British officials and twelve of whom were Cypriots. Of the latter, all of whom were popularly elected, three were Turkish Cypriots and nine were Greek Cypriots. In 1925, the Legislative Council was enlarged. Whereas Turkish Cypriot representation remained unchanged, that of the Greek Cypriots was increased to twelve, to conform more closely to the actual Greek Cypriot proportion of the island's population. But British representation was increased to nine, thus effectively preventing the Greek Cypriots from securing a majority of the seats. As a result, the Greek Cypriots felt just as powerless as before.[20]

But undoubtedly the greatest failing of the British colonial administration in Cyprus was its inability to raise the standard of living of the average Cypriot. As a matter of fact, the standard of living actually declined during the late 1920's and early 1930's, when the island underwent its own version of the Great Depression. Thousands of workers from the copper and asbestos mines were laid off; wages for those who were lucky enough to be employed were low;

---

19. "The Cyprus constitution was a sham gift", a British authority shrewdly remarked, "The giver gave nothing. The recipient received that which he did not want, and was unable to put to any good use. And the gift. . . had the fate of all shams. It. . . made the giver contemptible and the receiver ungrateful" (Kenneth Williams, *Britain and the Mediterranean*, London, n.d., p. 42).

20. The Governor (like the High Commissioner before him) had the tie-breaking vote in the Legislative Council. Because the Greek Cypriots continued to badger and intimidate the Turkish Cypriot minority on the island, the Turkish Cypriot members of the Legislative Council almost always supported the British, thus paralyzing that body. This, in turn, further antagonized the Greek Cypriots. Thus, the Legislative Council served the British as a means of furthering their divide-and-rule policy. For a good analysis of this policy, see Van Coufoudakis, ed., *Essays on the Cyprus Conflict* (New York, 1976), pp. 32-35.

the value of agricultural products dropped; debts mounted. Meanwhile, the colonial administration kept increasing taxes to meet escalating deficits.[21] By 1931, as many as 82 per cent of rural proprietors were in debt to a total extent of £1,800,000 sterling—a situation analogous to that in the Punjab. In 1924, the British founded an Agricultural Bank, charging low rates of interest on loans, with the hope of alleviating the peasantry's heavy burden of debt. However, in doing so, it undermined one of the most lucrative businesses in Cyprus—moneylending. In 1931, big moneylenders, often the political bosses in their districts, occupied five of the twelve Greek Cypriot seats in the Legislative Council. Therefore, by setting up the Agricultural Bank, the British alienated some of the richest and most influential men in Cyprus.[22]

While the problems which the British colonial administration in Cyprus faced grew in complexity, the quality of its personnel steadily declined, making it less able to meet new challenges. The first civilian commissioners appointed to run the island's six districts were scholarly men who spent many years at their posts and learned to speak fluent Greek and Turkish. But, gradually, bureaucrats, who were too rapidly rotated to become more than superficially acquainted with conditions in Cyprus, replaced them. Between the wars, Cyrpus, in the words of an acute observer, "was considered primarily as a good sanatorium for officials who had lost their health in West Africa".[23] Charles Foley, who, as founder and editor of the *Times of Cyprus*, was intimately acquainted with British officialdom in Cyprus, described it thus:

21. Doros Alastos, *Cyprus in History* (London, 1955), pp. 349-350.

22. Reginald Nicholson, "The Riots in Cyprus", *The Nineteenth Century*, Vol. CX, No. 658 (December, 1931), pp. 688-689. Nicholson was Colonial Secretary for Cyprus between 1926 and 1929.

23. Owen Tweedy, "Enosis: The Outbreak in Cyprus", *Fortnightly Review*, Vol. CXXX, No. 780 (December, 1931), p. 767.

They came and they went, a hundred or so officials, few knew
whence or whither, least of all why. They formed the top layer
of the Government, a British monopoly of the higher posts, and
they found it hard to realize that Cyprus, with a European
population of high literacy, was unlike any other colony they
had known. Here was the core of much of the trouble. It seemed absurd that the government should look to England for men
to fill scores of relatively minor posts when Cypriots had proven
their ability in every sphere outside the Civil Service. More than
a thousand were practising as lawyers, doctors, architects,
teachers. Yet in the Civil Service Cypriots had to put up with
lower pay and lower living standards than the British, many of
whom they knew to be less capable than themselves.

The British Civil Servants were the most isolated community
in Cyprus, and even the more understanding among them came
to feel, after many years of fighting against the current, that the
irresponsibility of the native justified the existence of the ex-
patriates.[24]

Therefore, Cypriots could expect little in the way of economic and political reform from the British colonial administration.

Being unable to alter the political status quo in Cyprus
by acting within the framework of British colonial institutions, Greek Cypriots sought to bring about the desired
changes by means of exerting pressure on these institutions
from without, and to that effect formed a variety of political organizations. The most powerful of these organizations
was the National Organization, founded in 1922. Its purpose was to mobilize all adult male Greek Cypriots to fight
for *enosis* by whatever means necessary. The Archbishop,
Cyril III, was its chairman; the bishops of Kition, Paphos
and Kyrenia headed its three regional branches. Its executive body, the Assembly, consisted of the Archbishop, the
three bishops and the twelve Greek Cypriot members of
the Legislative Council. The most dynamic of its leaders
was Nikodemos Mylonas, who was not only the Bishop of
Kition but also a member of the Legislative Council. In

---

24. *Legacy of Strife: Cyprus from Rebellion to Civil War* (Baltimore,
1964), pp. 20-21. Reprinted by permission of Longman Group Ltd.

1930 and 1931, National Youth Clubs were also founded throughout Cyprus for the purpose of harnessing the energies of the young on behalf of the nationalist ideal.[25]

Greek Cypriots, therefore, had the political organization necessary to sustain large-scale rebellion. All that was needed to set the island ablaze was the proverbial spark, and this was provided in 1931 by the governor, Sir Ronald Storrs. Storrs, a cultivated man, but an old-fashioned autocrat, had already become the subject of controversy because of his efforts to bring the island's educational system under the control of the British colonial administration and because of his insistence in 1928 on celebrating publicly the fifty year jubilee of the British occupation of Cyprus. Moreover, he had displayed his distrust of the Cypriots by asking the British Cabinet, in 1929, to approve a plan whereby the non-elective (i.e., British) portion of the Legislative Council would be further increased in size.[26] By 1931, his willful ways had provoked such widespread resentment in the Greek Cypriot community that civil war seemed imminent. On April 28 of that year, a very unusual event occurred: one of the Turkish Cypriot representatives in the Legislative Council sided with the Greek Cypriots in voting against a new tax proposal, thereby breaking the perennial deadlock in that chamber and causing the defeat of the bill. It was a major rebuke to the British colonial administration. But Storrs stuck to his guns and, using his legislative prerogatives, approved the offending bill by "Order in Council". This action was immediately condemned by the Cypriot press. It enraged the leaders of the Greek Cypriot community, but they could not agree among themselves as to which was the most effective way to demonstrate their disapproval of Storrs' latest display of arbitrariness. The Greek Cypriot members of the Legislative Council considered resigning *en masse*. However, this tactic had been tried

---

25. Alastos, *op. cit.*, p. 351.

26. *Ibid.*, p. 348; also Hill, *op. cit.*, Vol. IV, p. 542. The British Cabinet wisely rejected the plan.

before (the last time in December 1920)[27] without appreciable results. Instead, they decided to remain "on the battlements" and struggle against British intransigence from within the Legislative Council. This stand smacked of excessive timidity to the young activists of the National Organization who, on October 18, formed their own organization, the National Radicalist Union, which called for "the fanatical pursuit of the union of Cyprus with the Greek political whole".[28] On the same day, and possibly as a consequence of pressure from the latter group, the Bishop of Kition abruptly resigned from the Legislative Council and issued a manifesto advocating the violent overthrow of the British colonial administration. This unexpected move undermined the position of the remaining Greek Cypriot representatives who, accusing the bishop of "torpedoing" their unity, now felt compelled to resign too.[29]

In the afternoon of October 21, the National Radicalist Union held a meeting at the Commercial Club in Nicosia. Although small at the outset, the attendance gradually swelled until, by nightfall, a very large crowd had assembled. Some of the members of the Legislative Council who had just resigned spoke. Then, Dionysios Kykkotis, the chief priest of the Phaneromeni Church (the most important Orthodox place of worship in the capital), delivered an impassioned speech in the course of which he unfurled the Greek flag and called upon his audience to protect it. Finally, he announced, "I proclaim the revolution!" Soon there were cries of "to Government House!" and the crowd, led by the former Greek Cypriot members of the Legislative Council (who intended to personally hand in their resignations to Storrs) and by several priests, headed for the seat of government, a mere mile-and-a-half away. The mob, now

---

27. The Greek Cypriots had subsequently boycotted the elections of November 1921, and refrained from participating in the Legislative Council until the 1923 elections.

28. Alastos, *op. cit.*, p. 354.

29. *Ibid.*, pp. 352-353.

some 5,000 strong, picked up staves and rocks and converged on Government House, shouting *"enosis!"* and singing the Greek national anthem. In a frenzy of hate, it smashed all the windows, battered in the front door and set fire to the building. Storrs and his staff escaped unhurt, but the building was gutted. At first the police fought the rioters with clubs, but, as the demonstration got out of hand, several of the constables fired into the mob, fatally wounding one of the rioters. The next day disturbances broke out anew in Nicosia, and a riot erupted in Limassol, where the house of the British District Commissioner was burnt to the ground. By the following day demonstrations had spread to practically every part of the island. But the leaders of the insurgents lacked resolve and, in spite of the revolutionary organizations which they had at their disposal, were not able to build up a united front. Within ten days the riots had been suppressed by the British Army, and Cyprus' first uprising since the British occupation had come to an end.

The British inflicted severe penalties on the Greek Cypriots for their refractory behavior. Ten of the Greek Cypriot leaders, including the Bishops of Kition and Kyrenia, the Reverend Kykkotis, two former members of the Legislative Council, and the guiding spirits of the National Radicalist Union and the Communist Party,[30] were banished from the island. Many others were imprisoned, fined or forced to reside in small, out-of-the-way places on the island. At the same time, a collective fine of £25,000 was imposed on the Cypriot population, the Constitution was scrapped, the Legislative Council was suspended, municipal elections were abolished, political parties were made illegal, the press was placed under tight censorship, public meetings were banned, the police were given the right to search persons and their homes at will, rigid controls were established over

---

30. Although the Communists did little to instigate the riots, they eagerly joined ranks with the insurgents once the riots had started. See T. W. Adams, *AKEL: The Communist Party of Cyprus* (Stanford, Calif., 1971), pp. 18-19.

education, the teaching of Greek and Turkish history was restricted, and pictures of Greek and Turkish national heroes were removed from the walls of the schools.[31]

In 1933 an Advisory Council, consisting at first of six and later of eight Cypriots appointed by the Governor was set up to replace the Legislative Council and to act as a means of sounding out public opinion. Although the Legislative Council had had no real power, it had nonetheless functioned as a public forum in which grievances could be openly aired. In other words, the Cypriots had had a voice in their government, but nothing else. Now this voice was stilled.

The new system of colonial administration was deeply resented by most Cypriots. According to the British correspondent Arthur Merton, who visited the island in 1939, the Cypriots complained that it was "impossible for anyone to express his opinion freely", that measures directly affecting the inhabitants were "prepared without consulting even those whom the Government nominated as representatives of the people", and that the British officials charged with governing Cyprus tended to be "mediocre in capacity and standing" and evinced "little sympathy for or interest in the life of the people".[32]

The restoration of municipal elections in Cyprus in 1943, the Allied victory in World War II (in which thousands of Cypriots had fought in the British or Greek armies), the triumph of the Labour Party in the British elections of 1945, and the cession of the Dodecanese islands by Italy to Greece shortly thereafter, once more revived hopes among enosists that their national ambitions were about to be fulfilled.[33] They were, therefore, disappointed when the

31. The punishment by the British of the Turkish community, which had not taken part in the riots, can only be understood as a warning to discourage them from rioting in the future.

32. "Chastened Cyprus", *The Living Age* (March 1939), p. 62.

33. In his *Memoirs*, General George Grivas, who fought in the Greek Army, expressed the feeling of many Greek Cypriots who served in World War II. "Like every other Cypriot", he wrote, "I believed that we were also fighting for the freedom of Cyprus" (*The Memoirs of General Grivas*, ed. Charles Foley, New York, 1965, p. 2).

British elephant gave birth to another constitutional mouse. The new constitution, offered by the British government in 1948, merely granted internal self-government. The legislature was to be made up of four British officials and twenty-two elected members (including eighteen Greek Cypriot and four Turkish Cypriot representatives). But it was to be presided over by a chairman chosen by the Governor and was not to be allowed to discuss the status of Cyprus within the British Commonwealth. Furthermore, bills regarding finance, defense, external affairs, minorities and the constitution were not to be introduced in the legislature without the consent of the Governor. Finally, the Governor was to have the power to pass a bill or a motion rejected by the legislature if such action was deemed by him to be "in the public interest".

The constitution was so strenuously opposed by the Greek Cypriot leaders that it was never put into effect. The British Government's unwillingness to alter the status of Cyprus, which was again reflected in a constitutional proposal made in 1954, set the stage for the next act in the drama of *enosis*, namely the civil war. The outstanding Greek Cypriot leader in that struggle was Archbishop Makarios III (1913-1977). Born in humble circumstances in the village of Panayia, on the lower slopes of the Troodos mountains, he was enrolled at the well-known Kykko monastery at age thirteen. Shortly before World War II, he was sent to the Theological College at the University of Athens. In 1943, he returned briefly to Cyprus to teach at the Kykko monastery. In 1946, he traveled to the United States under the auspices of the World Council of Churches to further his studies at Boston University's School of Theology. In 1948, at the age of thirty-five, he was elected bishop of Kition and once more made his way home.

Back in Cyprus, Makarios at once assumed an active role as political leader and agitator for *enosis*. He was partly responsible for the rejection of the proposed 1948 constitution. In 1950, as the dominant personality in the Ethnarchy

Council, he organized an islandwide plebiscite to reinforce the demand for *enosis*. Every form of pressure was exerted on the Greek Cypriot population to produce an overwhelming majority in favor of union with Greece.[34] As a result, the vote was 95.7% for *enosis* (at least if one is willing to accept the figures released by the Ethnarchy Council). Although the plebiscite had no effect upon the attitude of the British government, it was nonetheless a good publicity stunt and, later that year, its architect was rewarded by being elected Archbishop of Cyprus and Ethnarch of the Greek Cypriot community.

As Archbishop, Makarios redoubled his efforts to enlist the support of the Greek government for *enosis*. Finding that *enosis* was a popular cause in Greece but that Greek officials were generally loath to antagonize Great Britain, a staunch ally in its struggle against the Communist guerrillas in the 1944-1945 and 1946-1949 civil wars, he did not hesitate to appeal directly to the Greek people. In the words of Sir Harry Luke, "He was thus able to stampede the Ministry of the moribund Marshal Papagos, politically none too sure of itself and without confidence in its ability to clamp down on mob passions kindled on a nationalistic issue".[35] In September 1953, Prime Minister Papagos raised the subject of *enosis* in a private meeting with the British foreign secretary, Sir Anthony Eden. However, the latter curtly dismissed the issue with a comment to the effect that as far as England was concerned the problem of *enosis* did not exist. Soon after this meeting, Eden's views were echoed by the colonial secretary who, in a speech in the House of Commons, declared with finality that Cyprus occupied a strategic position and that as such it belonged to that category of territories for which the principle of

34. According to Sir Harry Luke, "The signatures in favour of Enosis were openly displayed in every parish church and the penalty for not signing was excommunication" (*Cyprus: A Portrait and an Appreciation*, p. 180). The Turkish Cypriots denounced the plebiscite as a fraud and did not participate in the vote.

35. *Cyprus: A Portrait and an Appreciation*, p. 178.

self-determination could never apply. Then, in August, 1954, Greece raised the question of Cypriot self-determination at the United Nations, only to see the motion tabled by the Political Commission of the General Assembly.

By 1954, Makarios had become convinced that terrorism would have to be resorted to in order to dislodge the British, and he joined forces with George Grivas, a retired Greek military officer of Cypriot origin, who had long advocated violence as a solution to the Cyprus problem.

Grivas (1898-1974), the scion of a middle class family from the little town of Trikomo, in northeastern Cyprus, early in life opted for a military career. Upon graduating from the Pan Cyprian Gymnasium in Nicosia, in 1916, he was admitted to the Royal Hellenic Military Academy in Athens. An ardent Greek nationalist since his youth,[36] he joined a political organization which reflected his rightist and enosist views. He served as a lieutenant in the Greek invasion of Anatolia in the early 1920's. There he learned the rudiments of guerrilla warfare by observing how small detachments of Turkish troops, by operating far behind the Greek front, caused havoc with the Greek lines of communication.[37] As a lieutenant-colonel, he fought against the Italians in northwestern Greece in 1940. During the occupation of Greece by Axis forces, he organized a private army named X to resist the Germans, as well as to contain the Communist guerrilla bands which were becoming ever more numerous. In the postwar period, he participated in

36. "Mine was a happy childhood", he wrote, "and happiest of all when I marched behind the blue and white banners on some national day and felt the Hellenic passion for liberty burning in us all" (*op. cit.*, p. 3).

37. "It was in this rugged region that I had my first taste of guerrilla warfare and began to realise its possibilities", he reminisced, "I was fascinated by the ease with which a band of irregulars armed only with rifles successfully delayed our division near Nikomidia for a full day, even when artillery was brought up to shell their positions" (*ibid.*, p. 4.) Grivas also acquired a grudging admiration for Atatürk, to whose "brilliance and tenacity" he ascribed the Greek defeat (*ibid.*).

the struggle against the Communist-led popular front of EAM/ELAS, and tried unsuccessfully to transform X into a right-wing pan-Hellenic political party. By then he had become obsessed with the idea of leading a revolt in Cyprus. He formed a Liberation Committee, consisting of distinguished Greek citizens, for the purpose of raising funds and collecting weapons. He had several meetings with Makarios who, hoping to achieve *enosis* by peaceful means, at first endeavored to restrain him. Finally, he carried out two extended reconnaissances in Cyprus, where he laid the groundwork for his projected guerrilla war against the British.

Having at last obtained Makarios' support, Grivas established permanent headquarters in Cyprús in March 1954. There, taking the *nom de guerre* of Dighenis (the legendary folk hero of Byzantine times), he completed the formation of his clandestine revolutionary army, the *Ethniki Organosis Kypriakon Agoniston* (National Organization of Cypriot Fighters), better known by its acronym EOKA, the members of which were largely drawn from two organizations founded by Makarios, namely the Young People's Christian Orthodox Union (OXEN) and the Pan Cyprian Enosist Youth Organization (PEON). He then plunged the island into civil war. Displaying an unusual talent for revolutionary enterprise and the ruthlessness that usually accompanies it, he quickly became a major nuisance to the British colonial administration. But because EOKA was struggling to achieve not only independence from Great Britain but also *enosis*, it aroused the growing opposition of both the Turkish Cypriot community, which did not want to suffer the fate of other Turkish peoples in Greek-occupied territories, and the Turkish government, which did not want Greece to gain control of the eastern Mediterranean and the approaches to the southern littoral of Anatolia.[38]

---

38. For a detailed description of the Cyprus civil war, see Nancy Crawshaw, *The Cyprus Revolt* (London, 1978). For a detailed description of the negotiations for a settlement of the conflict, see Stephen G. Xydis, *Cyprus: Reluctant Republic* (The Hague, 1973).

CHAPTER IV
THE TURKISH COUNTERTHRUST

The Turks have a well-established reputation for ferocity, and the notion of the "terrible Turk" is deeply ingrained in the Western mind. What is, unfortunately, too little known is that during the nineteenth and twentieth centuries the Turks have much more often been the victims of aggression than they have been the aggressors. They have been involved in only two wars of aggression, namely the Second Balkan War of 1913, when they joined the Balkan League in the hope of recapturing Turkish territories seized by Bulgaria during the First Balkan War of 1912, and World War I, when they joined the Central Powers in the hope of recapturing Turkish territories seized by Russia during the nineteenth century. On the other hand, Turkey has been invaded numerous times: once each by Italy, France, England, Serbia, Bulgaria and Montenegro, and four times each by Russia and Greece.

Both Russia and Greece were determined to crush the Ottoman Empire, which Czar Nicholas I contemptuously called the "sick man of Europe", and, in the course of their conquests, caused widespread devastation. But because the Greeks tried to impose their rigid concept of religious and cultural uniformity upon a religiously and culturally diverse people, their ravages were even more extensive than those of the Russians. In this, the Greek War of Independence set the tone for all that was to follow. The Orthodox Greeks at once fell upon their Muslim neighbors and slaughtered them indiscriminately. To quote the distinguished historian, William St. Clair:

The Turks of Greece left few traces. They disappeared suddenly and finally in the spring of 1821 unmourned and unnoticed
by the rest of the world. Years later, when travellers asked
about the heaps of stones, the old men would explain, 'There
stood the tower of Ali Aga, and there we slew him, his harem,
and his slaves'. It was hard to believe then that Greece had
once contained a large population of Turkish descent, living in
small communities all over the country, prosperous farmers,
merchants, and officials, whose families had known no other
home for hundreds of years. As the Greeks said, the moon de-
voured them.

Upwards of twenty thousand Turkish men, women, and children were murdered by their Greek neighbours in a few weeks
of slaughter. They were killed deliberately, without qualm or
scruple, and there were no regrets either then or later. . . .

All over the Pelopponese roamed mobs of Greeks armed with
clubs, scythes, and a few firearms, killing, plundering, and
burning. They were often led by Christian priests, who exhort-
ed them to greater efforts in their holy work. . . . .

Within a few weeks of the outbreak of the Revolution, the
Turkish and Moslem Albanian population of the Pelopponese,
previously about a ninth of the whole, had ceased to exist as a
settled community. . . .

During April the inhabitants of the important islands of Hydra,
Spetsae, and Psara decided to join the revolutionaries. . . . They
armed their ships and began to attack traders flying the Turkish
flag. They ranged all over the Aegean and beyond. Many Turkish merchant ships were captured, their crews killed, or thrown
overboard, and the booty brought back to port. On several occasions ships crowded with Moslem pilgrims on their way to or
from Mecca were seized and the crews and passengers put to
death. . . . The crew of a Turkish corvette, fifty-seven men in
all, were brought back to Hydra in triumph and individually
roasted to death over fires on the beach.[1]

When Greece invaded Crete, in February 1897, Greek
Muslims were slaughtered by the thousands. In the district

---

1. *That Greece Might Still be Free: The Philhellenes in the War of
Independence* (London, 1972), pp. 1-2. Reprinted by permission of
Oxford University Press.

of Sitia alone, 851 persons (including 374 children) were killed.[2] The eighty Muslim villages of Central Crete were entirely destroyed.[3] The massacre was stopped only by the timely arrival of British and French military units. An eye-witness to the slaughter, a woman from the village of Rou-kaka, in the district of Sitia, gave the following deposition to French officials:

> Christians threw Halime, the pregnant wife of Hüseyin Meh-medakis, on the ground and slit open her belly, taking the fetus out. They also knifed Fatime, daughter of Mustafa Ömer Efen-dakis, cutting her open from her breasts to the middle of her back. They pushed the men into the mosque and, as they kill-ed them, hurled them from the minaret, which they then set ablaze with gasoline. Dogs were running all over the village car-rying half-burnt hands and feet. The children were stabbed to death, and a few were crushed beneath the minaret when it collapsed.[4]

When the Greeks occupied the İzmir region in 1919 and later, as they penetrated into central Anatolia, they carried out a policy of genocide on a grand scale. Typical was the Aydın massacre of June 25, 1919. Greek troops at first sub-jected the Turkish quarter of the town to an intensive artil-lery bombardment. All Turks who tried to escape were shot down by Greek soldiers or civilian auxiliaries. Then the Greek Army entered the quarter and continued its orgy of destruction. Some Turkish families were burnt alive when their homes were set afire. Others were gunned down in the streets. When four women who had barricaded themselves into a building were captured, they were impaled on wooden stakes. Altogether, an estimated 9,716 Turks were butcher-ed that day.[5]

2. Report from Consul Sir Alfred Biliotti to the Marquess of Salis-bury, dated July 20, 1897, in Turkey, No. 11 (1897), Great Britain, Parliament, Sessional Papers, 1898, Vol. CVI, No. 140.

3. Victor Bérard, Les affaires de Crète. Second Edition (Paris, 1900), p. 275.

4. Bérard, op. cit., pp. 247-248.

5. Salahi Ramadan Sonyel, The Turco-Greek Conflict (London, 1976), p. 20. Sonyel's account is based entirely upon official docu-ments in the Public Record Office. For the ravages of the Greek army, see also: Halide Edib, The Turkish Ordeal (London, 1926), pp. 313ff., 353,356,363,367-368,374 and Noëlle Roger, En Asie Mineure (Paris, 1930), pp. 208-209, 213.

The Greek and Russian conquests, as well as the depredations of the Serbians, Rumanians and Bulgarians, all of whom, like the Greeks, were pursuing their own dreams of national grandeur, resulted in a flood of Muslim immigrants into what was left of the Ottoman Empire. 1.4 million Tatars fled from the Crimea alone from 1854 to 1876.[6] Some 30,000 Muslims fled from Thessaly in 1897.[7] All of these refugees had to be given land or be otherwise economically accommodated by the Ottoman government—a fearful burden for an already impoverished nation.[8]

---

6. Shaw, *op. cit.*, Vol. II, p. 116.

7. Pierre Mille, *De Thessalie en Crète: impressions de campagne, avril-mai 1897* (Paris, 1898), p. 61. Jews were also driven out of Turkish territories seized by the Greeks. The fate of the Jews of Salonica was typical. According to Jacov Benmayor, an authority on the subject:

> In 1917 a great fire destroyed most of the town, leaving some 50,000 Jews homeless. The Greek government, which followed a policy of hellenizing the town, was ready to compensate the Jews whose houses were destroyed, but it refused to let the Jews return to certain parts of the town, causing many of them to leave the country. . . . In 1922 a law (no. 236) was enacted which forced all the inhabitants of Salonika to refrain from working on Sundays, thus causing another wave of emigration. . . . In 1932-34 the Campbell riots, which accompanied the elections and were anti-Semitic in tone, took place. An entire Jewish neighborhood was burned to the ground by hooligans, and most of the Jews who lived in the Campbell neighborhood emigrated after the riots ("Salonika", *Encyclopaedia Judaica*, Vol. XIV, pp. 703-704). See also Leon Sciaky, *Farewell to Salonica* (New York, 1946), pp. 213-235.

8. The Ottoman Empire also welcomed Christian victims of oppression. Polish refugees streamed into the Ottoman Empire after the uprisings of 1830 and 1863 in their country (see Adam Lewak, *Szieje emigracje polskiej w Turcji, 1831-1878*, Warszawa, 1935; and Z. F. Fındıkoğlu, "Türkiye'de Slav muhacirleri", *Sosyoloji konferansları*, 1964, pp. 1-30). Hungarians sought asylum in the Empire following their revolt against the Austrian government in 1848-49. Among them was the great revolutionary leader Louis Kossuth, whom the Turks refused to extradite (see Dénes Jánossy, "Die ungarische Emigration und der Krieg im Orient", *Archivum Europae Centro-Orientalis*, 1939, pp. 113-275).

The Ottoman Empire needed a dynamic new ideology with which to challenge both the aggressive nationalism of its neighbors and the disruptive nationalisms of its own minorities. But the task of devising such an ideology was by no means easy, for the Empire, having developed into a multi-national state, operated on the principal of ethnic inclusiveness—not exclusiveness. Even the once dominant Turks, by becoming a minority in their own Muslim *millet*, had lost their identity as a separate ethnic group, and the Turkish language, by becoming extensively Arabicized and Persianized, had lost much of its uniqueness.

Under these circumstances, one can understand why Ottoman statesmen, when faced with the need to devise a new ideology, picked *Osmanlılık* (Pan-Ottomanism), the goal of which was merely to strengthen the bonds between the various religious communities within the Empire. Pan-Ottomanism stressed the equality of all Ottoman citizens, and was buttressed by an impressive body of legislation (e.g., the Rescript of the Rose Chamber, of 1839, and the Illustrious Rescript, of 1856) which guaranteed the lives, properties and honor of the sultan's subjects, irrespective of creed or race. The essence of Pan-Ottomanism was captured to perfection by the Young Turk leader Enver in his famous speech delivered on the Hill of Liberty, in İstanbul, in 1909. "We are all brothers", he declared, "Under the same blue sky we are all equal; we all glory in being Ottomans".[9]

But Pan-Ottomanism was opposed by many Muslims and even non-Muslims who were reluctant to abandon the safeguards and special privileges which characterized the old Millet System.[10] It also failed to discourage the spread of nationalism among the minority *millets*. As Pan-Ottomanism

---

9. Louis A. Springer, "The Romantic Career of Enver Pasha", *Asia*, August 1917, p. 459.

10. Christians and Jews, for example, did not want to become so equal to the Muslim majority as to become eligible for military service and to lose their own courts of law.

proved increasingly lame as a national ideology, it was sup-
planted successively by *İslamlılık* (Pan-Islamism) and *Turan-
cılık* (Pan-Turanism).

Pan-Islamism was chiefly promoted by the strong, conservative sultan, Abdülhamit II (ruled 1876-1909). Abdülhamit felt that nationalism had made such deep inroads into the European provinces of his realm that they were all
but lost. What was now to be done was to forge a closer
union among his Asian subjects (most of whom were Muslims and had thus far remained steadfastly loyal), thereby
transforming Anatolia and the adjacent Arab provinces into a last bastion of strength. Pan-Islamism could also be
utilized by a spiritually revitalized Ottoman Empire as a
powerful weapon with which to launch a major counter-
attack against foreign nations which had come to regard
the sultan's dominions as a shipwreck fit for plunder. Just
as the Russians had been using the Orthodox peoples of
the Empire as agents of subversion, Turkey could now instigate widespread unrest among the Muslim subjects of
the Czar. It could also foment civil strife among the Muslims of India and North Africa if the need arose. Russia,
England and France were thus put on notice that they could
no longer annex Ottoman territory at will.[11] And the whole
world was reminded that the Ottoman sultan was the Caliph
of all Muslims, a title which, for expediency's sake, was
compared to that of Pope. Symbolic of the vitality of the
new ideology was the construction of the eight-hundred-
mile-long Hejaz railway (1901-1908), which greatly facilitated the traffic of pilgrims to the holy cities in Arabia and further enhanced Abdülhamit's prestige in the Muslim world.

But Pan-Islamism, in turn, proved inadequate as a national
ideology when, in the early years of the twentieth century,
such previously docile Muslim subjects of the Ottoman Empire as the Albanians, the Kurds and the Arabs began to

---

11. England occupied Cyprus in 1878 and Egypt in 1882. The
French occupied Tunisia in 1881.

struggle for their own independence. This left the Turks of eastern Rumelia and Anatolia as the mainstay of the regime. Thus, the Turks at last emerged from the shadows of anonymity and were able to develop their own feelings of cultural identity.

This nascent Turkish nationalism was encouraged by:

1) The works of European Turcologists (in particular the French historian Léon Cahun, 1841-1900, the British grammarian Arthur Lumley Davids, 1811-1832, and the Hungarian anthropologist and philologist Arminius Vambéry, 1832-1913), which revealed to the Turks the richness of their history, language and culture;

2) The writings of Russian Turkish scholars, such as İsmail Gasprinski (1851-1914) and Yusuf Akçura (1876-1933), which advocated the unification of all Turks—in other words Pan-Turanism—to meet the challenge of Russian nationalism and Pan-Slavic imperialism.

Turkish nationalism first flourished as a political ideology in the period immediately preceding World War I, when the Young Turks, who had overthrown Abdülhamit in 1909 and had first attempted to revive Pan-Ottomanism, championed Pan-Turanism as a means with which to unify the Turkish inhabitants of the Empire in the struggle to save the nation from disintegration.

Pan-Turanism gave the Turks, who were just acquiring an ethnic pride of their own, a sense of national mission and the hope of being able to emulate the heroic dreams of their ancestors. In his poem "Turan", the great philosopher Ziya Gökalp, reflecting the nationalist euphoria of his time, exulted:

The country of the Turks is not Turkey, not yet Turkestan,
Their country is a vast and eternal land: Turan![12]

----

12. Uriel Heyd, *Foundations of Turkish Nationalism: The Life and Teachings of Ziya Gökalp* (London, 1950), p. 126.

The Pan-Turanist wave crested in World War I, when the
Turks attempted to regain the initiative against Russia and
other countries which had long taken advantage of Turkey's
dire predicament of being the "sick man of Europe". Enver
himself became so dedicated a Pan-Turanist that he sacrific-
ed himself for that ideal in 1922, leading a band of Turkic
guerrillas in Central Asia in a desperate struggle against
overwhelmingly superior Soviet forces.

Enver's brave but suicidal act was symbolic of the futility
of Pan-Turanism as a national ideology, Indeed, it was as self-
destructive as the *Megali Idea*, Pan-Slavism and the other
nationalistic poisons for which it was supposed to serve as
an antidote, and Gökalp's poem is embarrassingly reminis-
cent of the sensational literature produced by the devotees
of Greek nationalism. In any case, the disasters of the First
World War doomed the movement and the Greek invasion
which followed it enabled Atatürk to make a fresh ideo-
logical start.

Having realized that the Ottoman Empire could not be
saved, Atatürk decided to make a clean break with the past.
Believing, like Gökalp, that language is "the touchstone of
nationality",[13] he created a new nation—modern Turkey—
out of those parts of the empire which were inhabited by a
majority of Turkish-speaking peoples. But, unlike Gökalp,
whose concept of Turkish nationalism imposed no definite
limit on the projected Turkish state, Atatürk relinquished
all of Turkey's territorial claims beyond Eastern Thrace,
Anatolia and the *sancak* of Alexandretta. "Rather than increasing the number of our enemies and their coercion
over us by chasing concepts which we cannot realize", he
recommended, "let us withdraw to our national and legitimate limits".[14] He also declared that the goal of his government was "to work within our national boundaries for the

---

13. *Ibid.*, p. 115.
14. From a speech by Atatürk, quoted in Frank Tachau, "The
Face of Turkish Nationalism as Reflected in the Cyprus Dispute",
The Middle East Journal, Vol. XIII, No. 3 (Summer, 1959), p. 265.

real happiness and welfare of the nation".[15] Thus, his political creed, *Türkçülük* (Turkism) was a fundamentally pacific ideology. As Lord Kinross has pointed out in his excellent biography of Atatürk, "peace at home and peace abroad" were his watchwords.[16] Atatürk's decisions to create a lay state and abolish the Caliphate acted as an additional brake on expansionism, for it discouraged any temptation to resuscitate the Pan-Islamic ideology of Abdülhamit.

Thus there is a fundamental difference in ideology between modern Greece and modern Turkey. Modern Greece was born out of a religious-sentimental dream of reconstituting the Byzantine Empire, and even though the Greek Government officially disavowed the *Megali Idea* after the Anatolian disaster it has nonetheless continued to push for its implementation in the case of the Dodecanese islands[17] as well as in that of Cyprus. Moreover, the Greeks, as we have seen, are still emotionally committed to that ideal. On the other hand, modern Turkey rose in opposition to such a dream—as a reaction to the folly of the Young Turks, whose military adventurism brought about the final collapse of the Ottoman Empire, and to the recklessness of the Greeks, who in their haste to fulfill the *Megali Idea*, tried to seize what was left of that Empire after World War I. This explains why the Turks made no claim to the Dodecanese

---

15. From a speech by Atatürk, quoted in George Lenczowski, ed., *The Political Awakening in the Middle East* (Englewood Cliffs, N. J., 1970), p. 87.

16. *Atatürk* (New York, 1965), p. 520. Although he was a general, Atatürk abhorred violence. Upon reading Hitler's *Mein Kampf*, he is said to have expressed horror at the 'meanness of his language and the madness of his thoughts' (*ibid.*, p. 522). It is interesting to note than on January 12, 1934, Eleftherios Venizelos, the most distinguished Greek statesman of modern times, wrote a letter to the Nobel Committee recommending Atatürk for the Nobel Peace Prize.

17. The Dodecanese islands, in the Aegean Sea, belonged to the Ottoman Empire until they were seized by the Italians in 1912, during the Italo-Turkish War. They were awarded to Greece by means of a treaty signed in Paris, on February 15, 1947. The largest and most important of the Dodecanese islands is Rhodes.

islands after World War II[18] and why they have never tried
to encourage feelings comparable to those for *enosis* among
the Turkish Cypriots. When, in December 1923, a group of
Turkish Cypriot leaders went to Ankara to press for the return of Cyprus to Turkey, Atatürk rejected their plea, re-
peating, in essence, what he had previously said in a speech
about the new nationalism:

> Although our nationalism loves all Turks. . . with a deep feel-
> ing of brotherhood, and although it desires with all its soul
> their wholesome development, yet it recognizes that its politi-
> cal activity must end at the borders of the Turkish Republic.[19]

But Atatürk's ideas nonetheless deeply influenced Turkish Cypriots—especially the young. As his eager disciples,
they began to think of themselves not just as Muslims (as
they had up to then) but as Turks, and they spontaneously
adopted many of his social reforms. Turkish ethnocentrism
in Cyprus was also encouraged by the discriminatory prac-
tices of the British administration and the bigotry of the
Greek Cypriots.

The British administration took Turkish Cypriot support
for granted and, at times, treated the Turkish Cypriot minority with even more harshness than it did the Greek Cypriot majority. On the pretext that the Muslims on the island had "no alternative arrangement" to replace the appointment of their religious head, the *Müftü*, by the Ottoman government, the British at once assumed this right.[20]
In 1921, they banned the importation of schoolbooks
from Turkey.[21] In 1927, they abolished the position of

---

18. In July 1944, the Turkish ambassador in Athens, referring to
the Dodecanese, reminded Prime Minister Papandreou that "it was
official Turkish policy to have no territorial claims" (Psomiades, *op.
cit.*, p. 56n).

19. Quoted in Tachau, *op. cit.*, p. 265.

20. Charles Fraser Beckingham, "Islam and Turkish Nationalism
in Cyprus", *Die Welt des Islams*, Vol. IV, No. 4 (1956), pp. 72-73.

21. Vehbi Z. Serter, *Kıbrıs Türk mücadele tarihi* (Nicosia, 1975),
Vol. I, p. 31.

Chief Judge. In 1928, they converted the Muslim pious foundations (*Evkaf*) into an agency of the colonial administration. In 1929, they eliminated the position of *Müftü* altogether and deprived the Turkish Cypriot community of any say in the administration of its own schools. In 1930, the *şer'î* courts were placed under the administration of the *Evkaf*.[22] In 1931, the Turkish Cypriot community, which had not participated in the riots, was forced to share in the punishment meted out to the Greek Cypriot community. When Atatürk died, in November 1938, the British authorities banned the film of his funeral from the island.[23] Meanwhile, the economic condition of the Turkish Cypriot community was steadily deteriorating. Already in 1913, the French traveller, Count Jean de Kergorlay, observed that "the Turkish element is becoming poorer, financially speaking, from day to day".[24] As a result, many Turkish Cypriots emigrated to Turkey and elsewhere. Between World Wars I and II, some 6,000 to 8,000 of them settled down in Turkey alone.[25] These included hundreds of students who, because of the limited educational opportunities under British rule, had no choice but to complete their studies in Ankara or İstanbul.

There was also a rise in anti-British sentiment, especially among students, the intelligentsia and the professional classes. The Islamic High School (*İslâm Lisesi*) in Nicosia, which was renamed the Turkish High School (*Türk Lisesi*) in the early 1930's, became such a center of anti-British agitation that in 1937 the colonial government dismissed four of the teachers, imposed a British headmaster and changed the school's name back to the Islamic High School.[26]

22. Beckingham, *op. cit.*, pp. 71-72; A. Suat Bilge, *Le conflit de Chypre et les Cypriotes turcs* (Ankara, 1961), pp. 9-12.

23. Merton, *op. cit.*, p. 63.

24. *Chypres et Rhodes* (Paris, 1913), p. 136.

25. Beckingham, *op. cit.*, p. 71.

26. Derviş Manizade, *Kıbrıs: dün, bugün, yarın* (İstanbul, 1975, p. 412.

At the same time, a literature of protest appeared. In September 1920, the journalist Remzi Okan founded the newspaper *Söz* (The Word), which criticized the British colonial administration and attacked religious leaders who were felt to be too pro-British. In April 1931, a lawyer by the name of Can Mehmet Rifat founded the newspaper *Masum millet gazetesi* (Newspaper of an Innocent Nation) to expose the legal abuses of the British colonial administration. The British repeatedly tried to suppress these newspapers, but succeeded only in closing them down for brief periods of time. The growth of nationalist and anti-colonialist feeling was also expressed in two important historical treatises, İsmet Konur's *Kıbrıs Türkleri* (The Turkish Cypriots), which was published in İstanbul in 1938, and Halil Fikret Alasya's *Kıbrıs Tarihi* (History of Cyprus), which was published in Nicosia in 1939.

During the 1930's and 1940's, several Turkish Cypriot popular leaders emerged. The two most distinguished of these were Dr. Fazil Küçük (1906—) and Rauf Raif Denktaş (1924—). Dr. Küçük, the son of a farmer, was born in Nicosia. After graduating from the Turkish High School in Nicosia, he studied medicine at the Universities of İstanbul, Lausanne and Paris. In 1937, he returned to Cyprus and started a practice. But soon his passion for politics led him away from his initial calling. When, in 1940, Remzi Okan, the publisher of *Söz*, died and the *Masum millet gazetesi* ceased publication, he decided to found his own newspaper, *Halkin sesi* (The Voice of the People), to "give voice to the many complaints of the Turkish Cypriot people against the British colonial administration".[27] However, because the British authorities were reluctant to issue the necessary publication permit, the first issue of this paper appeared only on March 14, 1942. Dr. Küçük was one of the founders of the *Kibris Adası Türk Azınlığı Kurumu* (Association of the Turkish Minority of the Island of Cyprus), better

---

27. Letter from His Excellency Dr. Küçük, dated June 3, 1978.

known by its acronym, KATAK, in April 1943. The purpose
of this political party was to promote the political, economic
and social interests of the Turkish Cypriot community. In
1944, because of disagreements with the other leaders of
KATAK, Dr. Küçük resigned from the party and founded
his own political organization, the *Kibris Türk Milli Birlik
Partisi* (Turkish Cypriot National Union Party). In 1946,
he established the first Turkish Cypriot trade union. Rauf
Denktaş, the son of a judge, was born in the small town of
Paphos, in Western Cyprus. After graduating from the English School in Nicosia, he worked briefly as a columnist for
the newspaper *Halkın sesi*. In 1944, he went to study law
in England and, in 1947, he was called to the bar at Lin-
coln's Inn. Upon returning to Cyprus shortly thereafter, he
embarked upon a highly successful career as a lawyer and
politician, swiftly becoming Dr. Küçük's chief aide and heir
apparent.

In 1948, Lord Winster, the Governor of Cyprus, bowing
to pressure from the Turkish Cypriot community, appointed a Committee on Turkish Affairs to examine and make
recommendations regarding the office of the *Müftü*, the
Evkaf, the *şeri* courts and, inasmuch as they affected the
Muslim population of the island, education and family
law. It was composed of eight members, all of whom were
Turkish Cypriots, and it included Rauf Denktaş. In 1949,
the Committee published its *Interim Report*,[28] outlining
its recommendations. Its members hoped that the British
colonial administration would implement their proposals
and would consult them concerning the drafting of the
necessary legislation. But the British quietly lost interest
in the project and the *Interim Report* was quickly shelved.
The Turkish Cypriot leaders regarded this as an affront.
They adopted the recommendations of the Committee as

---

28. *An Investigation into Matters Concerning and Affecting the
Turkish Community in Cyprus: Interim Report of the Committee
on Turkish Affairs* (Nicosia, 1949).

their program and "devoted much of their energy in the succeeding years to agitating for its enactment".[29] Finally, in the 1950's, the British relented and accepted a number of the proposals. As a consequence, resentment against British rule markedly decreased in the Turkish Cypriot community.

But by that time the Turkish Cypriots had become less concerned with the nature of their relationship with the British colonial authorities than they were with the incipient threat posed by Greek Cypriot bigotry and aggressiveness. This fear was heightened by the behavior of the Greek Cypriot members of the Municipal Councils, established by the British in 1944. Greek Cypriot politicians, who held a majority of seats in all the Municipal Councils, used these bodies to air their enosist views and to enact a program the purpose of which was the complete Hellenization of the island and the elimination of all traces of Turkish culture. The names of streets and squares which were Turkish were arbitrarily changed to Greek ones. The tombs of Turkish heroes were removed in the course of "street widening" projects. Only Greek flags were allowed to fly over the town halls. Finally, the needs of the inhabitants of the Turkish Cypriot quarters of the towns were deliberately neglected. By June 3, 1957, the eighteen Turkish Cypriot councilors were so disheartened that they resigned. This was an event of major importance, for it signalled the end of unified, bi-communal municipalities in Cyprus.[30]

As the nationalistic fervor of the Greek Cypriots soared to unprecedented heights of passion in the 1950's, causing the Turkish Cypriots to feel ever more isolated, it spurred a corresponding rise in national consciousness in the latter group. "Cyprus is Turkish" became a popular slogan in the Turkish Cypriot community. Reflecting that growing ethnocentrism, Dr. Küçük argued that if the British were to

29. Beckingham, op. cit., p. 76.
30. Personal interview with His Excellency Osman Örek, then Speaker of the Assembly of the Turkish Federated State of Cyprus, Nicosia, July 25, 1977; also Bilge, op. cit., p. 187.

withdraw from Cyprus, control of the island should revert to its previous owner, Turkey, and not to Greece, which had never owned it, and, in May 1955, he defiantly changed his party's name to *Kıbrıs Türktür Partisi* (Cyprus is Turkish Party).

Of primary concern to the Turkish Cypriot leaders was the safety of their community. Because EOKA's aim was to bring about *enosis* and the Turkish Cypriots stood in the way of the fulfillment of that goal, the Turkish Cypriots were convinced that sooner or later Grivas' campaign of terror would be directed against them. Thus, they organized an anti-terrorist militia. However, this poorly armed and widely scattered force (which bore the theatrical name of *Volkan*, or Volcano) was no match for EOKA, which was led by a professional army man (Grivas) and had a large arsenal of weapons smuggled in from Greece. An incident, which occurred on June 21, 1955, dramatically illustrated how vulnerable the Turkish Cypriot community was to acts of terrorism: a time bomb which had been planted in a letterbox at the entrance of the Nicosia Central Police Station in the Turkish Cypriot quarter, exploded, wounding thirteen of the inhabitants.

The Turkish Cypriots hoped to secure military assistance from Turkey. But in spite of the fact that the government of Prime Minister Adnan Menderes was profoundly disturbed by events in Cyprus and was under great pressure by the Turkish press to intervene in the conflict, it was reluctant to interfere in what it considered as essentially a British problem. It was preoccupied with the threat of Soviet expansion and was eager to make NATO (which Greece and Turkey had joined in February 1952) and the Balkan Pact between Greece, Turkey and Yugoslavia (which had been signed in August 1954) work smoothly, which necessitated maintaining harmonious relations with both Great Britain and Greece. Furthermore, it was convinced that the British would never willingly leave Cyprus, owing to its strategic importance, and that, consequently, they would spare no effort to crush EOKA. Therefore, all it did was state publicly that it was opposed to any change in the status of the island. Certain that only the British could provide for their safety and that of their families, many young Turkish Cypriots then enrolled as auxiliaries in the British Security Forces. This, in turn, only strengthened Greek Cypriot resentment against the Turkish Cypriots and made every Turkish Cypriot a potential target of EOKA hit men. Thus, by 1956, the civil war in Cyprus had become an inter-communal war as well as a war of liberation.

During the early months of the civil war, the British vigorously resisted the EOKA onslaught. In September 1955, Prime Minister Anthony Eden appointed a tough, battle-hardened military man, Field Marshal Jóhn Harding, governor of Cyprus. After attempting unsuccessfully to negotiate a settlement of the conflict with Archbishop Makarios (October 1955-January 1956), Field Marshal Harding launched a major offensive against EOKA strongholds. In March 1956, Makarios and three other high-ranking Greek Orthodox churchmen were deported to the Seychelle islands, in the Indian ocean. Later that year, several of Grivas' guerrillas were executed. But the bungled Anglo-French invasion of the Suez canal area in October 1956 dealt a deathblow to Harding's ambition of wiping out EOKA. After the Suez fiasco, the strategic importance of Cyprus to the British was substantially reduced, for there were no longer any British interests in the canal area to protect. Consequently, the British displayed a growing eagerness to come to terms with the Greek Cypriot leadership. In December 1956 the British government presented a plan for the partial autonomy of the island (the so-called Radcliffe Constitution) which was promptly rejected by Greece but which was nevertheless used as a basis for further negotiations. Under Harold Macmillan, who succeeded Eden as prime minister of Great Britain in early 1957, efforts to bring about a peaceful solution to the conflict were further intensified. In March 1957, Makarios was released (though not allowed to return to Cyprus) and in October of that year Harding was dismissed.

Needless to say, the Turkish Cypriots viewed these developments with alarm. By then, they had become deeply committed to the British cause and they had come to rely on Harding's Security Forces for protection. However, a speech made by the British colonial secretary, Alan Lennox-Boyd, in the House of Commons in December 1956 gave them at least a glimmer of hope that they might survive a British withdrawal from the island. Hoping to deflate Makarios' argument (which was forcefully echoed by the Greek government at the United Nations) that self-determination was the only fair solution to the Cyprus problem, Lennox-Boyd maintained that if the Greek Cypriots had the right of self-determination so did the Turkish Cypriots. He then proposed that Cyprus be partitioned between Greece and Turkey. The idea immediately struck a responsive chord in Ankara and the Turkish Cypriot quarter of Nicosia, and "partition or death" became the slogan of the Turkish Cypriots during the remaining months of the civil war. Although the Turks had no territorial ambitions, they could, by advocating partition (or *taksim*, as they called it), put pressure upon the Greek and Greek Cypriot leaders to abandon their demand for *enosis* and settle instead for a compromise solution, namely the creation of an independent, bi-communal Cypriot state—a solution which appealed to the Turks because

1) It seemed to offer the Turkish Cypriot community a better chance of survival as a separate ethnic group than *enosis* did, and

2) It would prevent Greece from gaining control of the eastern Mediterranean and the approaches to the southern Anatolian littoral.

During 1957 Turkey became ever more directly involved in the Cyprus civil war and was thus able to exert added pressure on the Greek and Greek Cypriot leaders to reach an agreement which would take into account the wishes of the Turkish government and the leaders of the Turkish Cypriot community. What convinced the Turks to give up their hands-off policy towards Cyprus was a sharp increase in the volume of military assistance from Greece to EOKA and continued efforts on the part of the Greek government to champion the cause of the Greek Cypriot revolutionaries at the U.N. As Stavrinides has pointed out, "The Greek Cypriot and Greek leaders succeeded in making Cyprus an international issue, and this brought Turkey on the scene".[31]

The Turks denounced *enosis* with increasing vehemence and threatened military action to prevent it. At the same time, they provided the Turkish Cypriot self-defense forces with both military advisors and modern weapons. In November 1957, a Turkish colonel by the name of Rıza Vuruşkan founded a new Turkish Cypriot anti-terrorist organization which he called *Türk Mukavemet Teşkilatı* (Turkish Resistance Organization), but which became better known by its acronym TMT. Its purposes were:

1) To fill the vacuum in Turkish Cypriot defenses, which was daily becoming more apparent as EOKA was growing in strength;
2) To unify all existing Turkish Cypriot underground forces and coordinate the activities of all the *mücahit*s (literally, "champions of Islam"; in this case, Turkish Cypriot partisans);
3) To form ties with sympathizers in Turkey;
4) To inspire confidence among the Turkish Cypriots.[32]

The intervention of Turkey in the Cyprus civil war determined its outcome, for it guaranteed a stalemate. The simple facts were that whereas EOKA was stronger than TMT, Turkey was stronger than Greece. Moreover, England did not wish to antagonize either power by favoring one over the other. Realizing that all hope of achieving *enosis* in the immediate future had vanished, Premier Constantine Karamanlis of Greece and Archbishop Makarios at last decided to enter into negotiations with the Turks and the

---

31. Stavrinides, *op. cit.*, p. 30.

32. Bilge, *op. cit.*, p. 174; also Rauf Denktaş's article "TMT" in Manizade, *op. cit.*, pp. 160-161, and Serter, *op. cit.*, p. 115.

Turkish Cypriots, which they had refused to do until then, and to scale down their demands to conform to the new realities of the power game in Cyprus.

During the civil war 84 Turkish Cypriots lost their lives. Moreover, the Turkish Cypriot population of 13 mixed villages and one Turkish Cypriot village were chased out of their homes by Greek Cypriots, becoming refugees in other Turkish Cypriot enclaves.[33] Finally, the Turkish Cypriots, after having been squeezed out of all bi-communal administrative and business organizations when these were Hellenized, were forced to establish their own municipalities (June 1958), chamber of commerce (October 1958) and import and export corporation (November 1958).[34]

The exodus of Turkish Cypriots from mixed and isolated villages which began at that time was ultimately to lead to the physical separation of the Turkish Cypriot community from the Greek Cypriot community. The establishment of separate municipalities was the first step in the creation of two distinct administrations. Therefore, during the civil war the Greek Cypriots did not move the island closer to union with Greece but towards division into two separate states.

---

33. See Annex I.
34. Bilge, *op. cit.*, pp. 226-231.

CHAPTER V
RISE AND FALL OF THE CYPRIOT REPUBLIC

At two conferences, which took place in Zürich and London in 1959, the prime ministers of Greece and Turkey, Constantine Karamanlis and Adnan Menderes, in consultation with the leaders of the Greek Cypriot and Turkish Cypriot communities, Archbishop Makarios and Dr. Küçük, negotiated a settlement of the Cyprus conflict. The so-called Zürich-London Accords, which were signed by the prime minister of Great Britain, Harold Macmillan, as well as by the above-mentioned leaders, on February 19, provided for the creation of an independent, bi-communal Cypriot republic and furnished guidelines for the framing of a constitution. A Joint Constitutional Commission, composed of legal experts from Greece and Turkey, as well as from the Greek Cypriot and Turkish Cypriot communities, and chaired by a Swiss professor of international law, Marcel Bridel, then drafted the new constitution, taking some eighteen months to do so. Finally, on August 16, 1960, the constitution was signed by all parties concerned and Cyprus became an independent country.

This arrangement constituted a victory for the Turks and the Turkish Cypriots: by signing the Zürich-London Accords, Makarios officially abandoned *enosis* and, by signing the Constitution of 1960, he provided the Turkish Cypriots with the legal protection they needed to survive in a highly ethnocentric society.

According to the Constitution of 1960, Cyprus was to be bilingual, the two official languages being Greek and Turkish. The executive branch of the government was to consist of a Greek Cypriot president and a Turkish Cypriot vice-president, both to be elected by their respective communities. They were to be assisted by a Council of Ministers, seven of whom were to be Greek Cypriots and three of whom were to be Turkish Cypriots. A Turkish Cypriot was to be given one of the key ministries of defense, foreign affairs or finance. The Council of Ministers was to vote by simple majority on matters within its purview, but its decisions in the realms of foreign affairs, defense or security could be vetoed by either the president or vice-president.

The legislative branch of the government was to consist of a House of Representatives. Its fifty seats were to be allocated in such a way that thirty-five of them (or 70%) would be occupied by Greek Cypriots and fifteen of them (or 30%) would be occupied by Turkish Cypriots. Both groups of representatives were to be elected by their respective communities. The president of the House was to be a Greek Cypriot and the vice-president a Turkish Cypriot. The House was empowered to legislate on any matter except those specifically reserved for legislation by the Communal Chambers. It was to vote by simple majority, except in cases dealing with taxes, municipal affairs and modification of the electoral law. In such instances, separate majorities from both the Greek Cypriot and Turkish Cypriot members were needed to pass legislation.

Besides this unicameral legislature, there were to be separate Greek Cypriot and Turkish Cypriot Communal Chambers, the members of which were to be elected by their respective communities. Each Communal Chamber had complete jurisdiction with regard to religious and cultural affairs, educational policy, questions of personal status (e.g., marriage and eivorce), community activities (including co-operatives and credit societies), and the assessment and collection of personal taxes and fees for communal services. The House of Representatives was to allocate at least two million pounds from the annual budget to the Communal Chambers (80% of which was to be allocated to the Greek Cypriot Communal Chamber and 20% of which was to be allocated to the Turkish Cypriot Communal Chamber). The president and vice-president of the Republic were obligated to sign into law the legislative decisions of the Communal Chambers and had the responsibility of enforcing them. But a provision was added to the Constitution to the effect that within four years of its promulgation the president and the vice-president of the Republic were to decide whether or not this system of separate Greek Cypriot and Turkish Cypriot Communal Chambers was to continue.

The five major towns (Nicosia, Limassol, Famagousta, Larnaca and Paphos) were each to have its own separate Greek Cypriot and Turkish Cypriot municipalities with their respective elected councils. A co-ordinating committee was to be established in each town. This committee was to consist of two members from each council and was to be chaired by a president acceptable to both councils. Each village was to be administered by a *muhtar* (headman). In mixed villages the Greek Cypriot and Turkish Cypriot quarters were each to elect its own *muhtar*. Matters of common concern were to be handled by a village commission consisting of the two *muhtar*s and the elders of the two quarters.

The civil service was to be shared in such a way that in all grades the Greek Cypriots were to be given 70% and the Turkish Cypriots 30% of the positions. The same ratio was to be applied to the police and gendarmerie, which were to total two thousand men. However, the army, which was also to number two thousand, was to be divided in the ratio of 60/40. It was stipulated that at least one of the commanders of these forces (police, gendarmerie or army) was to be a Turkish Cypriot.

A Supreme Constitutional Court was to be established to rule on questions arising out of different interpretations of the Constitution and cases involving alleged violations of the Constitution, to arbitrate conflicts between the House of Representatives and the Communal Chambers, and to review decisions by the House or the Council of Ministers viewed as discriminatory by the president or vice-president of the Republic. It was to consist of a Greek

Cypriot judge, a Turkish Cypriot judge and a neutral presiding judge who was not to be a Cypriot, a Greek, a Turk or an Englishman, and who was to be appointed jointly by the president and the vice-president of the Republic.

A court of appeals, the High Court of Justice, was also to be set up. It was to have the same type of neutral presiding judge as the Supreme Constitutional Court. But in this case there were to be two Greek Cypriot judges and only one Turkish Cypriot judge. On the other hand, the presiding judge was to be provided with two votes.

Finally, a Treaty of Guarantee between Great Britain, Greece and Turkey was signed to "ensure the recognition and maintenance of the independence, territorial integrity, and security of the Republic of Cyprus by preventing direct or indirect *enosis* or partition or annexation by any of the three guarantor states".[1] In case of a breach of this treaty, the guarantor states shared the collective responsibility of taking "the necessary steps to ensure observance" of the relevant provisions.[2] But in cases in which "common or concerted action [should] prove impossible" each of the guarantor states was given "the right to take action with the sole aim of reestablishing the state of affairs established by the present Treaty.[3] An additional guarantee of the status of the island was provided by a Treaty of Alliance between Cyprus, Greece and Turkey according to which 950 Greek and 650 Turkish soldiers under the command of a Tripartite Headquarters were to be stationed in Cyprus. The leadership of this joint force, which was also to train the new Cypriot army, was to be rotated annually among the three signatories.

When Cyprus became independent, there was every reason to be optimistic about its future: its agriculture was booming, with record quantities of carobs, cereals, citrus

---

1. Xydis, *Cyprus: Reluctant Republic*, p. 409.
2. *Ibid.*, p. 410.
3. *Ibid.*

fruit, potatoes and wine products being exported; its mining industry was thriving; the two large military bases which the British had kept on the island were providing jobs, as well as much needed foreign revenue; tourism was making a promising start. Even the Turkish Cypriots were, by and large, satisfied with their lot, believing that the guarantees built into the Constitution would protect them from further oppression. They were able to work and move about freely, they were rarely insulted or harassed by their Greek Cypriot neighbors, and they were able to profit from the general economic prosperity of the island.

But political dissension soon shook the new Cypriot Republic to its foundations. In 1960, Archbishop Makarios, who had been elected its first president, insightfully remarked that the Constitution, which he had helped to draft, had created a state but not a nation. As chief of state, it was Makarios' responsibility to develop a sense of nationhood among his people, and there is no doubt that he had the deft political touch necessary to reconcile the two long-feuding communities in his realm. Moreover, he had emerged from the civil war with a reputation for moderation, which would have been eminently useful to him had he chosen to be a man of peace.[4] But it quickly became obvious that he was still committed to bringing about *enosis*, and that he regarded the establishment of the Republic as a mere tactical maneuver in his struggle to attain this goal. Even before Cyprus celebrated her independence, he had begun to complain that he had been forced to sign the Zürich-London Accords, and to argue that, contrary to what some of his critics were saying, he had never wavered in his determination to achieve *enosis*. In a speech at Nicosia, on April 1, 1960, he had made the following controversial remarks:

---

4. His break with Grivas, which had become complete when the latter, on July 29, 1959, formally "dissociated" himself from the Zürich-London Accords, had reinforced belief in his relative mildness.

The realization of our hopes and aspirations is not complete under the Zürich and London Agreements. . . . The glorious liberation struggle, whose fifth anniversary we celebrate today, has secured for us advanced bastions and impregnable strongholds for our independence. From these bastions we will continue the struggle to complete victory.[5]

When Makarios chose the Greek Cypriot members of the Council of Ministers, the Turkish Cypriots were deeply disturbed to find that one of the most fanatical of the EOKA terrorists, Polykarpos Yorgadjis, had been named Minister of the Interior, with responsibility for internal security, and that another one, Tassos Papadopoulos, had been entrusted with the sensitive portfolio of Minister of Labor.

As president of newly independent Cyprus, Makarios continued to deliver inflammatory speeches which left no room for doubt as to his ultimate intentions. During a sermon at Kykko monastery on August 15, 1962, he stated that "Greek Cypriots must continue to march forward to complete the work begun by the EOKA heroes", and that "the struggle is continuing in a new form, and will go on until we achieve our goal".[6] In a speech in his native village of Panayia, on September 4, 1962, he made the even more ominous statement that "Unless this small Turkish community forming a part of the Turkish race which has been the terrible enemy of Hellenism is expelled, the duty of the heroes of EOKA can never be considered as terminated".[7] His cabinet ministers spoke in a similar vein. In 1962 Yorgadjis publicly declared that "There is no place in Cyprus for anyone who is not Greek, who does not think Greek and who does not constantly feel Greek".[8]

In order to inspire among the Greek Cypriots new heights of Hellenistic passion, Makarios made liberal use of the Greek Cypriot schools and the services of the Greek Cypriot-controlled Cyprus Broadcasting Corporation. In the schools, the British journalist Michael Wall informs us, children were

---

5. Stavrinides, *op. cit.*, p. 40.
6. Osman Örek, *Makarios on Enosis* (Nicosia, 1974), p. 22.
7. *Ibid.*
8. Letter to the Editor of the *Wall Street Journal*, by Nail Atalay, Representative of the Turkish Federated State of Cyprus at the United Nations, dated June 29, 1978.

taught that "Cyprus is Greek—and that the Turks are in-
truders", with the result that they emerged "more Greek
than they were".[9] As for the Cyprus Broadcasting Corporation, it regularly broadcast virulently anti-Turkish plays.
In one of the latter, a mother asks her son what he wants
to become, to which he replies "a hero". When she asks
him "what will you bring us?" he answers "I am going to
bring seven Turkish heads to you".[10]

The Greek flag flew over the Presidential Palace in Nicosia and on Makarios' official limousine.

Makarios hoped ultimately to present his case to the
United Nations and argue that the Zürich-London Accords
were invalid since they had never been submitted for approval to the Cypriot people, and that the only just solution
to the Cyprus problem would be to apply the principle of
self-determination, according to which the will of the majority would prevail. Inasmuch as the United States, the United
Kingdom, Greece and Turkey all upheld the status quo in
Cyprus, Makarios quickly realized that he could not expect
any support from the West at the United Nations. Therefore, he pursued an increasingly pro-Third World and even
pro-Soviet foreign policy. This was very much against the
wishes of Dr. Küçük, who had been elected vice-president
of Cyprus by the Turkish Cypriot community. Dr. Küçük
believed that the future prosperity and safety of Cyprus
could best be guaranteed by good relations with the Western
powers and NATO, to which Cyprus was linked through
its Treaty of Alliance with Greece and Turkey. But although
he had a constitutional right of veto in foreign affairs, Dr.
Küçük was unable to exercise any influence in that field.
Makarios insisted upon making all foreign policy decisions
on his own and controlled the Republic's chief outlets to
the outside world—the Minister of Foreign Affairs and the
ambassadors to the United Nations, the United States and

9. "Cyprus—Island of Hate and Fear", *The New York Times Magazine*, March 8, 1964, p. 93.

10. Telegram to the U.N. by Dr. Fazıl Küçük, dated November 24,
1978.

the United Kingdom, all of whom were Greek Cypriots. As a result, Dr. Küçük usually learned about important foreign policy decisions only by reading the newspapers, and the foreign policy of the nation remained one which had no other purpose but to gather support for *enosis*—in other words, the destruction of Cyprus as an independent nation.

Makarios felt confident that once he had obtained the backing of the United Nations for his scheme to bring about *enosis* through the application of the principle of self-determination, he would be able to crush the Turkish Cypriots without fear of outside intervention. This required extensive military preparations. Accordingly, Interior Minister Yorgadjis was ordered to organize a new EOKA-like secret army. In the words of the late Professor Richard A. Patrick, one of the outstanding authorities on modern Cyprus:

> The clandestine recruiting, training and organizing of the Greek-Cypriot 'secret army' began early in 1961. Although the EOKA organization of the 1955-1959 campaign had been disbanded, many of its weapons had never been handed over to the Cyprus police and the loyalties and obligations of its cells remained intact. These cells became the cadres of the new force. In 1962, weapons training for company-sized units was being conducted in the Troodos Mountains under the guidance of the Greek-Cypriot officer-cadets of the Cyprus Army and using arms 'borrowed' from government armories. By December 1963, there were up to 10,000 Greek Cypriots who had been recruited and trained to some extent.[11]

11. *Political Geography and the Cyprus Conflict: 1963-1971* (Waterloo, Ontario, 1976), pp. 37-38. There were also armed Greek Cypriot gangs who refused to be integrated into the "official secret army". Some of these remained loyal to Colonel Grivas, who lived in self-imposed exile in Greece. According to Patrick, the prime objectives of these gangs were "to exact revenge on Turk-Cypriots for events which occurred during the enosis campaign of 1955-1959, to indulge their fantasies for adventure, and to enhance their own local social and political positions" (*ibid.*, p. 36). These elements were probably responsible for setting five small bombs in two mosques in Nicosia on March 25, 1962 (Greece's Independence Day).

Overtures were made to the Karamanlis government to help supply this growing force. But Karamanlis, apparently fearing a strong Turkish reaction, refused to do so. Nonetheless, a large amount of war materiel was smuggled in from Greece, where there were still substantial arms caches dating from World War II and the civil war which followed it.[12]

At the same time, Makarios tried to wipe out all the advantages gained by the Turkish Cypriots at the conference table by blatantly violating many of the articles of the Constitution of 1960, which he had signed and which, as president of Cyprus, he was pledged to uphold. Because these articles were designed to protect the Turkish Cypriot community from official persecution, Makarios' actions were stubbornly resisted by the Turkish Cypriot leaders and led to a series of bitter controversies, the major ones of which were:

1) *The Security Services Controversy:* When independence was declared, the Makarios government at once dismissed hundreds of Turkish Cypriot policemen on the grounds that they were auxiliaries who had been hired only on a temporary basis during the civil war and that their number exceeded that allowed by the Constitution (which was 600, or 30% of the Security Services personnel). It then replaced them with Greek Cypriots, many of whom were former EOKA fighters. "Not only was the ratio not maintained", the distinguished British historian H. D. Purcell noted,

> but auxiliary Greek police were created far in excess of the 2,000 total for the Security Services which were permitted by the constitution. Many of the extra appointments here also went to ex-EOKA men, and both in the police and the gendarmerie many of those promoted had previously belonged to that organization.[13]

The leaders of the Turkish Cypriot community repeatedly complained about these abuses, but their words fell on deaf ears.

---

12. *Ibid.*, p. 38.
13. *Cyprus* (London, 1969), pp. 315-316.

2) *The Civil Service Controversy*: When Cyprus became independent, Greek Cypriots already held most of the positions in the civil service and they were reluctant to surrender any of these to their Turkish Cypriot neighbors. In order to implement the 70/30 ratio assigned to the civil service, a "Public Service Commission", consisting of seven Greek Cypriots and three Turkish Cypriots was set up. Realizing that it would take some time for this body to reorganize the entire civil service, Dr. Küçük agreed not to insist upon full compliance with the Constitution on the question of the ratio for a period of five months. However, it soon became unmistakably clear that the Greek Cypriot majority of the Commission had no intention of meeting this deadline. All sorts of excuses were found to delay implementation of the ratio. It was said, for example, that there were not enough qualified Turkish Cypriot candidates to fill the positions in question. But, according to the census of 1960, the Turkish Cypriots had more than their share of college graduates.[14] Moreover, to judge by the number of administrative posts left vacant during the years following independence, the Greek Cypriots themselves suffered from a shortage of trained civil servants. In spite of repeated demands by the leaders of the Turkish Cypriot community that the Commission get on with its work, the latter never completed its task, with the result that the 70/30 ratio mandated by the Constitution was never attained. Even those candidates whose appeals to the Constitutional Court were successful were frequently denied employment by means of various subterfuges, such as prolonging the term of service of the Greek Cypriot civil servants who were scheduled to be replaced.

3) *The Armed Forces Controversy*: According to Article 132 of the Constitution, "Forces which are stationed in parts of the territory of the Republic inhabited in a proportion

---

14. There were then 3,274 Greek and Turkish Cypriots with a university education, of whom 2,634 or 80.5% were Greek Cypriots and 640 or 19.5% were Turkish Cypriots.

approaching one hundred per centum only by members of one Community shall belong to that Community". To Dr. Küçük, this article mandated the formation of separate Greek Cypriot and Turkish Cypriot units, at least at the platoon and company levels. He felt that such a system was vital for the safety of his community. The fact that all 150 Greek Cypriot officers chosen for the force were ex-EOKA men led him to suspect that sooner or later the Cypriot army would be used against his people and he did not want to leave the many scattered and vulnerable Turkish Cypriot enclaves unprotected. He also believed that differences of language, religion and disciplinary standards would make a completely integrated force unworkable. But Archbishop Makarios insisted upon the formation of a monolithic force which he could control and, on October 20, 1961, he introduced a motion in the Council of Ministers to integrate the armed forces at every level. Because the Greek Cypriots had a majority of seats in the Council of Ministers, the motion was approved. This left Dr. Küçük with no option but to veto the measure. Because Makarios refused to accept any compromise, a stalemate ensued. As a consequence, no national army was created and the Greek Cypriot officers were used to train the secret army which was being readied for action against the Turkish Cypriot community.

4) *The Municipalities Controversy:* According to Evangelos Averoff-Tossizza, the Greek Foreign Minister at the time of the Zürich and London conferences, it was the Greek Cypriots who, during the negotiations, were the chief advocates of the creation of separate Greek Cypriot and Turkish Cypriot municipalities within the five major towns of Cyprus.[15] But after independence, Markarios, who was mandated by the Constitution to establish these separate municipalities, refused to do so on the grounds that it would amount to at least a partial endorsement of *taksim.*

---

15. Robert Stephens, *Cyprus: A Place of Arms* (New York, 1966), p. 176.   The reason for that stand was probably that the Greek Cypriots did not want to bear the economic burden of having to develop the generally poorer Turkish Cypriot neighborhoods. Stephens was the Foreign Editor and Diplomatic Correspondent of *The Observer.*

To the Turkish Cypriots separate municipal governments meant a guarantee that basic services would be maintained in the Turkish Cypriot quarters of the towns. Having been forced to form their own municipalities in 1958, the Turkish Cypriot townspeople had become used to managing their own affairs. They had also come to believe that the existence of separate municipalities was necessary to preserve their own cultural and social identity. As a foreign observer noted, for the Turkish Cypriots the retention of separate municipalities "became the main test of how far the Greeks genuinely accepted the separate identity of the Turkish community".[16] The issue was made complicated by the fact that the Constitution did not specify how the separate municipalities were to be organized. It merely stipulated that laws in this regard were to be promulgated within the first six months of the new administration. Generally speaking, there was a *de facto* territorial separation between the two communities in each of the major towns of Cyprus, for during the civil war the beleaguered Turkish Cypriot townspeople had formed self-contained and largely self-sufficient socio-political units with well-defined boundaries. To the Turkish Cypriots, therefore, the concept of separate municipalities could be understood only territorially. But Makarios regarded such enclaves as states within the state, and he proposed instead the setting up of a single municipal authority in each town based upon proportional representation of the Greek Cypriot and Turkish Cypriot population. In this he had the backing of the Greek Cypriot business community, for there were a number of Greek Cypriot-owned factories in the Turkish quarters of the towns, where cheap labor had traditionally been plentiful, and the owners did not want their plants to fall within Turkish Cypriot jurisdiction.

While these conflicting views were being debated, a bill was passed by the House of Representatives extending by three months the British-promulgated laws regarding municipal organization, which recognized the separate municipalities

---

16. *Ibid.*

established by the Turkish Cypriots in 1958 and which were to expire on December 31, 1960. Because of the failure of the contending parties to come to terms, this deadline was extended several more times after March 1961. In December 1962, Makarios abruptly announced his opposition to any further prolongation of the status quo. Even though he had not come to any agreement with the Turkish Cypriot leaders on the drafting of new legislation, he asserted that the granting of yet another extension of existing legislation would "lead to dangerous suspense which would be a permanent obstacle to finding a reasonable solution".[17] In the hope of overcoming this obstacle, the Turkish Cypriot Communal Chamber, on December 29, approved a measure designed to retain the Turkish Cypriot municipalities in the five major towns of Cyprus after January 1, 1963, and to establish an additional municipality in the predominantly Turkish Cypriot town of Lefka. Makarios at once denounced the measure. He proclaimed the abolition of all municipalities and ordered their replacement by government-appointed bodies. On January 2, 1963, the Council of Ministers voted to implement this decision by invoking a law enacted under British colonial rule empowering the government to declare any district to be an "improvement area" under the administration of an "improvement board" appointed by the state. Thus, the five major towns of Cyprus were designated as "improvement areas" and steps were taken to set up "improvement boards" to run local services. This was, naturally, unacceptable to the Turkish Cypriots. They refused to recognize the new boards and continued to manage their own municipal affairs independently of the central government. In this particular case, Makarios even defied his own Supreme Constitutional Court. As Dr. Christian Heinze, the assistant to the president of the Court, recalls:

---

17. *The Times* (of London), January 1, 1963. p. 9e.

When at last one of the violations of the Constitution by the Greek Cypriots of the gravest political consequence to the Turkish Cypriots, namely a violation of the Constitutional provision for separate Greek and Turkish municipal administration in the five towns, was brought before the Supreme Constitutional Court of the Republic of Cyprus, the Greeks lost their case. But even before, and all the more after the Judgment given in April 1963, the Greek part of the Cypriot government announced that they would ignore the decision. This meant that the violation of the Constitution had now become officially judicially notorious, and that the only independent instance in Cyprus before which disputes between Greek and Turkish Cypriots could be brought, the Supreme Constitutional Court, had been rendered impotent.[18]

5. *The Tax Controversy*: According to Article 78 of the Constitution, taxes levied on all Cypriots had to be approved by separate majorities of the Greek Cypriot and Turkish Cypriot contingents in the House of Representatives. The Constitution, therefore, gave the Turkish Cypriots the right to veto any proposed tax legislation. This was an important prerogative, for it was the only means by which the Turkish Cypriot leaders could exert any pressure on the Makarios regime to adhere to the Constitution. Under Article 188 of the Constitution, British tax laws could remain in effect until December 31, 1960, in order to give the House of Representatives sufficient time to prepare new laws. Inasmuch as no agreement on new legislation had been reached by that time, the deadline was extended for a three-month period. In March 1961 the Greek Cypriot representatives suggested a further three-month extension. But the Turkish Cypriot leaders, arguing that part of the revenue from taxation was being improperly spent to hire Greek Cypriot civil servants in excess of the ratio dictated by the Constitution and that another part of it was being unfairly apportioned as development aid so that their community's needs were being neglected, refused to extend the deadline for a full three-month period. However, they declared themselves

18. *The Cyprus Conflict*, Second Edition (Nicosia, 1977), p. 20.

willing to accept a two-month extension. As the Turkish Cypriot representative, Cemil Ramadan, explained:

> There are, according to the basic provisions of the Constitution, certain rights for the Turkish community, like the seventy: thirty and the geographical separation of the municipalities, which must not remain perpetually in abeyance. . . . When the three-month extension was granted, we were given the promise from those directly concerned that these problems would be solved. . . . Therefore, with this promise we voted for the extension. Unfortunately, the same situation exists today. In spite of these bitter truths, I am in favor of extending [the tax laws] for two months. This we are doing for the *last time* in order to show our good faith [and] to give time to those directly concerned to solve the pending problems.[19]

The Greek Cypriot leaders rejected this compromise proposal, for, in the words of the constitutional authority, Stanley Kyriakides, they felt that a shorter extension "would give the Turkish Cypriots an opportunity to bring pressures upon the solution of the other existing tension problems".[20] A deadlock ensued. Thereupon, Makarios illegally ordered the revenue collecting departments of the government to continue functioning after the March 31 deadline, and the Turkish Cypriot leaders reciprocated by urging all Turkish Cypriot importers to refuse to pay duties or taxes to the central government. Reflecting upon these events, the Greek Cypriot president of the House of Representatives, Glafkos Klerides, said:

> Some of the Honorable Turkish members demanded to parallel the matter of the tax extension with that of the seventy:thirty.... But I fail to see the connection between the seventy:thirty and the extension of the tax law. If there is a belief that some departments of Government do not abide by the Constitution, surely there is the proper mechanism in the Constitution through which the Vice-President and those whose interests and rights are violated to ask the Supreme Constitutional Court to decide about these matters.[21]

---

19. Quoted in Stanley Kyriakides, *Cyprus: Constitutionalism and Crisis Government* (Philadelphia, 1968), p. 86.

20. *Op. cit.*, p. 85.

21. Quoted in *ibid.*, p. 87.

But we have already seen that when the Turkish Cypriots appealed to the Supreme Constitutional Court in the matter concerning the establishment of the "improvement boards", the Makarios regime chose to ignore its decision.

A new crisis erupted in December 1961, when the Makarios government introduced an income tax bill in the House of Representatives. The Turkish Cypriot leaders agreed to support the bill on condition that the schedule of rates be reviewed annually or, at least, every two years. Otherwise, Dr. Küçük maintained, the Turkish Cypriots would lose "their last chance to remind their Greek brethren of their constitutional obligations towards the Turks".[22] But Archbishop Makarios was determined to deny the Turkish Cypriots any further opportunity of using their weapon of last resort—the veto. He rejected their proposal. Thereupon, the Turkish Cypriots, certain that by voting for the tax bill they would lose whatever influence they still retained over government policy, vetoed it. When he was informed of the Turkish Cypriot decision, Makarios angrily declared that, "taking into consideration the general interest of the people of Cyprus", he intended to "disregard any constitutional provision which, if abused, might obstruct the regular functioning of the state".[23] He also threatened to delay indefinitely the establishment of the new Cypriot army and the application of the 70/30 ratio in the civil service.[24] Finally, he launched a propaganda campaign to convince the world that by using their veto power to block tax legislation, the Turkish Cypriots were deliberately sabotaging all government activity and making a mockery of the Constitution—charges which the Turkish Cypriots were unable effectively to refute because the Greek Cypriots controlled not only all of the country's key diplomatic outlets but also the Cyprus Broadcasting Corporation. In an effort to circumvent the Turkish Cypriot

---

22. Quoted in Purcell, *op. cit.*, p. 313.

23. *Ibid.*

24. *The Times* (of London), December 23, 1961, p. 5b.

veto, Makarios ordered the Greek Cypriots to pay a special temporary tax through the Greek Cypriot Communal Chamber. The Turkish Cypriot leaders then reciprocated by ordering the members of their community to refuse to pay their taxes to the central government, but instead to pay an equivalent amount to the Turkish Cypriot Communal Chamber.

6) *The Constitutional Court Controversy*: In 1960, Archbishop Makarios and Dr. Küçük both approved the nomination of Dr. Ernst Forsthoff, a distinguished German jurist and a professor at the University of Heidelberg, as the neutral president of the Supreme Constitutional Court, and that of Dr. Heinze as his assistant. But these two jurists, because they condemned Makarios' violations of the Constitution, soon became major irritants to the Greek Cypriot leadership. Accordingly, a campaign of hate and rumor-mongering was launched to discredit them and force them to resign. Dr. Forsthoff was accused of having been a "minor Nazi official", and was characterized as "a second-rate professor of the University of Heidelberg".[25] Dr. Heinze was described as "living luxuriously on Turkish bribery money" and even received threats against his life.[26] Early in 1963, Dr. Heinze asked the attorney-general of Cyprus, Kriton Tornarides, to investigate these threats. When the latter refused to do so, Dr. Heinze resigned. Then, on May 21, 1963, Dr. Forsthoff, in turn, handed in his resignation. Looking back upon the 1960-1963 period, Dr. Heinze was to come to the following conclusion:

> Failure to achieve a joint legislation was not due to the incompetency of those concerned, but to the fact that the ruling group of Greek Cypriots made no serious effort to co-operate or arrive at a compromise, but insisted with growing determination on ignoring and abolishing the existing Constitution. For this reason the practicability of the Constitution could never be tested. The reason for its failure is rather due to lack of good will to make use of it.[27]

---

25. Purcell, *op. cit.*, p. 317.
26. *Ibid.*
27. Heinze, *op. cit.*, p. 25.

When inter-communal fighting broke out in December 1963
(see Chapter VI), Dr. Forsthoff observed to a U.P.I. correspondent in Heidelberg that "From the moment Makarios
started openly to deprive Turkish Cypriots of their rights,
the present events were inevitable".[28]

Once the Supreme Constitutional Court had been effectively neutralized, Makarios was able to devote all his energies to bringing about the complete dissolution of the Republic. There was no need to wait until the United Nations
had backed his demand for self-determination to bring
matters to a head.[29] Now that much of the world was willing to believe that the Turkish Cypriots had made the

28. Zaim M. Nedjatigil, *Cyprus: Constitutional Proposals and
Developments* (Nicosia, 1977), p. 72.

29. In any case, the idea of convincing the United Nations to back
up *enosis* was doomed to frustration from the very start owing to
the intrinsic weakness of Makarios' argument. As Professor Franz
Georg Maier, of the University of Frankfurt, has pointed out (*Cyprus
from Earliest Times to the Present Day*, London, 1968, pp. 142-143):
    The Greek sympathies of the majority of Cypriots do not in
    themselves justify the demand for Union with Greece. It is high-
    ly questionable whether, as so frequently claimed, they provide
    a historic and legal basis for Cypriot claims. Cyprus has never
    been part of Greece in the present-day sense, although it be-
    longed to the Greek-dominated empire of the Ptolemies in
    Alexander's reign and was again governed by a Greek ruling
    class in Byzantine times. But the modern Greek national state
    cannot plausibly claim to be the inheritor of these empires. A
    right to union derived from former membership of the Greek
    state therefore does not exist. . . .
    The champions of Enosis invoke the United Nations charter
    even more than historic links. As the majority on the island, so
    they argue, the Greek Cypriots should be granted Union with
    Greece. No water-tight foundation, however, exists anywhere
    in international law for the restitution of a colony to the coun-
    try whence the majority of its inhabitants originally came.
    Above all, we must ask whether the right to self determination,
    so loudly demanded, has any relevance to Cyprus, where the
    Turks, who amount to 23 per cent of the population, might
    well be considered a second nation rather than a minority.
It is also a fact that the Charter of the United Nations does not pre-
scribe the right of self-determination in any of its articles. For a discussion of this, see Linda B. Miller, *World Order and Local Disorder*
(Princeton, N.J., 1967), p. 132.

Constitution unworkable by their irresponsible use of the veto, the Constitution could be unilaterally altered, for the official purpose of eliminating such abuses but actually to achieve *enosis* by legal means. In order to implement this scheme, Makarios entrusted Polykarpos Yorgadjis, Tassos Papadopoulos and Glafkos Klerides with the task of formulating a secret plan of action. This plan, the famous "Akritas Plan", which was first published by the Greek newspaper *Patris*, on April 21, 1966, was signed by a person who identified himself, somewhat mysteriously, as "The Chief, Akritas", but was, in fact, none other than Yorgadjis, the very man who at that time was responsible for maintaining internal peace on the island. It was a blueprint for a coup within the government to achieve *enosis* and to wipe out all opposition before it had a chance to solidify. The first step in this process was to be the adoption by the government, on a unilateral basis, of a series of amendments to the Constitution. The amendments in question would seem "reasonable and just", but would actually deprive the Turkish community in Cyprus of its most cherished prerogatives. Although the Turkish Cypriots were not to be given the opportunity to reject these amendments, they were to be mollified by being made to feel that the Makarios regime was always "ready for peaceful talks". Should some of the Turkish Cypriots "react strongly", they were at once to be subdued by an overwhelming display of force. "If we show our strength to the Turks, immediately and forcefully", the plan asserted, "then they will probably be brought to their senses and restrict their activities to insignificant, isolated incidents". Speed would be of the essence in such a military undertaking, "since, if we manage to become masters of the situation within a day or two outside intervention would not be possible, probable or justifiable". It was also predicted that "the forceful and decisive suppressing of any Turkish effort will greatly facilitate our subsequent actions for further constitutional amendments, and it should then be possible to apply these without the Turks being able to show any reaction".

Should clashes become "widespread", the Greek Cypriots were not only to use all military means at their disposal to crush the dissenters, but were also to issue an "immediate declaration of *enosis*", because there would then be "no need to wait or to engage in diplomatic activity". However, should there be time for diplomatic endeavor, the whole world would have to be convinced that

1) The Zürich-London Accords were "not satisfactory or just",
2) The Zürich-London Accords were not "the result of the free will of the contending parties",
3) The demand for revision of the Accords does not arise from "any desire on the part of the Greeks to dishonour their signature", but from an "imperative necessity of survival for them",
4) "The co-existence of the two communities is possible", and
5) "The Greek majority, and not the Turks, constitute the strong element on which foreigners must rely".

The second point was especially to be stressed for, as the plan points out:

It has been an important trump card in our hands that the solution brought by the Agreements [Accords] was not submitted to the approval of the people; acting wisely in this respect our leadership avoided holding a referendum. Otherwise, the people would have definitely approved the Agreements in the atmosphere that prevailed in 1959.[30]

Faithfully adhering to the "Akritas Plan", Makarios, on November 30, 1963, submitted thirteen proposed amendments to the Constitution under the heading "Suggested Measures for Facilitating the Smooth Functioning of the State and for the Removal of Certain Causes of Inter-Communal Friction". According to these,

1) The president and vice-president of the Republic were both to lose their veto power,

---

30. A copy of the "Akritas Plan" is to be found in Stavrinides, *op. cit.*, pp. 135-143, and Nedjatigil, *op. cit.*, pp. 74-81.

2) The vice-president of the Republic was to stand in for the president in case of the latter's temporary absence or incapacitation,

3) The Greek Cypriot president of the House of Representatives and the Turkish Cypriot vice-president of that body were to be elected by the House as a whole,

4) The vice-president of the House of Representatives was to stand in for the president of that body in case of the latter's temporary absence or incapacitation,

5) Separate majorities for the enactment of certain laws by the House of Representatives were to be abolished,

6) Unified municipalities were to be established,

7) The administration of justice was to be unified,

8) The division of security forces into police and gendarmerie was to be abolished,

9) The numerical strength of the security forces and the army was to be determined by law rather than by the Constitution,

10) The proportion of Greek Cypriots and Turkish Cypriots in the civil service, the security forces and the army was to be modified to reflect the actual ethnic ratio of the Cypriot population,

11) The membership of the Public Service Commission was to be reduced from ten to five,

12) All decisions of the Public Service Commission were to be taken by simple majority vote, and

13) The Greek Cypriot Communal Chamber was to be abolished with no constraint on the Turkish Cypriot Communal Chamber to abolish itself as well.[31]

These demands, which seemed "reasonable and just" to many foreign observers who had been made to believe that Turkish Cypriot obstructionism was the principal cause of

---

31. For the full text of Makarios' proposed amendments, see Halil İbrahim Salih, *Cyprus: The Impact of Diverse Nationalism on a State* (University of Alabama, 1978), pp. 132-143.

the prevailing governmental paralysis, were, of course, unacceptable to the Turkish Cypriots. The projected amendments would have deprived them of the veto power which alone prevented the Greek Cypriot leaders from destroying the Republic and achieving *enosis* by legal means. They would also have stripped them of the only organization on which they could rely for protection in the towns, namely the separate municipalities. Finally, they would have given the Greek Cypriots complete control over the Public Service Commission.

The submission of the proposed amendments inevitably precipitated a major constitutional crisis which, in turn, led to renewed inter-communal fighting, as foreseen by the "Akritas Plan". This crisis came at a very inopportune time for the Turkish Cypriots: Adnan Menderes, the charismatic Turkish premier who had championed the cause of *taksim* during the civil war and had saved the Turkish Cypriots from certain disaster, had been overthrown in May 1960, and now, in December 1963, Turkey was facing a government crisis of its own as the aged İsmet İnönü was attempting to form a new cabinet; in Greece, Premier Karamanlis, who had exercised a restraining influence on Makarios, had resigned in June 1963; the United States was preoccupied with the trauma of President Kennedy's assassination.

The Turkish Cypriots were largely on their own and had to make the most of whatever political organizations they possessed. The most powerful of these was the Turkish Cypriot Communal Chamber. That body had become a Turkish Cypriot parliament in spite of itself. Originally, the Turkish Cypriots had hoped that the central government would minister to their needs and protect their rights as citizens. That is why they so steadfastly insisted on strict compliance with the provisions of the Constitution. But when the central government became mired in deadlock and the Makarios regime began to defy the Constitution ever more brazenly, they were forced to depend more and more on their Communal Chamber for basic services. Thus, the fulcrum of power in the Turkish Cypriot community shifted from the Council of Ministers and the House of Representatives to the Turkish Cypriot Communal Chamber. Two other factors accounted for the growing importance of this body: it had become the only tax collecting agency in the Turkish Cypriot community as a result of the failure of the House of Representatives to reach an agreement on tax legislation, and it was ably led by its president, Rauf Denktaş, who had been one of the chief architects of the Constitution and was now reluctantly assuming many of the responsibilities of a chief of state for his politically ostracized people.

The Turkish Cypriots were, therefore, not leaderless as they faced renewed turbulence. Nor were they entirely defenseless. As the clouds of civil war were gathering, TMT was revived and weapons were smuggled in from Turkey. But TMT remained essentially a local militia with very limited objectives. As Patrick wrote:

> Turk-Cypriot military planning. . . concentrated on preparations for sealing off Turk-Cypriot quarters in the larger towns from Greek-Cypriot mobs and snipers, fortifying Turk-Cypriot villages against Greek-Cypriot police patrols, and by being prepared to counter abductions and assassinations by reprisals in kind.[32]

---

32. *Op. cit*, p. 37.

CHAPTER VI
THE 1963-1964 CRISIS

In an interview published in a major Athenian daily, Lieutenant General George Karayannis, the Greek commander of the Cyprus National Guard during the 1963-1964 crisis, candidly stated: "When the Turks objected to the amendment of the Constitution, Archbishop Makarios put his plan into effect and the Greek attack began in December 1963".[1] But actually the fighting started even before the Turkish Cypriot leaders had had time to complete their study of the proposed amendments and draft an official reply.

Throughout December tensions steadily rose as the Greek Cypriots made their final preparations for the impending conflict and behaved in an ever more provocative fashion. Elias Kyrou, the correspondent for the Salonica newspaper *Ellinikos Vorras*, who was visiting Cyprus, was "warned of a coming all-out attack on the Turks",[2] and Interior Minister Yorgadjis, who had been entrusted with the task of organizing this attack, urged ex-EOKA Special Branch officers to assume a "tough and merciless attitude" towards their Turkish Cypriot neighbors.[3] Roadblocks were then set up by illegally armed Greek Cypriot civilians hired as "special constables" by Yorgadjis. There, Turkish Cypriot motorists were frisked and summoned (often to the accompaniment of blows and insults) to show their identification papers. These body searches were deeply resented by the Turkish Cypriots, especially when women were subjected to them.

---

1. *Ethnikos Kiryx*, June 15, 1965 (Quoted in Purcell, *op. cit.*, p. 323).

2. Purcell, *op. cit.*, p. 323.

3. *Ibid.*

In the early morning of Saturday, December 21, when Greek Cypriot "special constables" attempted to search a woman in the Turkish Cypriot quarter of Nicosia, an angry crowd formed. The "constables" thereupon fired their automatic weapons, nearly cutting the woman and her male escort in half. These murders were the opening salvo in the Greek Cypriot offensive.

Following the slaughter of the Turkish Cypriot couple, the "constables" stood on the street corners, firing randomly at passing vehicles. Other Greek Cypriot civilians then joined them, shooting from the windows of their cars as they sped through the Turkish Cypriot quarter. Groups of armed men also fired on the statue of Atatürk, near Kyrenia Gate, and into the offices of Rauf Denktaş. Alarmed by these acts of wanton aggression, Dr. Küçük and Osman Örek, who since 1960 had been serving as Minister of Defense, rushed to the Paphos Gate police station to complain to Interior Minister Yorgadjis. They were amazed to find the place already heavily fortified. Back home, the two Turkish Cypriot leaders issued a statement appealing for calm, but the Greek Cypriot manager of the Cyprus Broadcasting Corporation refused to broadcast the message.

Later that morning, shots were fired into the playground of the Turkish Boys' Lycée in Nicosia, injuring two boys, and at a car carrying eight Turkish Cypriot school children, aged five to seven. While these new outrages were being perpetrated, Dr. Küçük and the Turkish Cypriot cabinet ministers were at the Presidential Palace, urging Archbishop Makarios and Interior Minister Yorgadjis to bring an end to the bloodshed. Although Yorgadjis made the preposterous accusation that the Turkish Cypriots shot their own people, Makarios appeared to be in a conciliatory mood, which encouraged the Turkish Cypriot leaders to believe that he would act as a moderating influence. But after the meeting the Turkish Cypriot leaders learned to their dismay that Makarios had publicly reaffirmed his intention of amending the Constitution, unilaterally if necessary, and had declared the Treaty of Guarantee, which empowered Great Britain, Greece and Turkey to intervene in Cyprus to safeguard the constitutional status quo, as null and void. A general mobilization of all the Greek Cypriot elements of the police and gendarmerie ensued, with new firearms being distributed for the alleged purpose of "preventing new flareups". An effort was also undertaken to round up and detain all Turkish Cypriot policemen and gendarmes.

The Greek Cypriot forces were split up into several private armies. The largest of these by far was Yorgadjis', which was called simply The Organization. It was divided into 100-man companies and was armed with rifles, automatic weapons, mortars, grenades and armored bulldozers. A second army was led by Makarios' personal physician, Dr. Vassos Lyssarides. A third was led by the newspaper publisher Nikos Sampson, who during the civil war had headed the notorious Assassination Squad in Nicosia and boasted that he had killed someone for every year of his life.

Realizing that they faced a grave threat, the Turkish Cypriots took whatever measures they deemed necessary in order to insure their own immediate survival. Many of the families which lived outside of the Turkish Cypriot quarter of Nicosia or the predominantly Turkish Cypriot suburb of Omorphita (in Turkish, Küçük Kaymaklı) abandoned their homes and fled to safer neighborhoods. Meanwhile, the Turkish Cypriot leaders were organizing the rudiments of a citizens' army and all available weapons were being collected. They did not amount to much: the entire Turkish Cypriot arsenal in Omorphita, for example, consisted of six rifles, five Sten guns, two Bren light machine guns (only one of which was operative), some pistols and approximately one hundred shotguns, and there was very little ammunition (some of which dated from World War I).[4] But the Turkish

---

4. H. Scott Gibbons, *Peace Without Honour* (Ankara, 1969), p. 10. This unfortunately much-neglected work by a British journalist in Cyprus contains the most detailed and reliable account of the 1963-1964 crisis thus far published. Quotations from it in this and later chapters are by permission of the author.

Cypriot leaders were still hoping that restraint and cool-
headedness would act as a deterrent to further Greek Cypriot
aggressiveness. Therefore, through the Turkish language press
they called upon the members of their community "to act
calmly and peacefully, and restrain themselves from resorting to extreme measures which will only serve the Greeks
in the realization of their aims".[5] This concern was also
uppermost in the mind of Rauf Denktaş when, on Sunday,
December 22, he spoke at the funeral of the couple slain
on the previous day. In his remarks, he warned that any re-
vengeful action would be a "betrayal of our just cause".[6]

That night Greek Cypriot terrorists subjected the Turkish
Cypriot quarter of Nicosia and Omorphita to heavy firing
from the roofs of nearby buildings. All telephonic and tele-
graphic communications between the Turkish Cypriot quarter of Nicosia and the outside world were severed. On the
Kyrenia road, Turkish Cypriot-owned vehicles were raked
with machine gun fire; one man was killed and several other
persons were wounded.

On Monday morning, a group of *mücahits* (TMT militiamen) gathered together the Greek Cypriot families which
had been left behind in Omorphita and escorted them out
of harm's way to the Greek Cypriot lines, telling them,
"This is a gesture to unarmed civilians".[7] At noon, Dr.
Küçük and the Turkish Cypriot cabinet members had another meeting with Makarios. The Archbishop denied any
complicity in the ongoing massacre and agreed to join Dr.
Küçük in making a public appeal for peace. But when the
message was broadcast on the radio it was followed by a
statement in Greek calling upon Greek Cypriots to keep
struggling for the "materialisation of our aspirations—
Enosis".[8] Needless to say, the effect of this new peace initiative was nil. Quite to the contrary, terrorist activity
greatly increased that afternoon and evening:

5. *Ibid.*, p. 11.
6. *Ibid.*, p. 12.
7. *Ibid.*, p. 15.
8. *Ibid.*, p. 25.

In Nicosia, a Turkish Cypriot architect was shot in cold blood. In a separate incident, a Turkish Cypriot male nurse at the Nicosia General Hospital and a just-discharged patient were machine-gunned to death.

In the suburb of Çağlayan, southeast of the city walls, some six hundred Turkish Cypriots were gradually forced to retreat into a small cluster of houses along the Famagousta highway by sniper fire. The abandoned houses were promptly looted and burned. During the flight an old man was felled by bullets.

In Larnaca, two Turkish Cypriots were wounded in an exchange of fire.

In the village of Peristerona, between Nicosia and Lefka, a Greek Cypriot policeman wounded one of the Turkish Cypriot villagers.

Omorphita, where fighting had been going on since dawn, sustained two major assaults. At midday a large number of Nikos Sampson's men made an all-out charge against the Turkish Cypriot positions. They armed three bulldozers with steel plates and with these makeshift tanks tried to break through the Turkish Cypriot defenses. But six Turkish Cypriot sharpshooters successfully picked off several of Sampson's men through cracks in the armor plating, causing the rest of the attackers to flee in panic. That evening, Sampson's force was strengthened by units of the 950-man mainland Greek contingent of the Tripartite Force stationed in Cyprus and these, in turn, attempted to wipe out the Turkish Cypriot positions with light anti-aircraft machine guns. Although they were not able to eliminate all resistance, they nonetheless inflicted heavy losses on the defenders of the town.

That night the 208 Turkish Cypriots in the mixed village of Mathiati, in the district of Nicosia, were also attacked. Over a thousand Greek Cypriot youths, accompanied by some uniformed policemen, suddenly rushed into the Turkish Cypriot quarter and started shooting. In Gibbons' words:

Three Turks were seriously wounded in the first few minutes. As the other Turks rushed from their little, white matchbox houses, the mob, cursing abuse and shrieking with laughter, kicked and punched them along the street.

As the terrified Turks shuffled along, cowering from the blows from rifle butts, the mob rushed into the houses, dragged the blazing logs from the fireplaces and threw them at curtains and on beds. The wooden roof beams, dried out over many years, smoked then crackled into flames.

Along the blazing street the Turks were driven, dragging their wounded; women, many in their night dresses and bare feet, sobbing, clutching babies awakened by the noise and starting to wail, children old enough to walk holding tightly to trouser and blue striped pajama legs.

The youngsters fired hysterically into the houses, yelling themselves hoarse in their frenzy. Before some of the buildings had fully caught fire, groups of them dashed inside, smashing furniture and dishware, grabbing valuables and stuffing them into their pockets.

Terrified noises from behind the houses drew the attention of the attackers to the Turkish livestock.

Breaking into the barns, they machinegunned milk cows, goats and sheep. Hens were thrown into the air and blasted by bullets as they squawked and fluttered, their pathetic bodies exploding in feathered puffs. The mob roared in blood-crazed delirium.

The Turks were driven out of the village, along the freezing open road. Near the next village, Kochatis, an all Turkish area, the tormented refugees were left.

While the Turks of Kochatis rushed out to help their neighbours, the mob . . . returned to Mathiati to continue their orgy of shooting, burning and pillaging.[9]

At 10 p.m. Archbishop Makarios once more agreed to join Dr. Küçük in an appeal for a cease-fire, but Makarios' message, when it was broadcasted, included the following ambiguous remarks:

It is with satisfaction that I have found that the appeal which I have made jointly with the Vice-President at noon today has already met with a response.[10]

9. *Ibid.*, p. 31.
10. *Ibid.*, p. 34.

On Christmas Eve yet another meeting took place between the Greek Cypriot and Turkish Cypriot leaders. This
time, the U. S. Ambassador and the acting British High
Commissioner, as well as their military attachés, were invited to attend. It was decided that the following measures
would be taken:

1) A new appeal for a cease-fire would be broadcast,
2) Glafkos Klerides and Defense Minister Örek, accompanied by armed police units of Greek Cypriots and
   Turkish Cypriots in equal numbers, would make their
   way to the various trouble spots in Nicosia and there
   arrange for the removal of the sick and wounded and
   for the provisioning of those who, because of the
   fighting, had not been able to get any food for several
   days,
3) Armed police units of Greek Cypriots and Turkish
   Cypriots in equal numbers would be posted at each
   spot where fighting had taken place to enforce the
   cease-fire, and
4) A committee of Greek Cypriots and Turkish Cypriots
   in equal numbers, together with an advisory body of
   independent experts, would be set up to effect a return to normalcy.[11]

But the Greek Cypriot leaders made no effort to implement this agreement. Later that day, the Nicosia Divisional
Commander of the Police, when pressed for an explanation
as to why the joint police units were not being created, replied that he had just received an order from Makarios to
the effect that the Turkish Cypriots were first to surrender
unconditionally.

Meanwhile, the Greek Cypriot offensive was reaching
new heights of destructive frenzy:

In the Greek Cypriot quarter of Nicosia, the twenty-one
remaining Turkish Cypriot patients at the Nicosia General
Hospital, many of whom were recovering from surgery,
were dragged out of their beds; their bandages were ripped
off and they were driven away never again to be seen.

11. *Ibid.*, p. 67.

Taking advantage of the fact that the Greek Cypriots were concentrating their forces in the Omorphita sector, the hard-pressed inhabitants of Çağlayan piled up in the few available cars and managed to reach Kyrenia Gate on the outer fringes of the Turkish quarter of Nicosia without loss of life. However, all their possessions had to be left behind.

An attempt was also made to evacuate Omorphita, for the defenders there were running out of ammunition. Because the town was constantly under fire, this was a risky operation and had to be carried out at night. But nonetheless some 3,000 out of the 5,000 Turkish Cypriot inhabitants had been safely escorted into the Turkish quarter of Nicosia by Christmas morning. Two of the *mücahit*s who were protecting the evacuees were killed in the course of the operation.

During the day, an old shepherd who was grazing his flock in a meadow near the city walls was attacked by a gang of youths and riddled with bullets in full view of the British High Commission building.

In the evening, Greek Cypriot terrorists raided two Turkish Cypriot communities northwest of Nicosia. In the mixed village of Ayios Vasilios, armed men who had come by truck from the direction of the capital, attacked the 120 Turkish Cypriot inhabitants of the Turkish quarter. What followed has been vividly described by Gibbons:

> Shots rang out, rifle butts smashed against locked doors, people were dragged into the streets.
>
> A 70-year old Turk was awakened by the sound of his front door splintering. Tottering out of his bedroom, he found several young armed men inside the door.
>
> "Have you any children?" they asked. Bewildered he replied, "Yes".
>
> "Send them outside", he was ordered.
>
> His two sons, 19 and 17 years old, and his granddaughter aged 10, hastily dressed and followed the gunmen outside.
>
> They were lined up outside the cottage wall. The gunmen machinegunned them to death.
>
> In another house, a 13-year old boy had his hands tied behind his knees and was thrown on the floor. While the house was

being ransacked, his captors kicked and abused him. Then a pistol was placed at the back of his head and he was shot.

Altogether, 12 Turks were massacred that evening in Ayios Vasilios. The others were rounded up and kicked and punched along the highway to Skylloura, to seek refuge with the Turks there. In night attire and bare feet, they stumbled along in the cold, the Greeks shooting after them in the darkness.

Then the gunmen turned their attention to the Turkish houses. They looted and destroyed, and finally, exhausted, they set the houses on fire.

. . . .

In isolated farmhouses in the same region, nine more Turks were murdered.[12]

In Kumsal, near Ortaköy, two R.A.F. officers witnessed an equally savage attack on the Turkish Cypriot community there. The wife and three children of a major in the Turkish army contingent were machine gunned to death in the bathroom of their house, where they had taken refuge. The landlady, who had locked herself in the lavatory of the same house, was also killed. The terrorists then turned their wrath on the remaining Turkish Cypriot villagers. To quote Gibbons once more:

Gunmen smashed down doors and charged into Turkish houses, clubbing and beating, cursing and punching.

The retreat from Kumsal began. Once again, like Europe reeling under the onslaught of the Nazis, the families were dragged from their homes into the cold streets, bewildered, terrified, the crash of rifles, the rattle of automatic fire echoing loudly in their ears.

They ran, slipping, falling, grabbing each other.

In the streets, the cry of a woman was heard, "Will nobody help us, please?"

159 of the Turkish inhabitants of Kumsal did not escape that night. Four others besides the four in the bath and the landlady, died. 150 were taken hostage. Some of the hostages were never seen again.[13]

That night seven of the leaders of the Turkish Cypriot community in the northern seaport of Kyrenia were also

12. *Ibid.*, p. 73.
13. *Ibid.*, p. 76.

arrested, as were all the Turkish Cypriot policemen of that town and the Gendarmerie's district commander.

While these events were taking place, the Greek Cypriot-controlled radio station in Nicosia was unceasingly broadcasting inflammatory propaganda to the effect that the Turkish Cypriots (all of whom were huddling together in their various ghettoes) were revolting against the government and had embarked upon a wholesale slaughter of the Greek Cypriot population. These accusations served not only to further encourage Greek Cypriot militancy but also to misinform the outside world as to the true nature of the massacre which was then underway on the island. On Christmas Eve, the following communiqués were issued:

> For the fourth day running... Turkish fanatics continued their unprovoked attacks on security forces and on Greek civilians.
>
> Security forces have launched a mopping up operation in Nicosia following the daylong heavy attacks on unarmed Greek families by Turks in Omorphita.[14]

Interior Minister Yorgadjis unwittingly came close to the truth when at a press conference he declared:

> The endurance, perseverance and courage of the officers and men of the police and gendarmerie is unparalleled. They have succeeded in keeping the situation under control and confining the armed Turks to the positions they held from the moment they started their orgy of lawlessness. At no point were the Turks able to move forward from their original positions. The Turks themselves now show signs of fatigue.[15]

That the Turkish Cypriots were unable to get out of their ghettoes, and that they were showing signs of fatigue were certainly undebatable. The beleaguered Turkish Cypriot enclaves in and around the capital, crowded as they were with refugees, had had no food or medical supplies since the beginning of hostilities. There was also such a shortage of arms that the defenders rushed from sector to sector with the few weapons they possessed to fool the Greek Cypriots into thinking that they were well armed. In all of Nicosia, the Turkish Cypriots had only one Bren gun.

---

14. *Ibid.*, p. 112.
15. *Ibid.*, p. 111.

In Omorphita, the situation was even more desperate than in the Turkish Cypriot quarter of Nicosia. The town had not yet been entirely evacuated by Christmas day. Yet, the defenders had run out of ammunition. Making the most of this opportunity, Nikos Sampson and his men redoubled their efforts to seize the town and, finally, overwhelmed the Turkish Cypriot positions. The 70-year-old *imam* (religious leader) and his crippled son were shot on sight, as were two other men. The 550 people who had remained in the town were then brutally dragged out of their homes and herded behind the Greek Cypriot lines. The mosque was shattered with bazookas and all the houses in the Turkish Cypriot quarter were looted or burned.

The Turkish Cypriot inhabitants of Omorphita were taken to the Kykkos School, on the airport bypass, where they were interned together with the inhabitants of Kumsal.

That day an old woman who had refused to be evacuated from her home in a predominantly Greek Cypriot area in Nicosia was shot by youths who were target practicing from the roof of the Ledra Palace Hotel, and a young man from Lefka was ambushed and killed on his way to work.

Sampson was the hero of the day. He was lavishly praised by the Greek Cypriot press and hailed as the "Conqueror of Omorphita". He was also warmly congratulated by Brigadier General George Perides, the Greek Tripartite Headquarters commander, who had become the chief planner of the Greek Cypriot onslaught.

However, in spite of the fall of Omorphita, the Greek Cypriots had very little cause for rejoicing on that Christmas day. Their plan depended upon speed for success. They had hoped to capture the Turkish Cypriot quarter of Nicosia in three hours and Omorphita in six hours, and then present the outside world with the *fait accompli* of Turkish Cypriot capitulation. But four days had already elapsed and they still had not smashed Turkish Cypriot resistance in Nicosia. By Christmas day even the fabrications of the Cyprus Broadcasting Corporation and Makarios' phony appeals for a cease-fire had lost their effectiveness as smokescreens, and the whole world was being fully informed about the atrocities by a battery of foreign correspondents in Nicosia. Understandably, it was in Turkey that news of the Cyprus massacres had the greatest impact. The Turkish government promptly appealed to the governments of Great Britain and Greece, the other two guarantor states, to make a common effort to restore peace on the island. As a result, on December 24, the three governments issued a joint statement offering their good offices to the two communities. This appeal was repeated on the 25th. For added emphasis, Prime Minister İnönü of Turkey sent three jet planes to buzz Nicosia in what he described as "warning flights" and the 650-man-strong Turkish army contingent of the Tripartite Force was ordered to leave its barracks at Wayne's Keep and settle down at strategic points along the Kyrenia road. At last, on December 26, Archbishop Makarios, fearing unilateral Turkish intervention, accepted the offer of the guarantor states. It was agreed that a mixed peace-keeping force would be established. It was to consist of the forces of the United Kingdom, Greece and Turkey which were already stationed in Cyprus by virtue of the Treaty of Establishment[16] and the Treaty of Alliance, and was to be led by Major General Peter Young, the commander of the British troops on the island. However, because the Greek and Turkish contingents of the Tripartite Force had already taken sides in the inter-communal struggle, British troops formed the backbone of the force.

On December 26, the Makarios government also asked for an emergency meeting of the U. N. Security Council to air charges that Turkey had committed "acts of a) aggression, b) intervention in the internal affairs of Cyprus by the threat and use of force against its territorial integrity".[17]

---

16. The agreement which enabled the British to retain the sovereign bases of Akrotiri and Dekelia when Cyprus became independent.

17. Thomas Ehrlich, *International Crises and the Role of Law: Cyprus, 1958-1967* (London, 1974), p. 57.

But at the meeting, which took place on December 27, the Cypriot delegate at the United Nations, Zenon Rossides, was unable to substantiate either charge. Consequently, the meeting was adjourned without any action being taken.

While Makarios was appealing to the Security Council for protection, the reign of terror against the Turkish Cypriots was continuing. On December 26, a hundred Greek Cypriot irregulars attempted to dislodge a small group of *mücahits* from their strategic location astride the Kyrenia pass, killing one of the defenders before being forced to retreat.

On December 27, the first British units began to stream into Nicosia from the sovereign bases. By December 30, a neutral zone had been agreed upon by all parties concerned and British troops occupied a string of sandbagged posts all along the cease-fire line (also known as the Green Line)[18] between the Greek Cypriot and Turkish Cypriot quarters of the capital. Thus the British were able to impose what *Newsweek* called a "sullen and tenuous truce"[19] in Nicosia.

On December 29, a political committee consisting of the British High Commissioner (at that time Sir Arthur Clark), the Greek and Turkish ambassadors and representatives of the Greek Cypriot and Turkish Cypriot communities, was organized for the purpose of giving guidance to the joint peace-keeping force. Then, on January 2, 1964, it was announced that an agreement had been reached to hold a conference in London with the participation of the three guarantor states and the two communities to explore possible solutions to the crisis. Simultaneously, the governments of Greece, Turkey, Great Britain and Cyprus jointly requested the Secretary-General of the United Nations to appoint a representative to act as U. N. observer in Cyprus and report on the progress of peace-keeping efforts there. Finally, the British government despatched Duncan Sandys, the Secretary of State for Commonwealth Relations, to Nicosia

---

18. So-called because General Young had traced it on a wall map with a green army map marker.

19. Issue of January 20, 1964, p. 27.

in the hope that his skill as a mediator might be put to use in bringing about a lessening of tension on the island.

Shortly after his arrival, Sandys was able to secure the release of the Turkish Cypriot hostages at the Kykkos School, but they were not allowed to return to their villages. He also succeeded in making the necessary arrangements for the evacuation of fifty seriously wounded Turkish Cypriots to Turkey for treatment, and talked the Greek Cypriots into dismantling many of their roadblocks.

By tolerating the presence of British troops on Cypriot soil and by making a show of collaborating with the peace-keeping efforts of the guarantor powers, Makarios had ably parried the threat of unilateral Turkish intervention. Indeed, as long as British troops were guarding the island it seemed highly unlikely that the Turks would ever resort to force in an attempt to bring an end to the crisis. On the other hand, the British troops could not be everywhere at once. There were still many possible targets for aggression, especially in the countryside. Thus, under the cover of the peace-keeping force, Makarios was able to continue his attacks on isolated pockets of Turkish Cypriot resistance. In early January, the correspondent of *The Observer* reported:

> Eight days after the big battles at Christmas, Cyprus is still an island of anarchy. In the Nicosia suburb, Omorphita, correspondents watched Greek arsonists burn Turkish houses under the eyes of the local Greek police. I have spoken with the Turkish hospital matron who saw a nurse and patient shot cold-bloodedly in her drawing room. I have talked with an English girl from Ealing who saw a man machine-gunned to death by uniformed police in front of her flat and I have visited houses in the Turkish quarter which are almost carpeted with blood.[20]

By the end of December 1963, the Turkish Cypriot inhabitants of twenty-two villages had fled from their homes as their villages were being attacked.[21] In January, the Turkish Cypriot inhabitants of fifty-five more villages joined the growing stream of refugees.[22] As Giorgio Bocca, the correspondent of *Il Giorno*, reported:

---

20. Issue of January 5, 1964.
21. See Appendix II.
22. See Appendix III.

Right now we are witnessing the exodus of the Turks from their villages. Thousands of people abandoning homes, lands, herds; Greek terrorism is relentless. This time, the rhetoric of the Hellenes and the busts of Plato do no suffice to cover up barbaric and ferocious behavior. At four o'clock in the afternoon, curfew is imposed on the Turkish villages. Threats, shootings and attempts at arson start as soon as it becomes dark. After the massacre of Christmas that spared neither women nor children, it is difficult to put up any resistance.[23]

At Arediou, in the district of Nicosia, five Turkish Cypriots were killed when the Turkish Cypriot quarter was attacked. As Mrs. Gülsün Salih recalls:

It was a cold evening in January 1964, when there was a knock on the door. Before we could open it, the door was kicked open and about a dozen Greek Cypriots armed with rifles and automatic guns rushed in. They grabbed my husband, Salih Mehmet, aged 60, and took him away, saying that they would be taking him to Nicosia. That was the last I saw of my husband and nothing has been heard of him since then. Four other Turkish Cypriot men, Naim Hüseyin, Kemal Hüseyin, Niyazi Cemal, and Şevket Cemal, from the same village, were taken away in the same manner on the same night and nothing has been heard of them either since then.[24]

Thousands of refugees flocked to Nicosia and other towns with a substantial Turkish Cypriot population. In these towns the Turkish Cypriots were living in a state of siege, receiving food from Turkey or from international relief and welfare organizations. Many Turkish Cypriot villages were also swollen with refugees from nearby areas. Gibbons tells us that the village of Hamit Köy, in the district of Nicosia, which, in 1960, had a population of 418, was flooded with some 3,500 refugees.[25]

During this period Makarios repeatedly tried to use the peace-keeping force to further his own political aims. General Young was astonished to learned that he was expected to assist the "legal state forces", namely Yorgadjis' private

23. Issue of January 14, 1964.

24. *News Bulletin*, May 26, 1977, p. 4.

25. *Op. cit.*, pp. 128-129.

army, in disarming the *mücahit*s and taking over the Turkish Cypriot enclaves. When he balked, Makarios became angry and threatened once more to abrogate the treaties. But he had to backtrack when Commonwealth Secretary Sandys, in turn, threatened to withdraw all British troops from the Republic and Turkey again began to "talk ominously of intervention",[26] Relations between Makarios and the British further deteriorated during the weeks that followed as, with increasing frequency, British troops rushed to help Turkish Cypriot villagers in distress. As the correspondent of *Newsweek* observed:

> The British. . . were coming under increasing verbal fire from the Greek Cypriots, who accused British troops of fostering partition of the island by putting themselves between the combatants and escorting fleeing Turks from mixed villages to Turkish-held communities.[27]

Makarios vented his ire in a note to Acting High Commissioner Cyril Packard requesting that the British force take no action without the approval of the Cypriot government, which would have given the Greek Cypriots veto power over all peace-keeping operations.[28]

The London Conference, which opened on January 15, took place in an atmosphere so emotionally charged that it was doomed from the very start. The Greek Cypriot representatives (Glafkos Klerides, Spyros Kyprianou and Kriton Tornarides) merely repeated Makarios' non-negotiable demands for amending the Constitution, which left the Turkish Cypriot representatives (Rauf Denktaş and Osman Örek) with no choice but to ask for partition of the island into two separate ethnic zones. Duncan Sandys, who headed the British delegation, did his best to effect a compromise, but

---

26. *Newsweek*, January 13, 1964, p. 29.

27. *Newsweek*, March 9, 1964, p. 36.

28. The United States also became the object of a hate campaign in the Greek Cypriot press because of its support of British peace-keeping efforts. In early February, two bombs exploded in front of the U.S. Embassy in Nicosia and Ambassador Fraser Wilkins organized an airlift of U.S. dependents to Beirut.

it quickly became obvious that no agreement could be reached as long as the violence on the island continued. To complicate matters, England, which since December had become bogged down in a struggle to suppress the National Liberation Front in Aden, no longer could bear the burden of policing Cyprus, as a consequence of which a new peace-keeping force had to be organized. Furthermore, both the Greek and Turkish governments had become highly agitated by the Cyprus controversy, creating a rift within NATO.[29]

In the hope of cooling tempers in Athens and Ankara, General Lyman L. Lemnitzer, the Commander-in-Chief of NATO forces, flew to the two capitals. Meanwhile, the British devised a plan to prevent a recurrence of inter-communal fighting in Cyprus. This plan called for the formation of a 10,000-man force to be drawn from NATO countries (including some 2,000 troops from the United States). It was to remain in Cyprus for a period of not more than three months, during which time the governments of Greece and Turkey were to desist from exercising their right of unilateral intervention under Article IV of the Treaty of Guarantee. Great Britain, Greece, Turkey and the two Cypriot communities were also to appoint a mutually acceptable mediator to assist in the search for a resolution to the conflict. The plan, which was presented on January 31, 1964, was accepted by Greece, Turkey and the Turkish Cypriot leadership, but it was rejected by Makarios as "totally unacceptable". What Makarios wanted was to scrap the Zürich-London Accords, which prevented him from changing the Cypriot Constitution at will. A NATO force, he felt, would only reinforce the status quo. The only peace-keeping force he was willing to accept was one under U.N. sponsorship, for the U.N. was in no way committed to uphold the Zürich-London Accords and its Secretary-General, U Thant, was known to be of the opinion that the Cyprus problem was first and foremost a matter for the Cypriot government (i.e.,

---

29. The Turks manifested their displeasure by undertaking naval maneuvers in the waters between southern Anatolia and Cyprus. The Greeks reciprocated by gathering their fleet around Crete.

Makarios) to solve. At the U.N., moreover, Russia exerted considerable influence, and Makarios had been actively cultivating the friendship of that nation, hoping to use it as a lever against the treaty guaranteeing states. He had frequent meetings with the Soviet ambassador, Pavel Yermoshin, and the Soviet Premier, Nikita Khrushchev, openly supported him in the ongoing civil war, publicly chastising the U. S. and Great Britain for intervening in the internal affairs of Cyprus. But the U.S. and British governments were opposed to the establishment of a U.N. peace-keeping force because they feared that by appealing to the U.N. Makarios would embroil the Cyprus problem in the politics of the Cold War.

This impasse gave the Greek Cypriots the opportunity to once more intensify their campaign of aggression. Having taken advantage of the January lull in fighting to import large quantities of arms from Russia and Czechoslovakia, they launched a new wave of assaults against Turkish Cypriot enclaves throughout the island. Their first target was the village of Khoulou, in the Paphos district. As a survivor described the incident:

> On 3rd February 1964 the armed Greeks launched a surprise attack against the Turkish quarter of Hulu [Khoulou]. They took away 20 of our brothers as prisoners. The attackers were the Greek inhabitants of our village. They were supported by groups from nearby villages. On the first night of this inhuman attack we secretly ran away from our village through the forest under the cover of darkness. We had to leave behind four elderly and disabled persons: Ismail Emin (90), Halil Abdullah (95), Cemaliye Ali Kamber (100) and Mehmet Yusuf (75). They were tortured to death by the attackers.
>
> That night we managed to take refuge at Akkargı [Pitargou]. Two days later, on 5th February, the Greeks attacked Akkargı as well. Together with the people of Akkargı we had to flee to a safer village, Aksu [Akhylou]. The prisoners taken by the Greeks from Hulu were returned to us with the help of the British soldiers.
>
> We could stay at Aksu for only two months. In this small village the Turkish refugees of four villages, Falya [Phalia], Pitargu [Pitargou], Hulu and Kurtağa [Kourtaka], were facing great difficulties. Hunger was a common problem. Nobody

could go out to work in fields or orchards. The Greeks were firing at the village every day in order to obstruct the Turkish shepherds and farmers from going out into the fields. On 23rd February 1964 the Greeks caught a Turk, Şerifali Salih, while he was cutting wood and fatally shot him. His body was brought to the village by the British. There were 27 bullet wounds on his body.

On 4th April 1964, pressed by hunger and the Greek oppression we had to take refuge at another Turkish village in the area, Aydoğan [Stavrokono]. Before we had left the village of Aksu, the Greeks had even cut off the water of this Turkish village, adding thirst to hunger.[30]

On February 6, units of the Greek Cypriot gendarmerie and some armed Greek Cypriot civilians attacked the Turkish Cypriot quarter in the mixed village of Ayios Sozomenos, in the district of Nicosia. The attack was in retaliation for an incident which had taken place earlier that day. A Land-Rover carrying seven armed Greek Cypriots from the nearby village of Potamia had been fired upon by Turkish Cypriot militiamen defending Ayios Sozomenos. The Greek Cypriots later claimed that the occupants of the Land-Rover had merely intended to open a water pump which serviced their village. But the Turkish Cypriot quarter of Ayios Sozomenos had been in a state of siege since December 22. Tensions had been kept at the boiling point by a series of arrests, abductions and murders of Turkish Cypriots who had ventured out to tend to their crops or to graze their sheep, and on one occasion a gendarmerie patrol had even forced its way through the Turkish Cypriot defenses. Understandably, therefore, when early on February 6 the Land-Rover filled with armed Greek Cypriots had approached the village, the defenders had thought that they were being attacked. It is, however, just as certain that when the Greek Cypriots had suddenly found themselves surrounded by *mücahit*s they had concluded that they were being ambushed. It is not known who fired first, but shots had been exchanged and two of the Greek Cypriots had

30. *Special News Bulletin*, January 20, 1979, p. 1.

been killed. The Greek Cypriot attack which followed was one of the most brutal of the entire civil war. *Time* correspondent Robert Ball, who witnessed the assault, cabled the following description of it:

> The bitterest fighting was at the western edge of the village, where the attacking Greeks had the cover of gnarled olive trees. In one mud-brick hut, where nine Turks had taken refuge, a window was blasted by a bazooka-type rocket, and the second floor literally sieved with bullet holes. In desperation, one Turkish shepherd tried to flee to the riverbed, but was cut down a few feet from the door. Another grabbed a pitchfork, made a futile, one-man assault on the Greek position and was mowed down at once.[31]

The Turkish Cypriots lost seven dead and several wounded. But, oddly enough, the Greek Cypriots suffered heavier losses. This was partly due to the fact that at the height of the battle two groups of Greek Cypriots had mistaken each other for Turkish Cypriots and had mowed each other down. The next day the Turkish Cypriots evacuated both Ayios Sozemenos and Potamia.

On February 12, George Ball, the United States Under-Secretary of State, arrived in Nicosia in an endeavor to persuade Archbishop Makarios to accept a revised version of the British proposal for a NATO peace-keeping force. According to the new scheme, most of the troops were to be drawn from British Commonwealth countries. But Makarios again rejected the plan. In the course of their meeting, the much-exasperated American diplomat accused Makarios of turning Cyprus into his "private *abattoir*".[32]

On February 13, a large Greek Cypriot force attacked the Turkish Cypriot quarter of Limassol. "This morning, in the early hours", General Young reported,

> the Greek side launched a deliberate attack supported by a home made tank, armoured bulldozers, and assorted weapons such as bazookas and, it is alleged, mortars. We were forewarned the evening before, but I was assured that it would not take place by a very senior minister in the government.[33]

---

31. Issue of February 14, 1964, p. 23.

32. Laurence Stern, *The Wrong Horse* (New York, 1977), p. 84.

33. Gibbons, *op. cit.*, p. 147. General Young's failure to prevent the attack or his candidness resulted in his being relieved of his command a few days later.

Once the fighting started, the British did not attempt to interfere on the grounds that this might have endangered the
hundreds of servicemen's families which lived in the town.
The following impressions of the struggle were despatched
by *Newsweek*'s correspondent on the scene:

> For three days last week a bitter battle raged in the seaport
> town of Limassol where in happier times 31,000 Greek Cypriots
> and 6,000 Turkish Cypriots had lived peaceably side by side.
> From the yellowed stone battlements of Limassol Castle, where
> in the days of chivalry Richard the Lion-Hearted courted Prin
> cess Berengaria of Navarre, Greek Cypriots poured fire into the
> city's Turkish quarter. A Turk making a zigzag run for shelter
> was brought down with a single sniper's shot. Three more Turk
> ish bodies were piled on the top of bloodstained sandbags in
> the gutted remains of the Magic Bar and Grill, a Turkish-owned
> restaurant which once served Limassol's best food.
>
> Greek casualties in Limassol were two dead while the unofficial
> Turkish toll was 50 dead and 100 wounded—a figure which the
> Greek Cypriot press greeted with the exultant headline, HAIL
> TO THE HEROES—WE'VE WON. Snipers seemed to be on
> every roof, and a Greek Cypriot youth snickered as submachine-
> gun fire reverberated through the narrow streets. "He likes the
> sound of automatic weapons", a Greek Cypriot policeman ex
> plained.[34]

John Law, the correspondent of *U.S. News & World Report*,
who visited the Turkish quarter of the city during a lull in
the struggle, reported:

> My first view of the Turkish quarter was not a pretty sight.
> Houses were riddled with gaping holes. Whole walls had been
> blasted off many of them.
>
> There were many dead—some still lying where they had been
> killed.
>
> The Turks were getting ready for more trouble. Everyone was
> withdrawing into a smaller stronghold. Women, some carrying
> small children, were scurrying out of the houses and moving
> into the reduced bastion being set up.
>
> Practically all of them were crowding into the only two places
> left where there was room for them to spend the night—a
> mosque and a movie theater.

34. Issue of February 24, 1964, p. 39.

> In the narrow streets, Turks were feverishly piling up barricades. Men, women and children were passing concrete building blocks from hand to hand to erect the barriers.
>
> . . . .
>
> The Turks didn't know how many had been killed during the day because they had not been able to collect their dead.[35]

On February 14, Greek Cypriot irregulars attacked the Turkish Cypriot quarters of Paphos and Polis, in western Cyprus. At Paphos, five persons were killed; at Polis two. Altogether, between February 2 and February 14, the Turkish Cypriot inhabitants of sixteen villages fled to safer areas, permanently abandoning their homes.[36]

On February 15, Britain gave up hope that its plan for a NATO peace-keeping force would ever be accepted by Archbishop Makarios and took the Cyprus issue to the United Nations. On March 4, the Security Council authorized the establishment of a U.N. peace-keeping force under the control of the Secretary-General, with financing by voluntary contributions. Thus Makarios had scored a major diplomatic triumph. Lieutenant General Prem Singh Gyani of India, who since January had been serving as U.N. observer in Cyprus, was named head of the new peace-keeping force by U Thant. Later, Sakari Severi Tuomioja of Finland was also sent to Cyprus. As U.N. Mediator, his mission was to bring an end to the fighting by diplomatic means.

During this period, Makarios announced plans for the creation of a new 5,000-man, Greek-officered National Guard, to function as an auxiliary police force, in open violation of the Constitution of Cyprus which limited the police to 1,200 (including its Turkish Cypriot contingent). The official purpose of the new force was "to disarm all citizens illegally carrying guns".[37] But its real aims probably were:

---

35. Issue of February 24, 1964, pp. 77-78.
36. See Appendix IV.
37. *Newsweek*, March 9, 1964, p. 35.

1) To absorb the various private armies, which had become increasingly unmanageable, and consolidate all Greek Cypriot fighting men in one official police force under the leadership of Makarios, and
2) To give the Greek Cypriot irregulars an official status in the hope that the U.N. peace-keeping force (UNFI-CYP) would recognize them as the only legitimate security force in the country and assist them in subduing the *mücahits*.

The Greek Cypriots then launched yet another offensive against the Turkish Cypriots—this time for the apparent purpose of improving their position before the arrival of U.N. forces.

On March 5, a force of 200 Greek Cypriots attacked the Turkish Cypriot quarters in the mixed villages of Kazaphani and Temblos, near Kyrenia, killing two men, and in Nicosia five persons were injured when a bomb exploded in the Turkish Cypriot Communal Chamber.

On March 7, the leaders of the two communities agreed to an exchange of hostages. When only 49 out of 225 known Turkish Cypriot hostages were released, however, it became obvious that the 176 remaining hostages had been killed.

On the same day, a Turkish Cypriot postman in Paphos was shot by a sniper while making his rounds. The Turkish Cypriots retaliated by firing into the Greek Cypriot quarter of the town. Soon, there was a heated exchange of fire between the two quarters and both sides started taking hostages. Upon hearing of this incident, General Gyani rushed to the scene and succeeded in arranging a truce as well as a new exchange of hostages. By the time the shooting had ceased, six Greek Cypriots and one Turkish Cypriot had been killed. Several of the Greek Cypriot casualties were persons who had been shopping in the municipal market place and had been caught in the cross-fire between the two quarters.

On March 8, the Greek Cypriots, seeking revenge for their heavy losses, decided to make an all-out attack against the Turkish Cypriot quarter in Paphos. They barricaded all roads leading to that town to delay the arrival of British troops and then stormed the Turkish Cypriot defenses with mortars, bazookas and automatic weapons. The assault continued until the 9th, when British units were finally able to reach the town and impose a truce. By that time, 14 more Turkish Cypriots and 11 more Greek Cypriots had been killed, 78 shops and 85 houses in the Turkish Cypriot quarter had been wholly or partly destroyed, and the 3,500 inhabitants of that quarter had been hemmed into an area which Ward Just, the *Newsweek* correspondent, described as "not much larger than Yankee Stadium".[38]

On March 7, there were also Greek Cypriot attacks on Lapithiou, in the district of Paphos, and on the Turkish Cypriot quarter of Mallia, in the district of Limassol. In Lapithiou, the Turkish Cypriot population was forced to flee to nearby Anadiou. In Mallia, which since the end of January had served as a place of refuge for over 200 inhabitants from the neighboring villages of Prastio and Kithasi, the entire population was forced to retreat into the local school building, where it was besieged for three days. When British troops intervened on the 10th, a cease-fire was agreed upon, the savagely mauled Turkish Cypriot garrison agreeing to surrender its weapons. Five Turkish Cypriots were killed in the struggle for Mallia. Patrick writes that allegedly "most of these casualties were unarmed and occurred when the cease-fire was supposed to be in effect".[39]

By March 13, fighting had spread throughout the island and the Greek Cypriots had taken many more hostages. On that day, the Turkish government issued an ultimatum to the Makarios regime. It demanded that

> All individual or collective assaults and acts committed against the Turkish community in Cyprus such as murder, pillage, robbery, arson, rape, torture and the like be stopped forthwith; that an immediate cease-fire all over the island be established and all existing cease-fire agreements and the Green Line agreements in Nicosia be observed completely and without exception; that all sieges around any Turkish locality be lifted forthwith anywhere; that the liberties of complete movement, communication and correspondence be immediately restored and that the Turkish hostages and the bodies of those murdered be returned to the Turkish community without delay. Otherwise, the Government of the Turkish Republic declares that it will use the right to take unilateral action conferred upon it by the Treaty of Guarantee of 16th August, 1960.[40]

---

38. *Newsweek*, March 23, 1964, p. 37.
39. *Op. cit.*, p. 62.
40. See Gibbons, *op. cit.*, p. 152.

To underline the point, troop transports were filled with battle-ready units of the Turkish Army at İskenderun. As tensions mounted, the U. S. Sixth Fleet approached Cyprus, Russian submarines converged on the area and the Security Council met in an emergency session to discuss the latest developments. But when, on the 14th, an advance party of the Canadian UNFICYP contingent reached the island, the Turkish government once more backed down, resuming its policy of watchful nonintervention.

On March 26, the Finnish contingent of UNFICYP reached Cyprus and, on the next day, General Gyani finally declared the U.N. force to be fully operative. 1,000 British troops, under the leadership of Major General R. M. P. Carver, who had succeeded General Young, were absorbed into UNFICYP. They were stationed at Limassol, in the vicinity of the sovereign base of Akrotiri. By June 8, Den-FICYP comprised 6,238 men from Austria, Canada, Denmark, Finland, Ireland and the United Kingdom. In addition to the peace-keeping force, a U.N. police force of 173 men was constituted, to which Australia, Austria, Denmark, New Zealand and Sweden contributed policemen. This force had the responsibility of conducting inquiries into incidents involving loss of life. Then, on May 10, Galo Plaza Lasso of Ecuador was appointed by U Thant as his special representative in Cyprus to undertake negotiations towards achieving a lasting peace on the island.

The Turkish Cypriots fervently hoped that the U.N. would at last re-establish order in Cyprus, but they were to be profoundly disappointed. UNFICYP, like the British peace-keeping force, could not be everywhere at once, and the Greek Cypriots, as the aggressors, could choose their objectives at will. Moreover, UNFICYP was basically powerless. According to its mandate, it could fire only in self-defense. Its only deterrent was its presence. As a result, the Greek Cypriots quickly acquired the same contempt for it that they had had for the similarly hamstrung British force and there was no letup in their efforts to break the back of Turkish Cypriot resistance. As the *News Bulletin* describes the situation:

The Greek Cypriots continued to build up their arms and war equipment by purchasing heavy weapons, ammunition, aircraft and vehicles from abroad. . . . The Turkish communities remained surrounded by the overwhelming Greek forces and were constantly subjected to all kinds of abuse, vexations and pressure. Freedom of movement on the island was totally denied to the Turks; their economic situation continued to deteriorate rapidly, as they were not allowed to sell their produce in the markets, to cultivate their fields, to graze their flocks and to go to their jobs in areas dominated by Greeks. In the villages which the Turks had abandoned in the face of Greek attacks, the houses were put on fire, the properties looted and the harvest confiscated. From March to June the Turkish Cypriots continued to be murdered and the Greeks did not give up their abhorrent method of taking hostages among the innocent people.[41]

On March 19, several hundred Greek Cypriot irregulars attacked the Turkish Cypriot village of Gaziveran, on Morphou bay, possibly because of its strategic location astride the Morphou-Xeros road. The population of the village, swollen to 600 by refugees from neighboring communities, was protected by some 50 *mücahit*s armed mostly with shotguns. As in Mallia, the villagers were forced to seek shelter in the schoolhouse into which the attackers fired their mortars and bazookas. By the time a cease-fire had been arranged, six of the villagers had been killed.

On March 26, the Makarios regime refused to allow Rauf Denktaş, who had been the spokesman of his community at the emergency session of the Security Council, to return to Cyprus.

During the first week of April, the Greek Cypriots carried out a series of raids in the Tylliria region, in northwestern Cyprus. Three Turkish Cypriots lost their lives in these attacks, the apparent aim of which was to gain control of the coastal road, which passed through the Turkish Cypriot villages of Limnitis, Mansoura and Kokkina.

On April 6, four Turkish Cypriots from Limassol were stopped at the Famagousta Gate in Nicosia by some Greek

---

41. Issue of February 11, 1977, p. 2.

Cypriot armed men. They were promptly taken to a nearby field and machine-gunned. Luckily, two of the victims, though badly wounded, managed to crawl to a British post. Some time later, the bullet-riddled bodies of the two slain Turkish Cypriots were delivered to the Turkish Cypriot quarter in Nicosia with death certificates signed by the Registrar of Births and Deaths indicating that they had died from "natural causes".[42]

At 3 a.m. on April 25, a force of some 300 Greek Cypriot irregulars attacked St. Hilarion Castle, near Kyrenia, which was defended by two dozen *mücahits*. By the morning of the 27th, six of the defenders had been killed and six more had been wounded. But the Turkish Cypriots still clung to this vital stronghold. General Gyani vehemently protested to Makarios concerning the "pre-planned" nature of the attack, and U.N. Secretary General U Thant gave orders to the U.N. peace-keeping force to take more vigorous action to stop armed flare-ups.[43]

In April, Archbishop Makarios and Premier Papandreou met in Athens and agreed that their "basic orientation" was *enosis*. Papandreou also promised to ship troops and arms to Cyprus clandestinely to strengthen Makarios' forces and "raise the cost of a Turkish landing".[44] Thus bolstered, Makarios, in a speech at the village of Yeroskipos, in the district of Paphos, on May 6, once more publicly reaffirmed his desire to achieve *enosis* at any cost, using the following words: "We declare once again that the Parthenon is the final goal of our struggle and we shall reach that goal irrespective of the obstacles we might encounter".[45]

On May 11, three Greek army officers and a Greek Cypriot policeman, probably as an act of bravado, drove through the walled Turkish Cypriot quarter of Famagousta.

42. Gibbons, *op. cit.*, p. 158.

43. *Newsweek*, May 11, 1964, p. 40.

44. Andreas Papandreou, *Democracy at Gunpoint* (New York, 1970), p. 132.

45. Örek, *Makarios on Enosis*, p. 25.

Turkish Cypriot policemen motioned them to stop as they were about to exit. The occupants of the car replied by firing at the Turkish Cypriot policemen. The latter fired back. Two of the Greek officers and the Greek Cypriot policeman fell dead. The third Greek officer was wounded. A Turkish Cypriot bystander was also killed. News reports of this incident in the Greek Cypriot press and radio were so biased that it appeared to Greek Cypriots that the Turkish Cypriot policemen had deliberately massacred some Greeks who had strayed into the Turkish quarter. This inspired all manner of Greek Cypriot extremists to seek immediate revenge. Within two days, 32 Turkish Cypriots were kidnapped and shot as reprisal for this act of "terrorism". Major E. F. L. Macey, the British contingent of UNFICYP, was given the task of investigating the kidnappings. On June 7, both he and his driver were, in their turn, abducted and murdered.[46] During this crisis, the Turkish Cypriot population of the mixed villages of Syngrassis and Monarga, near Famagousta, fled to that city.

Shocked by the Famagousta kidnappings, the Turkish government once more began preparations for a landing in Cyprus. This compelled Makarios, whose efforts to incorporate the existing private armies into his new National Guard had met with failure, to fill the ranks of the latter with draftees. Accordingly, on June 1, he ordered the conscription of all able-bodied Greek Cypriot men between the ages of 18 and 50. Lieutenant-General Karayannis, of the Greek Army, was appointed commander of the force.

On June 5, President Johnson, in a blunt message to Premier İnönü of Turkey, warned the Turkish government not to intervene in Cyprus, pointing out that the use of American weapons on the island would violate bilateral agreements between Washington and Ankara. This letter,

---

46. Major Macey had fought in Greece against the Germans during World War II and against the Communist insurgents in the civil war which followed, and he had been decorated for bravery by the Greek government.

which was prompted by fear that a Turkish landing in Cyprus would trigger a war between Greece and Turkey, and thus a conflict within NATO, effectively dissuaded the Turkish government from coming to the assistance of the destitute Turkish Cypriot community in the early summer of 1964, although it was clearly entitled to do so according to Article IV of the Treaty of Guarantee. Makarios thereby received a timely reprieve. But by that time Premier Papandreou of Greece had come to seriously doubt Makarios' ability as a leader. So, on June 14, he sent Grivas, by then a lieutenant-general in the Greek Army, to Cyprus for the purpose of coordinating future military actions against the Turkish Cypriots. He also made good on his promise to smuggle in troops from mainland Greece. He entrusted Defense Minister Peter Garoufalias with the responsibility of directing this operation. According to the noted journalist Taki Theodoracopulos,

> Garoufalias managed to pull off a magnificent coup. Under cover of darkness, using only small yachts and fishing boats, 9,000 men and 950 officers, fully equipped and heavily armed, landed in Cyprus.[47]

These troops became the backbone of the new National Guard. At the same time, whole shiploads of arms entered the country through Limassol. "Before dawn each day", Newsweek's correspondent in Cyprus reported,

> the great iron doors of the port of Limassol are slammed shut. Turkish Cypriot dockers are sent home. United Nations guards are barred. A few hours later, the doors swing open and covered lorries, weaving on heavily overloaded springs, roar out of the port and head northward towards the Troodos mountains.[48]

All this was of doubtful value to Makarios. He loathed the old rightist fanatic from Trikomo and the appointment threatened to sour his harmonious relations with the Kremlin. Grivas' only official position was commander of the Greek Army contingent in Cyprus. But, as Makarios feared, he quickly assumed leadership of the National Guard

---

47. *The Greek Upheaval* (New Rochelle, N.Y., 1978), p. 138.
48. Issue of July 27, 1964, p. 40.

as well, leaving General Karayannis with no other alternative but to resign, on August 15. Although he regarded himself as answerable to the Greek General Staff in Athens rather than to Makarios, Grivas usually acted independently of any authority. Thus, by mid-summer 1964, both Makarios and Papandreou had, to a great extent, lost control over the Greek forces in Cyprus.

Meanwhile, President Johnson was making renewed efforts to put an end to the fighting in Cyprus. In late June, he invited the Greek and Turkish premiers, George Papandreou and İsmet İnönü, to Washington for separate talks in the course of which he urged them in emphatic terms to exercise a restraining influence on the leaders of the Greek Cypriot and Turkish Cypriot communities on the war-ravaged island. He also suggested to U.N. Secretary-General U Thant that Greek and Turkish delegates meet at his Camp David retreat under the chairmanship of former Secretary of State Dean Acheson to work out a solution to the Cyprus conflict. U Thant approved the proposal but on condition that the meeting take place in Geneva and under the chairmanship of U.N. mediator Sakari Tuomioja. The Turkish government immediately agreed to send a delegation to Geneva. However, the Greek government at first refused to do so. It was only when President Johnson warned Premier Papandreou that his policy would lead to war with Turkey and that in that eventuality the United States would do nothing to protect Greece that the Greek government at last relented.

At the Geneva Conference, which convened in July, Dean Acheson, in his capacity as President Johnson's informal observer, offered a series of guidelines for a projected peace settlement. According to this plan, Cyprus was to be given a choice between independence and *enosis*, but

1) There was to be a Turkish enclave or military base on the Karpas peninsula which was to be an indivisible part of Turkey,
2) The tiny isle of Kastelorizon, on the southern littoral of Turkey, was to be ceded to that country, and

3) The Turkish Cypriots who lived in the Greek Cypriot part of Cyprus were to be given the right of local self-administration.

The Greek and Turkish delegates at once accepted the Acheson Plan, but in early August both the Greek government and Archbishop Makarios rejected it, even as a basis for further negotiations. The Greek and Turkish governments then submitted their own plans which, as could be expected, were mutually unacceptable, and the conference reached a complete deadlock.[49]

As Greek and Greek Cypriot statesmen were ostensibly debating the merits of the Acheson Plan, General Grivas and his staff were planning a series of large-scale military operations in northern Cyprus by the National Guard. To soften up the Turkish Cypriot enclaves, the Greek Cypriot government banned the delivery of all Red Crescent (Turkish Red Cross) supplies. Then, on August 1, the National Guard subjected St. Hilarion Castle and other Turkish Cypriot strongholds on the Kyrenia range to an intensive military bombardment. But the barrage was interrupted by the arrival of U.N. troops.

Grivas next concentrated a large force in the Tylliria hills, in northwestern Cyprus. It consisted of 2,000 National Guardsmen armed with six 25-pounder guns, two 4-barrelled Oerlikon 20mm. guns, several mortars and some armored cars. When General Kodendera S. Thimayya, who had succeeded General Gyani on July 8, complained to Archbishop Makarios about the troop buildup, the latter reassured him, asserting that no attack was being planned. However, on August 6 Grivas launched a major offensive against the Turkish Cypriot-held Kokkina salient, and Makarios announced that the struggle for *enosis* had entered its "final phase".[50]

The Kokkina salient included the little port of Kokkina, as well as the villages of Mansoura, Alevga, Selain t'Api and

---

49. For the full text of the Acheson Plan, see Salih, *op. cit.*, pp. 47-48.

50. *Newsweek*, August 17, 1964, p. 37.

Ayios Theodoros Tyllirias. It had great strategic importance, for it controlled the vital coastal road and was the principal entry point of supplies from Turkey to the hard-pressed *mücahits*. The enclave was defended mostly by 500 youths who had been studying in Turkey and England and who had just returned home via Kokkina because they had been denied entry through Kyrenia and other harbors in Greek Cypriot hands.[51]

As the attack began, the U.N. observation posts in the area were speedily overrun, and the officers and men of the peace-keeping force were compelled to run for their lives. Grivas was determined not to allow the United Nations to stand in the way of total victory this time. On August 7, the bulk of Grivas' army advanced towards Kokkina from the village of Pakhy Ammos, on the northwestern fringes of the salient. All day long Grivas' artillery shelled Turkish Cypriot villages, and that evening a patrol boat opened fire on Kokkina and Mansoura from the sea. However, Grivas, by not pressing his attack with sufficient energy, lost precious time, enabling his adversaries to summon outside help. The Turkish government was thoroughly aroused by the Tylliria offensive for, in Turkish eyes, the National Guard, led as it was by Greek officers and containing at least 9,000 Greek soldiers, was a Greek force. Hoping to discourage any further advance by the National Guard in the Kokkina salient by a mere show of strength, the Turkish leaders ordered warning flights to be made over the area. Accordingly, on the evening of August 7 four Turkish F-100 fighter planes buzzed concentrations of National Guardsmen and fired rockets into the sea. But the next day the National Guard continued to tighten its grip on the dwindling Turkish Cypriot enclave. Makarios and Grivas were still utterly confident that world pressure would prevent the Turks from becoming militarily involved in the Cyprus conflict. Hence, when General Thimayya implored Makarios to put an end

51. Gibbons, *op. cit.*, p. 167.

to the slaughter, he was rebuffed, and his commander in the Tylliria region, Colonel Jonas Waern, was not even able to arrange a temporary truce to allow some of his own men, as well as a group of Turkish Cypriot women and children, to be evacuated from an area under constant bombardment.

By the afternoon of August 8, all the villages in the salient had fallen except Kokkina, which was crowded with some 700 refugees and was being shelled from both land and sea. It was now clear to the Turkish leaders that the warning raid of the previous evening had not had any effect and that more vigorous steps would have to be taken to save the population of Kokkina and its defenders. Consequently, a fleet of jets was once more despatched to Tylliria, but this time with orders to fire in earnest. The National Guard's positions around Kokkina were blasted with rockets, machine gun fire, bombs and napalm, and one of the patrol boats which had been shelling the Turkish Cypriots was spotted from the air and sunk.

In a radio broadcast that evening, Archbishop Makarios, in an emotional speech, claimed that thousands of innocent Greek Cypriot civilians had been killed in the Turkish raid. Premier Papandreou, upon hearing of the latest developments, became fearful that the conflict would now spread. He pleaded with Makarios to "cease immediately" all military operations in northern Cyprus. However, Makarios defiantly replied that the Greek Cypriots would fight "till death".[52]

On August 9, a new wave of Turkish aircraft bombed the National Guard's positions and several Greek Cypriot villages where reinforcements were being gathered for a final assault on Kokkina. This raid at last stopped the Greek Cypriot offensive. It also destroyed the Greek Cypriot leaders' dream of achieving *enosis* by means of a quick, dramatic victory. While the air raid was in progress, Makarios, in a paroxism of grief and frustration, threatened that unless the Turkish Air Force left the scene within half an hour he

52. Hal Kosut, ed., *Cyprus: 1946-68* (New York, 1970), p. 136.

would order the massacre of the entire Turkish Cypriot population. But when the horrified U.N. officials threatened, in turn, to order the immediate departure of the peace-keeping force, which would have left the island at the mercy of the Turks, he withdrew his ultimatum. Later, when he visited the morgue of the General Hospital at Paphos and saw the bodies of nine young Greek Cypriot soldiers killed in the Turkish raids, he wept openly. But, as the *Newsweek* correspondent observed, "It was somewhat late for tears".[53]

That night the Security Council in New York called for an immediate, island-wide cease-fire. This time Makarios consented. Thus the fighting had at last come to an end. The battle of Kokkina cost the Greek Cypriot side 53 dead and 125 wounded. The Turkish Cypriots' casualty toll was 12 dead, 4 missing and 32 wounded.[54]

According to official records, 364 Turkish Cypriots and 174 Greek Cypriots were killed during the 1963-1964 crisis. In a vast exodus, upwards to 25,000 Turkish Cypriots fled from their homes, often leaving all their belongings behind. These comprised 18,667 inhabitants from 103 Turkish Cypriot and mixed villages, as well as several thousand who fled from villages which were only partially evacuated.

The 1963-1964 crisis was a most unusual phenomenon: it was not a revolution by a downtrodden minority against an arrogant, oppressive majority, but a revolution by an arrogant, oppressive majority against a downtrodden minority. Makarios tried to compel the Turkish Cypriots to accept constitutional changes which would have deprived them of their political rights by launching a campaign of terror against the various Turkish Cypriot enclaves and by forcibly disarming the TMT militiamen who were protecting them. But all he succeeded in doing was to frighten the Turkish Cypriot population of many isolated and mixed villages into leaving their homes and seeking shelter in the larger Turkish Cypriot enclaves, which his ill-organized and incompetently-led forces were unable to overrun. Thus his attempts to

---

53. *Newsweek*, August 24, 1964, p. 35.
54. Gibbons, *op. cit.*, p. 171.

carry out the Akritas Plan almost completed the physical separation between the two communities. The Greek Cypriot leaders angrily accused the Turkish Cypriot leaders of having encouraged the process of demographic consolidation. However, the Turkish Cypriots needed no prompting to desert their burning homes or abandon villages where they lived in constant fear of being massacred. It must be added that it was in the interest of the Greek Cypriot villagers to force their Turkish Cypriot neighbors to move since they could then seize their homes, fields and orchards, and that consequently many of them did their best to encourage the exodus.[55]

Throughout the crisis, the Greek Cypriot leaders displayed amazing shortsightedness in their dealings with the Turkish Cypriot community and Turkey. In an attempt to explain this shortcoming, Professor Kyriacos C. Markides, the noted Greek Cypriot political scientist, wrote:

Makarios's intuitions were the principal guiding antennas of the island's external relations. Not a single committee of experts was established for the rational and systematic study and analysis of data relating to internal Turkish Cypriot and Turkish politics. . . . Thus the appraisal of Turkish politics was guided more by stereotypes and prejudices learned in the high schools than by rational study.[56]

---

55. For a detailed psychological study of the impact of the traumatic events of 1963-1964 on the Turkish Cypriot refugees, see Vamik D. Volkan, *Cyprus—War and Adaptation* (Charlottesville, Va., 1979).

56. *The Rise and Fall of the Cyprus Republic* (New Haven, 1977), p. 53.

CHAPTER VII
THE 1967 CRISIS

The Tylliria debacle did not lessen Makarios' determination to bring about *enosis*, and he continued to advocate it—at times with great vehemence—in public speeches throughout the island. For example, in an address at Rizokarpasso, on May 26, 1965, he declared:

> Either the whole of Cyprus is to be united with Greece or [it will] become a holocaust. . . . The road to the fulfillment of national aspirations may be full of difficulties, but we shall reach the goal—which is Enosis—alive or dead.[1]

But, in spite of the threats implied in many of his utterances, he no longer believed that *enosis* could be achieved by force. Instead, he devoted his energies to winning over the nations of the world to his point of view and to making life as unpleasant as possible for the Turkish Cypriots in the hope that they would emigrate or bow to his will.

The principal obstacle to Makarios' attempts to sell *enosis* to the world was an all-out effort on the part of Turkey to improve relations with its neighbors. The Johnson letter had heightened Turkey's feelings of isolation and strengthened its resolve to mend its fences with the Soviet Union and the Balkan nations. Russia, eager to drive a wedge into NATO, had for some time been trying to woo Turkey. Therefore, it responded favorably to Turkish overtures for a rapprochement. There followed a series of official visits: Turkish Foreign Minister Erkin to Russia, in October 1964; Soviet President Podgorny to Turkey, in January 1965; Soviet Foreign Minister Gromyko to Turkey, in May 1965; Turkish Premier Ürgüplü to Russia, in August 1965; Soviet Premier Kosygin to Turkey, in December 1966; and Turkish Premier Demirel to Russia, in September 1967. As a

---

1. Örek, *Makarios on Enosis*, p. 30.

result, the Soviet Union gradually withdrew its political and military support from the Makarios regime and leaned increasingly towards a "two communities" solution of the type advocated by Turkey. It stopped shipping arms to Makarios and criticized Czechoslovakia for continuing to do so.[2] Symptomatic of the deteriorating relationship between Makarios and the Soviet regime was the discovery, in March 1967, of a Russian spy network in Nicosia, as a consequence of which a Russian Embassy attaché and the Aeroflot representative were both expelled from the country.

The loss of Russian support was a very serious diplomatic setback for Makarios. He attempted to make up for it by establishing more cordial relations with the United States. There, the Greek Lobby had already been hard at work for several years putting pressure on officials to declare themselves for *enosis*. So successful had this campaign been that by 1964 as many as thirty-seven senators, thirty-six representatives and four state governors had made statements in favor of *enosis*.[3] Makarios now authorized the CIA to use the British airfield at Akrotiri as a base of operation for its U-2 spy planes, to set up radio monitors in Cyprus to eavesdrop on communications between Middle East and Iron Curtain countries, and to install secret antennas for its electronic intelligence network. He apparently even accepted a $1 million yearly retainer from the CIA.[4]

Makarios also scored major triumphs at the Cairo Conference of non-aligned countries, in October 1964, and at the U.N. At the Cairo Conference, the forty-seven heads of state present signed a common declaration stating that

> Cyprus, as an equal member of the United Nations, is entitled to and should enjoy unrestricted and unfettered sovereignty and independence, allowing its people to determine freely, without any foreign intervention or interference, the political future of the country, in accordance with the Charter of the United Nations.[5]

---

2. Feroz Ahmad, *The Turkish Experiment in Democracy, 1950-1975* (London, 1977), pp. 407-409; Adams, *op. cit.*, pp. 160-161.
3. Purcell, *op. cit.*, p. 357.
4. Stern, *op. cit.*, pp. 106-107.
5. Purcell, *op. cit.*, p. 356.

Galo Plaza of Ecuador, who succeeded Sakari Tuomioja as U.N. Mediator on September 28, 1964, rapidly fell under the influence of Makarios. He minimized the suffering of the Turkish Cypriots at Kokkina, even though General Thimayya had described conditions there as "scandalous" and "degrading",[6] and his final report, issued in March 1965, displayed such a callous disregard for the welfare of the Turkish Cypriot community in Cyprus that the Turkish government promptly called for his resignation. He characterized the trend towards bi-zonality, which in Turkish Cypriot eyes appeared to be the only hopeful development in recent Cypriot history, as "a desperate step in the wrong direction";[7] he questioned the wisdom of retaining such guarantees as the treaties of 1960, which the Turkish Cypriots regarded as vital; and he recommended that "special measures... applied in order to ensure to the members of the minority community a proper voice in their... communal affairs and... an equitable part in the public life of the country as a whole" be strictly "transitional".[8] The U.N. General Assembly displayed a similar anti-Turkish bias. On December 18, 1965, it voted in favor of a resolution which, like the Cairo declaration, stated that Cyprus was "entitled to, and should enjoy, full sovereignty and complete independence without any foreign intervention or interference".[9] The Greek Cypriot leaders felt that this resolution would effectively deter Turkey from intervening in Cyprus in the near future. But by June 1966 much of the support which Makarios had mustered at the U.N. had eroded because of his intransigence. At that time, seven of the states that had voted for the U.N. resolution of the previous December (Nepal, Uruguay, Lebanon, Syria, Gabon, Ethiopia and Ghana) gave vent to their dissatisfaction by publicly announcing that their vote was in no way to be construed as an endorsement of *enosis*.[10]

---

6. *Ibid.*, p. 355.
7. *The Galo Plaza Report*, paragraph 155.
8. *Ibid.*, paragraph 163.
9. Purcell, *op. cit.*, p. 366.
10. Purcell, *op. cit.*, p. 367.

The same stubborn streak which Makarios displayed in his dealings with Cypriot affairs at the U.N. and which so disconcerted his friends there was clearly manifest in his treatment of the Turkish Cypriots at home, whom he politically ostracized and relentlessly drove to the brink of starvation. As soon as the fighting started, during the 1963-1964 crisis, the Greek Cypriots took over the government and dismissed all Turkish Cypriot officials. In the words of Vedat A. Çelik, the former foreign minister of the Turkish Federated State of Cyprus,

> With the pre-planned armed attack on the Turkish Cypriot Community on December 1963, all the governmental machinery and public services were seized by the Greeks. The Turkish civil servants, Turkish members of the police and the Cyprus army, and other Turkish Cypriot government employees, whose places of work were in Greek sectors, were chased away by threat of armed force (some of them were actually killed or abducted) and their salaries and remunerations were stopped as of that date. All public services were denied to the Turks and all public funds of the Republic were seized and used for the benefit of the Greek Community only.[11]

Even the freely-elected Turkish Cypriot representatives were ousted from office and when, in July 1965, they attempted to make their way into the House of Representatives they were informed that "unless the Turkish deputies agreed to the abrogation of the constitution and endorsed the unconstitutional laws enacted in their absence by their Greek counterparts, their return would be prevented by force".[12] As a consequence, the Turkish Cypriots became to all intents and purposes, stateless persons without any civil rights. Children born to Turkish Cypriots were not recorded in the State Register of Persons. Turkish Cypriots could not get passports.[13] No Greek Cypriot was prosecuted for any crime committed against Turkish Cypriots.

---

11. *Statement Made Before the Special Political Committee of the United Nations General Assembly*, October 29, 1974, A/SPC/ PV. 922, p. 32.

12. *Ibid.*

13. An exception was made for Turkish Cypriots who wished to emigrate. These were at once given a passport.

By the end of the summer of 1964, the plight of the Turkish Cypriots had become acute. 527 houses belonging to Turkish Cypriots in 109 villages had been destroyed and 2,000 others had been damaged. In Omorphita alone, 50 houses had been destroyed and 240 more had been damaged. Apart from losses incurred in agriculture and industry, the Turkish Cypriot community had lost other sources of income, including the salaries of over 4,000 persons who had been government employees or who had worked for public or private concerns located in Greek Cypriot areas. Besides the 25,000 refugees already mentioned, there were 23,500 unemployed persons and 7,500 dependents of missing persons or persons who had become disabled as a result of the fighting. Thus, more than 50% of the total Turkish Cypriot population had been made indigent by the Greek Cypriot onslaught.

To add to the Turkish Cypriots' woes, the Makarios regime subjected them to an economic blockade. The rationale behind this scheme was that "economic sanctions, unlike the deaths caused by military confrontations, would not offer a dramatic justification for a Turkish invasion".[14] After the Tylliria offensive, Makarios prevented all movements of people and supplies into the Turkish Cypriot enclaves of Nicosia, Lefka, Limnitis and Kokkina. On September 5, the blockade was extended to the Turkish Cypriot quarters of Famagousta and Larnaca. Within a week the population of these towns was close to starvation. The U.N. vehemently protested, U Thant observing that the restrictions "which in some instances have been so severe as to amount to a veritable siege, indicate that the Government of Cyprus seeks to force a potential solution by economic pressure as a substitute for military action".[15] Finally, the U.N. and the Red Cross convinced Makarios that his policy of starving out the Turkish Cypriots would damn him in

---

14. Patrick, *op. cit.*, p. 106.
15. U.N. Document S/5950, paragraph 222.

the eyes of the world. He, thereupon, granted permission
for a list of essential foodstuffs, based on a calorific minimum, to be brought to the besieged Turkish Cypriot enclaves. Gibbons, who checked the list, concluded that
"the calorific minimum allowed to Turks was below the
standards applied in the prisons of many civilised countries".[16] Later, when Makarios realized that the blockade
was solidifying support for the most militant of the TMT
leaders in the Turkish enclaves, the food quotas were gradually relaxed. But the following measures remained in effect:

1) The Makarios government continued to maintain its
strict blockade of Kokkina until November 1967.

2) Until March 1968, the Makarios government prohibited the importation of many "strategic materials"
into the Turkish Cypriot enclaves. The list of these
was continually growing and finally came to include
the following items: accumulators, cables, circuit
testers (galvanometers), electrical detonators, mine
detonators, safety fuses, exploders, explosives, shot-
gun cartridges, telephones, radios, wire (including
barbed wire), wire cutters, ammonium nitrate, sul-
phur, angle irons, thick steel plates, cement, sand,
crushed metal, crushed stone, iron pickets, iron poles
and rods, lead and plastic pipes, timber, automobile
spare parts, motorboats, Land-Rovers, trucks, tractors,
tires, fuel in large quantities, rubber boots, leather
shoelaces, studs for boots, leather jackets, gloves,
raincoats, socks for men, woolen clothing (if capable
of military use), khaki cloth, camouflage netting, tent
material, bags, thermos bottles and fire extinguishers.[17]
These restrictions severely affected all building activity, impeded transportation and throttled industrial
production.

3) The Makarios government surrounded the Turkish
Cypriot enclaves with fortifications and established

16. *Op. cit.*, p. 174.
17. *News Bulletin*, February 25, 1977, p. 2.

roadblocks on all the roads leading to them. The official purpose of the roadblocks was to prevent the smuggling of arms and war materiel into the Turkish Cypriot enclaves. But they became a means by which to harass the Turkish Cypriots and further restrict their economic activity. As U Thant contended, there were "too many cases of close bodily searches and lengthy interrogations which [did] not appear to be justified by the need to look for arms and strategic materials".[18] According to the correspondent of *Time* magazine, "At some roadblocks Turkish Cypriot truck drivers [were] stopped for tedious 'searches', in which their cargoes of fruit or vegetables [were] unloaded on the ground and sometimes damaged beyond use".[19] Passing Turkish Cypriots were constantly insulted. Occasionally, they were even robbed.[20]

4) The Makarios government imposed a 20% tax on the grain sold by the Turkish Cypriots through the Grain Commission as "compensation for Greek land under Turkish cultivation", even though much more Turkish Cypriot land was under Greek Cypriot cultivation. This tax caused considerable hardship because it effectively prevented the Turkish Cypriots from selling any more of their grain through the Grain Commission.[21]

5) Starting in December 1963, the Makarios government stopped paying social insurance benefits to Turkish Cypriots.

6) Until October 1966, the postal service between Greek Cypriot and Turkish Cypriot areas was interrupted. When it was reestablished, the Turkish Cypriot mail was subjected to censorship.

---

18. U.N. Document S/7191, paragraph 91.
19. Issue of March 26, 1965, p. 27.
20. Purcell, *op. cit.*, p. 358.
21. *Ibid.*, p. 369.

7) The Makarios government forced Turkish Cypriots to pay hard currency (which had to be imported from Turkey) for Cypriot money which they needed to purchase goods from Greek Cypriot stores.

As a result of these restrictions, the Turkish Cypriot economy remained stagnant. In December 1966, the United Nations estimated that approximately one-third of the entire Turkish Cypriot population still needed some form of relief.[22] The Red Crescent and the Turkish government offered all the help they could. By 1966, the sum contributed by Turkey to the Turkish Cypriot community had reached the equivalent of £8,000,000 *per annum*.[23] Dr. Volkan, who visited Cyprus in the summer of 1968, wrote that in Nicosia

> The contrast between one side of the green line and the other was impressive. The Turkish side looked as though it were in ruins; the streets were pitted, and poverty was evident everywhere. I learned that the delivery of building material to the Turkish sector had been forbidden for a long time lest the Turks use it to fortify their enclaves, so nothing had been repaired.[24]

As an authority on the psychological problems of refugees, Dr. Volkan concluded that the Turkish Cypriots were

> interim survivors who had withstood the terrible stress of bloody days only to face dislocation, a reduced lifestyle, and the loss of loved ones and property. They had become prisoners, in spite of the fact that their 'prisons' lay within the neighborhoods of their own people in which it was possible to conduct some semblance of normal life.[25]

During this time, the Greek Cypriot community was booming. Whereas the *per capita* gross domestic product of the Turkish Cypriot community declined from £188 in 1963 to £160 in 1968, that of the Greek Cypriot community increased from £218 to £302 during the same period.[26] Indeed, Spyros Kyprianou was later to refer to these years as "the happy years".

---

22. Patrick, *op. cit.*, p. 108.
23. *Ibid*.
24. *Op. cit.*, p. 82.
25. *Ibid*., p. 89.
26. Patrick, *op. cit.*, p. 109.

But these were also troubled years. Grivas was contemptuous of Makarios' policy of achieving *enosis* by economic strangulation. He tenaciously clung to the belief that only brute force would bring the Turkish Cypriots to their knees and he was determined to increase military pressure on the Turkish Cypriot enclaves in spite of Makarios' orders to the contrary. This controversy caused a major rift in the Greek Cypriot community. Makarios, who was supported by his own Patriotic Front, as well as by AKEL (the Communist Party) and its labor union, the Pan Cyprian Federation of Labor, regarded Grivas as a dangerous egomaniac, whose recklessness would provoke another military confrontation with Turkey. In early 1966, Makarios accused Grivas of trying to start a civil war and asked the Greek government to limit his powers. He also dismissed pro-Grivas government officials and reduced the allocations for the National Guard. Then, to bolster his own forces, he added £ 200,000 to the budget of the Greek Cypriot police, recruited an additional 500 constables and created a new paramilitary police force.[27] To arm this force, he purchased 1,000 rifles, 1,000 sub-machine guns, 20 rocket-launchers, 20 mortars, and 20 armored cars from Czechoslovakia, but pressures from Turkey, Greece and the United Nations prevented the Czechs from delivering the armored cars, and most of the small arms which reached the island were kept in storage. Grivas, who was supported by many ex-EOKA leaders and fighters, retaliated by accusing Makarios of betraying *enosis* and by launching a campaign of terror aimed mostly at AKEL and the Pan Cyprian Federation of Labor.

Because of Grivas' aggressiveness and insubordination, Makarios' policy was doomed from the very start. Not only did the National Guard act on its own, causing increasingly serious incidents, but many Greek Cypriot villagers, encouraged by Grivas' bellicosity and inspired by his fiery oratory, also joined the fray, setting booby traps and taking pot shots at Turkish Cypriot villages. The Turkish Cypriots

---

27. By 1967, Makarios' regular police force consisted of more than 2,200 men and his para-military police force had reached battalion strength.

protected themselves as well as possible by fortifying their villages. Because of the lack of cement, these fortifications could not be as elaborate as those of the Greek Cypriots. Nonetheless, soon every Turkish Cypriot enclave was surrounded by a protective network of trenches, barricades and dugouts, which spilled into the surrounding countryside and sometimes almost touched the outer perimeter of the Greek Cypriot fortifications. The Turkish Cypriots also closed some of the roads which passed through their villages.

On February 19, 1965, the National Guard opened fire on a group of unarmed Turkish Cypriot fighters who were cutting a tree on their own side of the cease-fire line at Kokkina, killing one of the men.

On March 12, 1965, a major shooting incident occurred in the neighborhood of Turkish Cypriot-held Lefka, when the National Guard occupied two strategic hills between that town and three Turkish Cypriot villages. In the course of the fighting that ensued and that lasted for several days, one Greek Cypriot and one Turkish Cypriot lost their lives.

On September 25, 1965, a group of Greek Cypriot policemen and National Guardsmen searching for arms raided the Turkish Cypriot quarter of the mixed village of Kato Polemidia, in the district of Limassol, looting many of the homes, confiscating some weapons and arresting three of the villagers.

On November 2, 1965, a National Guard patrol was fired upon when it entered a Turkish Cypriot orchard in Sakarya, a suburb of Famagousta. The National Guard responded by carrying out an immediate attack on Sakarya and neighboring Karakol, as well as upon the Turkish Cypriot quarter of Famagousta. In two days of bitter fighting, one Turkish Cypriot was killed and five were wounded. Six National Guardsmen were also wounded.

At the end of 1965, the National Guard seized the Umm Harâm, near Larnaca, the most important Muslim shrine on the island, and, in May 1966, declared the place off-limits to Muslims. This outrage shocked the world. But it was in keeping with the Greek Cypriot policy of total Hellenization, which had already led to the destruction of the mosque and shrine of Bayraktar, in Nicosia, the mosque of Omar in Kyrenia, the mosques of Ağa Ca'fer and Seyyid Mehmet Ağa in Lapta, the mosque of Zuhûrî in Larnaca and other places of worship during the 1963-1964 crisis.[28]

On January 22, 1966, the National Guard fired on a group of Turkish Cypriots who were cutting wood in the Kyrenia range, wounding three.

In early June 1966, the Makarios government closed off the Turkish Cypriot quarter of Nicosia for three days, prohibiting all Turkish Cypriots from entering or leaving the area.

On July 24, 1966, an attack by the National Guard on the villages of Mora, in the district of Nicosia, and Melousha, in the district of Larnaca, was thwarted by the arrival of a UNFICYP detachment.

On August 12, 1966, a seventeen-year-old Turkish Cypriot sentry was killed by a Greek Cypriot para-military policeman.

On September 9, 1966, a Turkish Cypriot villager was shot dead while cycling home in the mixed village of Arsos, in the district of Larnaca.

On the same day, two Turkish Cypriot villagers were ambushed and killed as they were passing by the Kykko Village Fair area, in the district of Nicosia.

By 1967, Grivas obviously felt a new surge of self-confidence. His forces were stronger than ever. Although the 1960 Treaty of Alliance limited the number of Greek troops on the island to 950, as many as 20,000 of them had infiltrated into Cyprus.[29] In addition, there was the Greek-officered National Guard, which comprised 10,000

---

28. Purcell, *op. cit.*, p. 367; also Emel Esin, *Turkish Art in Cyprus* (Ankara, 1969), p. 32.

29. *The New York Times*, November 19, 1967, p. 14f.

active soldiers and 20,000 reserves.[30] These forces were well-armed with automatic weapons, artillery and armored vehicles, and their battle readiness had been tested in large-scale military maneuvers in the summer of 1966. In comparison, the Turkish Cypriot side was practically defenseless. The Turkish Army contingent still comprised only the 650 men allowed by the Treaty. TMT had 5,000 men and was led by a small cadre of highly competent Turkish Army officers smuggled in for the purpose. But they were armed mostly with shotguns and their commander, the legendary "Bozkurt" ("Grey Wolf"), whose real name was Kemal Çoşkun, was abruptly recalled to Turkey in February 1967, when allegations of financial improprieties were made against him.[31] The military strength of the Turkish Cypriot community was further undermined by the departure for Turkey of 512 students in January 1966 and 438 more students in May 1967, which substantially reduced the number of potential fighters. It seemed like an ideal time to increase military pressure upon the Turkish Cypriot enclaves, and Grivas did not hesitate to do so. This, in turn, provoked a rise in the number of individual acts of terrorism by Greek Cypriot villagers against their Turkish Cypriot neighbors, compelling TMT to respond in kind. Thus, more than 600 shooting incidents took place in Cyprus during the year 1967.[32]

---

30. As a step towards achieving *enosis*, Grivas had done his best to transform the National Guard into a purely Greek force. As U Thant reported (*Report on U.N. Operations in Cyprus*, S/7969, paragraph 29):

Over the past few months UNFICYP has noticed increased signs of a tendency to identify the Cyprus National Guard with the Greek Army. These include the widespread use of the Greek Army cap badge by the National Guard and the use of the Greek royal crown in flags and sign boards at many National Guard camps, while the oath taken by recent National Guard recruits on enlistment now incorporates allegiance to the King of Greece.

31. According to *Time*, already in March 1965 the Greek Cypriots had an edge in military hardware which was 20 to 1 (issue of March 26, 1965, p. 27).

32. U.N. Documents S/7969 & S/8286.

On April 8, a National Guard unit comprising two armored cars, a Land-Rover mounted with a heavy machine-gun and a truckload of infantrymen stopped in front of the village of Mari, in the district of Larnaca, and began firing. During the four hours of the barrage, at least 40 two-pounder shells and 1,000 rounds of ammunition were fired by the armored cars alone. But, miraculously, none of the villagers were killed. For 15 days afterward, no one was allowed to leave the village. Only a truckload of oranges and lemons sent by the United Nations prevented outright starvation.

In the same month, there were six booby trap explosions around the village of Ambelikou, near Lefka. One Turkish Cypriot was killed; two British tourists and one Turkish Cypriot were wounded.

On April 21, a group of colonels seized power in Athens and established a military dictatorship. This dramatic political development greatly complicated the relationship between the Greek and Greek Cypriot governments. Even in the best of times this relationship had been strained owing to the following factors:

1) Most Greek prime ministers had insisted that Athens, being the *ethnikon kentron* (national center), should lead the fight for *enosis*. Makarios had been repeatedly warned that because Greece would have to bear the burden of defending Cyprus in case of Turkish intervention, he should take no initiative of his own.

2) Makarios had been haunted by the fear that the Greek government might negotiate a compromise peace settlement with the Turkish government without consulting him.

Now, in addition, Makarios was faced with a Greek government with which he was ideologically out-of-step. He loathed the junta's authoritarianism and rigid anti-communism. The junta just as vehemently disliked his leftist sympathies and independent-mindedness. Makarios might also have been personally disappointed, for if (as is alleged) he had entertained hopes of becoming the leader of a unified Greek nation comprising both Greece and Cyprus, these must now have been dashed.

As Greek nationalists, the military leaders of Greece believed in *enosis*. General Gregory Spandidakis, the deputy Prime Minister and Defence Minister, made the point quite clear in an address in Nicosia in October 1967, when he described Cyprus as part of southern Greece. But being more pragmatic than Makarios on this subject, the Colonels knew that it could not be achieved without compromise. Furthermore, they desperately wanted to solve the Cyprus problem to increase their popularity and reduce the cost (estimated at 10 million pounds sterling *per annum*) of maintaining forces in Cyprus. Consequently, they became increasingly impatient with Makarios' unyielding attitude. On July 2, they issued an official statement castigating the Makarios regime for its intransigence. It urged the dismissal of leaders who "on the eve of decisive developments", set "groundless conditions and subversive prerequisites". It labeled these as "deserters" and "hypocrites", and mourned the fact that "among them, unhappily, there are persons who hold the highest posts in the state and influence the leadership of the Cypriot people". Those who belonged to that category of leaders were invited to "step down and make room for those who. . . possess the realistic spirit needed for a final solution that will be both profitable to the nation and generally acceptable".[33] Unlike the Papandreou government, which had given Makarios assurances that no steps would be taken towards achieving a permanent settlement without his approval, the junta tried to arrange a separate peace with Turkey. It initiated a series of negotiations with the Turkish government which culminated in a summit meeting of the Greek and Turkish prime ministers on the Greco-Turkish boundary in early September 1967. There are conflicting reports as to what was offered by the two sides in the way of a compromise solution to the Cyprus problem. However, neither side was apparently willing to go far enough to accommodate the other, for the conference ended in failure.

33. *The Times* (of London), July 3, 1967, p. 5f.

Although Grivas' private war in Cyprus, using Greek officers and men, jeopardized Greece's seemingly sincere efforts to come to terms with Turkey and to disentangle itself from the Cyprus problem, the junta was reluctant to discipline him because he was still immensely popular in Greece and because he was the only person through whom it could exercise any control over Archbishop Makarios. Thus, it gave him *carte blanche* to continue his campaign of intimidation and aggression against the Turkish Cypriot enclaves.

In May 1967, the National Guard ousted UNFICYP from several of its observation posts which overlooked Scala (İskele), the Turkish Cypriot quarter of Larnaca, and there established heavily fortified strong points.

On June 18, a National Guardsman shot and killed a Turkish Cypriot militiaman at Ambelikou.

On July 23, a Greek Cypriot motorist, while passing through the village of Koloni, in the district of Paphos, stopped his car and shot two Turkish Cypriots to death; one of them was an 80-year-old man. The case was taken to court. The Greek Cypriot court condemned the murderer to four years in prison. But shortly thereafter Makarios pardoned him and gave him a government job.

On July 25, two Turkish Cypriots were battered to death in a dry river bed between the villages of Ayios Ioannis and Stavrokono, in the district of Paphos.

On August 6, a Turkish Cypriot woman and her ten-year-old son were shot to death by two Greek Cypriot men near Kourtaka, in the district of Paphos.

On August 12, a bomb exploded in the Turkish Cypriot quarter of the mixed village of Alaminos, in the district of Larnaca, killing one man, two youths and two children. It also blinded a small boy. A week later, a car driven by a Turkish Cypriot was blown up by a mine between Alaminos and Kophinou. The driver and a passenger were both severely wounded.

On August 18, a Turkish Cypriot mine worker was shot to death at the Limni Mines.

Early on October 31, Rauf Denktaş, who had been banished from Cyprus since 1964 by the Makarios regime, attempted to land secretly near Ayios Theodoros, on the Karpas peninsula, with two companions. But, owing to a navigational error, the trio set foot at the wrong place and were apprehended by the Greek Cypriot police. The captives were then taken to Nicosia and incarcerated there. As concern for Denktaş's safety mounted in the Turkish Cypriot community, tensions rose to fever pitch. At first the Greek Cypriot government seemed intent upon trying him for "criminal offenses against the state" for his activities during the 1963-1964 crisis (which consisted mostly of organizing the defenses of the Turkish Cypriot quarter in Nicosia). However, on November 12, after the United Nations, the Western powers and Turkey had urged his release, he and his companions were sent back to Turkey. This was widely regarded as a conciliatory move by Makarios. But, if such was the case, its effect was at once nullified by Grivas' savage attacks on Ayios Theodoros[34] and Kophinou, in the district of Larnaca.

In these attacks, Grivas was exploiting an already existing controversy, namely that of the police patrols. One of the ways by which the Greek Cypriot government asserted its authority was by means of police patrols which passed through most of the villages on the island on an average of twice weekly. But when some shooting incidents had occurred in the village of Ayios Theodoros on July 20-21 and 29-30, the Greek Cypriot police had wisely decided to refrain from patrolling the road which passed through the Turkish Cypriot quarter of that village until tensions had subsided. In early September, the Greek Cypriot police had announced its intention of resuming the patrols. However, the Turkish Cypriot leaders had refused to allow them to pass until the Greek Cypriot government had removed its strong points overlooking Scala. Inasmuch as both sides had been determined to get their way, this issue had rapidly escalated into a major controversy, and the United Nations had tried to effect a compromise. By the beginning of November, there were clear indications that the Turkish

---

34. There are several villages by that name in Cyprus.

Cypriot leaders were prepared to reconsider their stand as regards the patrols and were on the point of agreeing to a time-table put forward by UNFICYP for their gradual resumption. But before a final agreement could be reached, Grivas decided to force the issue and at the same time make a show of strength by sending through Ayios Theodoros a series of police patrols escorted by units of the National Guard. Thus, in the afternoon of November 14, two police patrols reinforced by National Guardsmen converged on the village, one from the north and the other from the south. Grivas himself directed the operation. Taken by surprise and not yet aware of Grivas' intentions or of the fact that he had usurped command of the Greek Cypriot police, the Turkish Cypriot militiamen in the village made no attempt to stop the force from passing through. Next morning, Grivas again sent a patrol through the village. Once more, it was unopposed. But when yet another patrol tried to make its way through the village that afternoon, the Turkish Cypriots, who now realized that they were being deliberately taunted, placed a tractor and a plow across the road. When the National Guardsmen accompanying the patrol tried to remove these obstacles, they were fired upon. Grivas then unleashed a well-planned attack upon the Turkish Cypriot quarter of Ayios Theodoros, as well as upon the neighboring all-Turkish Cypriot village of Kophinou, where the inhabitants had occasionally demanded gas from passing motorists because they were deprived of fuel by Makarios' blockade. The two villages were first sprayed with heavy machine guns, 2-pounder guns, mortars and bazookas, and then taken by storm. In the battle, which lasted seven hours and in which as many as 40 Greek Cypriot armored cars participated, all the Turkish Cypriot positions were overrun and 27 of the defenders were killed. An eighty-year-old man was wrapped in a gasoline-soaked blanket and burned alive. In the course of the operation, all U.N. troops in the area were forcibly disarmed and their wireless disabled. A witness, a middle-aged woman by the name of Mevhibe Ali, has given us a poignant account of the attack on Kophinou:

It was 2.10 p.m. on the 15th November, 1967. I heard a series
of loud explosions while I was shoveling loaves of dough into
the earthen oven. I froze and dropped the loafshovel. These
were not the usual sounds we were accustomed to hearing in
the village. Judging also by the villagers' running in the streets
it was evident that we were being attacked by the Greeks. In
fifteen minutes, gunfire spread to the east of the village. The
villagers panicked and ran for their children stranded in the
fields. I myself quickly searched for and found three of my
sons aged 8, 10 and 14 years. I had received no news about my
other two sons, who were defending our village together with
other villagers against the attacking Greeks. They were more
numerous than us and had far superior weapons at their disposal. Against their artillery fire our men had to battle with
simple rifles. The enemy pounded our village continually for
seven hours with mortars and artillery fire. Our fighters had to
respond with bullets. At the end of seven hours of resistance
our village fell. It was about 9.00 p.m. when we heard Greek
spoken in the village. 'Alas, they must have murdered our defenders, our sons and husbands, to enter the village' I thought
shuddering but was reluctant to give up hope. You could hear
people shouting and crying in the streets. Barbaric Greeks were
entering Turkish houses one by one, taking the villagers as hostages and moving them out of the village. At about 9.30 p.m.
I heard the voice of the Greek soldiers. Suddenly they broke
into our house and took my husband, my three sons and myself to the spot where the other prisoners were kept. On our
way we were horrified at the sight of the body of the eighty
year old Mehmet Emin burning like a torch at his doorstep. I
was so utterly shocked at this sight that my anxiety about my
other two sons' fate augmented. We had to spend the night at
the hospital and in the bar of the village, cordonned off by the
armed Greeks. It was the longest night of my life. It was un-
bearable.

The next day, when the men were released, Mevhibe Ali
looked for her two elder sons:

Among the men released I could spot one of my elder sons.
Amongst the people reuniting I searched for my eldest one. No
one seemed to know his whereabouts, but from the grim face
of my husband it was obvious that something terrible had happened. I was probably the last one in the village to learn the
tragic news of the death of my eldest son. It was hard, very hard
to accept the fact that my son at the prime of his life was dead.[35]

35. Lâtife Birgen, *The Cyprus Tragedy* (Nicosia, n.d.), p. 21.

Another mother, Ayşe Hasan Emir Mustafa, lost three sons at Kophinou.

The attacks on Ayios Theodoros and Kophinou had dire implications. As the correspondent of *Newsweek* observed:

> Since the end of the civil war that racked the island in 1963-64, the Turks have steadfastly refused to come out from behind the weed-covered sandbags and rusting barbed-wire barricades that hedge their scattered villages and urban enclaves. 'The Greeks', explained a Turkish Cypriot leader in Nicosia recently, 'are like a hunter who has chased the rabbit into a bush; they are standing there with their fingers on the triggers waiting for us to come out'. Now, however, the hunter was apparently no longer content to wait; he was coming in shooting.[36]

The capture of Ayios Theodoros and Kophinou also had strategic significance, for it effectively cut off the Turkish Cypriots in the south of the island from those in the north.

The Turkish reaction to these new outrages was swift. On the evening of November 15 Turkish Foreign Minister Çağlayangil called on UNFICYP to bring about an immediate cease-fire. On the morning of the 16th, the Turkish government warned that it would intervene militarily if the shooting continued. On the 17th, the Turkish Parliament authorized the government "to go to war with Greece itself if necessary should the Cyprus situation deteriorate further"[37] and the president of Turkey, Cevdet Sunay, announced his country's intention "to solve the Cyprus problem once and for all, from the roots upward".[38] Having decided to by-pass Archbishop Makarios, the Turkish government then sent the junta an ultimatum making the following demands:

1) General Grivas was to be recalled immediately.
2) All Greek troops on the island in excess of those permitted by the Treaty of Alliance were to be withdrawn.

---

36. Issue of December 4, 1967, p. 37.
37. Salih, *op. cit.*, p. 58.
38. *Ibid.*

3) The Greek Cypriots were to be disarmed.

4) The Greek Cypriot government was to compensate the victims of the attacks on Ayios Theodoros and Kophinou.

5) All economic restrictions on the Turkish Cypriot community were to be lifted.

6) Effective guarantees were to be given against any further assaults on the Turkish Cypriot enclaves.

To emphasize the gravity of the situation, the Turkish Air Force made a number of sorties over Greek Thrace and troops were concentrated on the Greco-Turkish border and in the seaport of İskenderun, within easy reach of Cyprus. The major cities of Turkey were also blacked out and anti-aircraft batteries were deployed around them.

It was now quite clear that the Turks were willing to go to war over the Cyprus issue and that Grivas had grossly underestimated the determination of the Turks to protect the Turkish Cypriot community. Indeed, Grivas' timing had been atrocious. In October 1965, Turkey's Justice Party had acquired a majority of seats in the Grand National Assembly, putting an end to a period of weak coalition governments. The new premier, Süleyman Demirel, was determined to act decisively if provoked by some blatant act of aggression against the Turkish Cypriots, and he was under growing pressure to adopt a firm policy towards the Makarios regime from the Turkish Army, the Turkish press and a large part of the Turkish population which favored a military solution to the Cyprus problem. The Turkish government was also tired of bearing the heavy financial burden of relief for the economically crippled Turkish Cypriot community. Turkey had staunchly supported the peace-keeping efforts of UNFICYP and it had hoped that this force would be given the authority to disarm and arrest troublemakers and to ban the importation of weapons into Cyprus. But this now seemed unlikely ever to happen. It must be added that never before had the Turks such ample legal justification for intervention:

1) The Greeks had broken the Treaty of Alliance by sending to the island a number of troops which was far in excess of that allowed.
2) Makarios continued to defy the Constitution of 1960, which Turkey was pledged to uphold according to the Treaty of Guarantee, by politically ostracizing the Turkish Cypriot community.
3) Grivas was openly violating the Security Council's injunction "to refrain from any action or threat of action likely to worsen the situation in Cyprus or endanger international peace".

Grivas had overestimated the strength of the Greek junta's commitment to him. Although they were ardent enosists, the early leaders of the junta were cautious men who did not want to provoke a military confrontation with Turkey, especially at a time when Greece could expect no support from her allies or sympathy from the United Nations because, as Professor Thomas Ehrlich, of the Stanford Law School, put it, "the crisis had been triggered by a premeditated Greek attack, led by a Greek general, in violation of Security Council resolutions and arrangements with the United Nations Force commander".[39] Therefore, the junta, which had already ordered Grivas to withdraw from the occupied villages before the ultimatum, now finally mustered the courage to recall the aging hero on November 19. However, this did not satisfy the Turkish government. It insisted that its other demands be met as well, and continued its preparations for war.

At this point, President Johnson once more intervened in the Cyprus conflict. On November 22, he despatched Cyrus R. Vance, a distinguished lawyer and a former Deputy Secretary of Defense, as his special envoy with instructions to help the two United Nations mediators, Jose Rolz-Bennett and Manlio Brosio, negotiate a settlement. Using the kind of "shuttle diplomacy" later made famous by Henry Kissinger, Vance convinced the governments of Greece and Turkey to accept a compromise solution. This agreement provided for:

39. *Op. cit.*, p. 113.

1) The withdrawal from Cyprus within 45 days of all Greek and Turkish troops in excess of those permitted by the Treaty of Alliance.
2) The dismantling of Turkey's war preparations on a step-by-step basis to coincide with the withdrawal of the Greek troops from Cyprus.
3) The dissolution of the National Guard.
4) Compensation to the Turkish Cypriot victims at Ayios Theodoros and Kophinou.
5) Expansion of the size and powers of UNFICYP.
6) The dismissal of General Grivas (already then an accomplished fact).

Greece did its best to comply with the agreement and withdrew its forces from the island. But Makarios cunningly succeeded in scuttling three of its provisions, with the result that the National Guard was not disbanded, UNFICYP's size and powers were not extended and the victims of Grivas' military campaign received no compensation. Makarios was also strengthened by the departure of his chief rival for power, Grivas. But his chances of ever again presiding over a unified, bi-communal government had become much more remote, for the Turkish Cypriots had been forced to form their own separate administration.

Having been reduced to the status of stateless persons during the 1963-1964 crisis, the Turkish Cypriots had had to organize themselves to survive the economic blockade that followed. Thus, a patchwork government had been set up. It consisted of the Vice-President of the Republic, the three Turkish Cypriot cabinet ministers, the Turkish Cypriot members of the House of Representatives, the members of the Turkish Cypriot Communal Chamber and a few others— all of whom formed a body known as the General Committee. But when Grivas embarked upon his campaign to overrun the Turkish Cypriot enclaves, the Turkish Cypriot leaders realized that a more efficient administrative machinery was required. Thus, on December 28, 1967, a Provisional Turkish Cypriot Administration (*Geçici Kıbrıs Türk Yönetimi*) was established. Under its "Basic Provisions", the

the executive functions of the administration were to be
performed by an Executive Committee. The vice-president
of the Republic (at that time Dr. Küçük) was to serve as
chairman of the committee and was to appoint its members.
The legislative functions were to be performed by a Legislative Assembly, comprising the 15 Turkish Cypriot members of the House of Representatives and the 15 members
of the Turkish Cypriot Communal Chamber. The judicial
functions were to be performed by independent Turkish
Cypriot courts. A Supreme Court was to be vested with the
jurisdiction which had previously been vested in the Supreme
Constitutional Court and the High Court of Justice.[40]

With the formation of the Provisional Turkish Cypriot
Administration, the separation between the two communities became complete. Hence, the splitting up of Cyprus
into two ethnically-homogeneous, self-governing states was
not achieved by the Turkish armed intervention of 1974,
as is commonly believed, but by Makarios and Grivas in
the 1960's.

---

40. Rauf R. Denktaş, *The Cyprus Problem* (Nicosia, 1974, p. 35.
On August 23, 1974 the name of this administration was changed to
Autonomous Turkish Cypriot Administration (*Otonom Kıbrıs Türk
Yönetimi*).

THE TURKISH CYPRIOT ENCLAVES IN THE LATE 1960'S

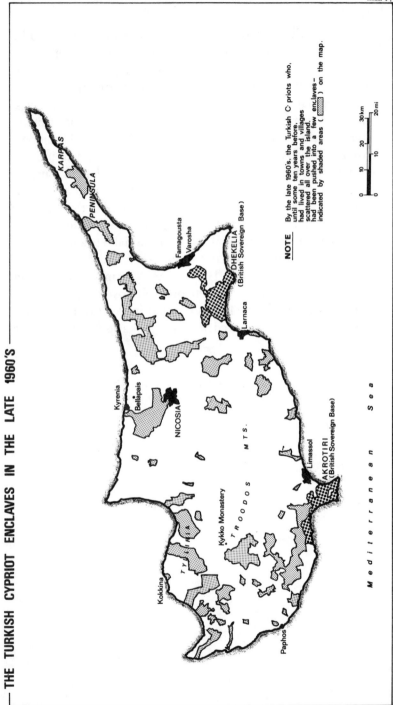

KARPAS

PENINSULA

Kyrenia

Bellapais

NICOSIA

Kokkina

Kykko Monastery

T R O O D O S   M T S.

Paphos

Limassol

AKROTIRI
(British Sovereign Base)

Larnaca

DHEKELIA
(British Sovereign Base)

Famagousta
Varosha

M e d i t e r r a n e a n   S e a

NOTE By the late 1960's, the Turkish Cypriots who,
until some ten years before,
had lived in towns and villages
scattered all over the island,
had been pushed into a few enclaves—
indicated by shaded areas (▨) on the map.

0   10   20   30 km
0   10   20 mi

L. e. ramann

CHAPTER VIII
THE FIRST PEACE OPERATION

The 1967 crisis convinced Archbishop Makarios that *enosis* was at best a distant goal. As he said in October 1970: "I have always been in favor of union with Greece. I realize, though, that because of extraneous difficulties such a solution is not attainable now".[1] He thereby joined a growing number of Greek Cypriots who were for making the most of Cyprus' independent status.

The increasing materialism that resulted from improved living conditions and exposure to moves and television had done much to dampen enthusiasm for the traditionalist, religion-oriented enosist point of view. Fears that *enosis* would transform Cyprus into "another remote and neglected province of Greece"[2] and the realization that it would subject the Cypriots to the arbitrary rule of a police state had also contributed to the erosion of pan-Hellenist sentiment on the island. Finally AKEL (the Communist Party) had convinced many erstwhile enosists to change their minds. AKEL, which was the largest political party in Cyprus, opposed union with Greece because the Communist Party was outlawed in that country and because such a union would have tied Cyprus more closely to NATO.

By the end of 1967, only a small minority of Greek Cypriots still felt strongly enough about union with Greece to be willing to fight for it. These die-hard enosists were mostly social and political reactionaries, such as clergymen, EOKA

---

1. Statement to Albert Coerant, representative of Dutch and Belgian Radio and Television, October 18, 1970 (Orek, *Makarios on Enosis*, p. 34).

2. Markides, *op. cit.*, p. 78.

veterans, old-fashioned, Greek-trained school teachers and businessmen who sympathized with the junta in Athens. But what this group lacked in size it more than made up for in vehemence. Its members violently criticized Makarios for having weakened his stand on *enosis*. Some even regarded him as a traitor. After the 1967 crisis, they formed an opposition party called the Democratic National Party (DEK). But when its candidate for president was overwhelmingly defeated in the presidential election of 1968,[3] the new party floundered and enosists turned increasingly to terrorism to express their dissatisfaction with the Makarios regime. Soon a handful of terrorist organizations made their appearance upon the scene, the principal of which were the National Front, the Organization of Akritas, the Enosist Youth Phoenix, the National Youth of Paphos and the Organization of National Salvation. One of the prime movers of the opposition to Makarios was none other than Polykarpos Yorgadjis, the former EOKA hero who had been serving as minister of the interior since 1960 and had been packing the Cypriot police force with ex-EOKA fighters. Makarios dismissed him in 1969. Thereafter, he devoted all his energies to activities of a revolutionary and conspiratorial nature. Another dedicated enemy of Makarios was the fiery newspaper publisher Nikos Sampson.

The various terrorist organizations vented their rage against the government through a rash of bombings and assassinations. On March 8, 1970, Makarios' helicopter was fired upon by gunmen from the roof of the Pan Cyprian Gymnasium in Nicosia just as he was taking off to attend a memorial service for an EOKA leader who had lost his life in the struggle for independence. But the Archbishop escaped injury. Suspicion immediately centered on Yorgadjis, who was placed under house arrest. One week later Yorgadjis was murdered under mysterious circumstances. The fact that Makarios failed to condemn the murder damned

---

3. He got only 2% of the votes cast.

him in the eyes of Yorgadjis' followers and strengthened their resolve to bring his government down by any means available.

On May 23, 1970, the National Front carried out a spectacular coup. Twenty terrorists belonging to that organization occupied the Central Police Station at Limassol, capturing £15,000 worth of arms and ammunition.

In September 1971, General Grivas returned secretly to Cyprus and formed a new underground organization, which he called EOKA-B, the purpose of which was to further energize the struggle for *enosis*. A political party, the Unified Committee for the Enosist Struggle (ESEA), was then established to serve as a political front for EOKA-B.

In 1972, the bishops of Kition, Kyrenia and Paphos—all of whom felt that fighting for *enosis* was the sacred duty of every man of the cloth—demanded that Makarios resign as president of Cyprus. When he refused to do so, they defrocked him. However, Makarios declared their decision to be null and void. He claimed that only a Supreme Synod of his peers, i.e., the other Greek Orthodox archbishops and the patriarchs, could sit in judgment upon him and he invited them to Nicosia to air their views. The Supreme Synod met in the summer of 1973, and on July 14 declared the three bishops guilty of schism.[4] The latter, who had boycotted the deliberations of the Synod, were then, in turn, defrocked. But they did not give up the fight: they continued to conduct religious services in "catacombs", or makeshift churches, throughout the island and they gave their wholehearted support to EOKA-B.

By the beginning of 1974, there was widespread unrest in Cyprus and the government seemed unable to stem the rising tide of violence. The main reasons for the government's impotence were the following:

1) Greek Cypriot politicians were afraid of the terrorist organizations. They all vividly remembered that during the struggle for independence more Greek Cypriots

---

4. The Patriarch of İstanbul declined the invitation to attend the Synod.

had been executed by EOKA for "betrayal" than British officers and soldiers had been killed in the fighting.

2) Many Greek Cypriot politicians had relatives or close friends who belonged to the terrorist organizations.

3) Greek Cypriot politicians feared that the taking of strong measures against the terrorists would remind the Greek Cypriots of those used by the British during the struggle for independence.

4) Outright condemnation of Grivas and EOKA-B was difficult because:

   a) Grivas was still a legendary hero in Greek Cypriot eyes.

   b) The saga of EOKA was an integral part of the national epic.

   c) Makarios had been one of the founders of EOKA.

   d) As ethnarch, Makarios was protector of Hellenism in Cyprus and upon his election to that office had pledged to uphold the same values which Grivas and EOKA-B were now preaching.

   e) While fighting EOKA-B, Archbishop Makarios, as father of the nation, was continually attending memorial services for dead EOKA heroes and eulogizing their achievements and idealism.

   f) Holidays celebrating the victories of Grivas and EOKA during the struggle for independence constantly reinforced their image as great patriots.

5) Because as ethnarch Makarios had to promote traditional values and champion *enosis* and as a liberal politician he tended to favor left-of-center political ideologies and (increasingly so) independence for his country, his policies and statements were often contradictory and he was not able to deal forcefully with the growing anarchy.

6) The government had no reliable police force. The Cyprus Police had been heavily infiltrated by ex-EOKA men during Yorgadjis' lengthy tenure as Minister of

the Interior, and the National Guard had successfully resisted all efforts by Makarios to control it and had become one of the chief agencies of subversion. The latter had also become the principal recruiting ground for terrorists.

Makarios attempted to curb terrorism by the following means:

1) In April 1971, he revived the Pan Cyprian Enosist Youth Organization (PEON). This organization, which advocated *enosis*, traditionalism and anti-communism,[5] was intended to lure the Greek Cypriot youth away from the more militant terrorist organizations. But its ideology was so obviously insincere that it had little success.

2) In 1972, he created a new auxiliary police force, the Tactical Reserve Force. Its purposes were to protect the presidential palace, the Nicosia radio and television stations, the international airport and all telecommunication facilities, as well as to apprehend the guerrillas. But it was never strong enough to present an effective challenge to the terrorist organizations.

3) He also relied on the irregular paramilitary organization of his personal physician, Dr. Lyssarides, the head of the Socialist Party (EDEK). But he dared not lean too heavily on this force lest he antagonize the rightist members of his administration and religious Greek Cypriots in general.

These measures were clearly inadequate. To make matters worse, Makarios made no attempt to arouse the Greek Cypriot population and mobilize its energies on his own behalf. Nor did he seriously try to involve other officials in the struggle against subversion. Finally, sentences meted out to terrorists in his courts were so light that punishment did not act as a deterrent to crime. All of this suggests either that Makarios had reached a point of total exhaustion or

---

5. For PEON's program, see Markides, *op. cit.*, p. 158.

that he was suffering from a paralysis of the will. In any case, the results of inaction on his part were disastrous: the morale of his administration rapidly sank, rightist members of his administration and conservative newspapermen shifted their allegiance to the more forceful General Grivas and EOKA-B was free to extort money from the peasantry and force Greek Cypriots to pay lip service to *enosis* by flying Greek flags over their homes.

One happy consequence of Makarios' political troubles was that he now felt it necessary to make peace with the long-abused Turkish Cypriot community. In 1968, the economic restrictions were lifted and Rauf Denktaş was allowed to return to the island. Makarios then initiated a series of inter-communal meetings to explore possible solutions to the Cyprus problems. For six years, Glafkos Klerides, representing the Greek Cypriot community, and Rauf Denktaş, representing the Turkish Cypriot community, met on a weekly basis in an effort to achieve a settlement. There were many persons in both communities who wanted the talks to fail. On the Greek Cypriot side, there were those who argued that the Greek Cypriots already had everything they wanted, since they had a monopoly of all the agencies of government and wallowed in prosperity. The establishment of a new bi-communal government, they argued, would lead to the dismissal of hundreds of Greek Cypriot public servants and revive the nightmare of Turkish Cypriot "obstructionism". Leftists were suspicious that Klerides, a conservative, would make a deal too favorable to the Western powers and NATO. Enosists opposed any settlement with the Turkish Cypriots on the grounds that it would inevitably entail the final rejection by the Greek Cypriots of *enosis*. On the Turkish Cypriot side, there were those who maintained that the Turkish Cypriot community was doing well enough as it was, since it had achieved *de facto* separation and, thanks to Turkey, it was provided with enough food for subsistence and protection against would-be aggressors. Moreover, they asserted, there was everything to gain by adopting a wait-and-see atittude inasmuch as the Greek Cypriot government seemed on the verge of complete collapse. It should be added that Makarios' propensity for making pro-enosist public pronouncements in the vain hope of assuaging his detractors continually threatened to disrupt the negotiations. Nevertheless, the talks proceeded and the representatives of the two communities remained optimistic of future progress. Already by 1969, relations between the Greek Cypriots and the Turkish Cypriots had so dramatically improved that when a tornado struck the Turkish Cypriot quarter of Limassol Makarios inspected the damage and promised the victims that his government would provide them with all that was needed to rebuild their homes.

However, while relations between the Greek Cypriot and the Turkish Cypriot communities were improving, those between the Greek Cypriot and Greek governments were steadily deteriorating. The main reason for this is that there was a fundamental difference of opinion between them as to how to solve the Cyprus problem. There is every reason to believe that the junta was willing to settle for a "double *enosis*" solution of the type proposed by Dean Acheson in 1964, whereby Turkey would have been offered an enclave or large military base on the Karpas peninsula, in northern Cyprus, in exchange for *enosis*, and it appears that at the summit conference of September 1967 it actually proposed such a solution. But Makarios refused even to consider any plan which would have resulted in a loss of territory. On the other hand, on the question of *enosis* the junta held much more rigid views than Makarios. The junta was determined to achieve *enosis*: the acquisition of Cyprus would crown its rule with glory and legitimize its continued existence. But Makarios now seemed willing to barter it away for the sake of effecting a rapprochement with the Turkish Cypriot community and restoring the unity of his long-divided nation. To the junta, therefore, Makarios was a traitor who had to be overthrown at the earliest possible opportunity.

To that end, the junta encouraged the formation of terrorist organizations, sent Grivas and other officers to Cyprus
to organize EOKA-B and recruited fighters for this new
underground force through the Greek-officered National
Guard. It also financed a press campaign against Makarios
in Cyprus and engineered several attempts against his life,
probably including the spectacular one of March 1970.[6] In
1972, when Makarios formed his Tactical Reserve Force and
ordered Czechoslovak weapons for it, the junta demanded
that the weapons be handed over to UNFICYP. During the
same year, it sent Makarios a provocative note requesting
the dismissal of government ministers who were not dedicated enosists and supporters of the Greek government's
policies.

Makarios was bolder in facing the junta than he was in
coping with dissidents at home. This was probably because
his pride as the leader of an independent nation was at
stake and he never imagined that the junta would be so
reckless as to topple him from power by means of a military coup d'état. He rejected Athens' demand that he re-
shuffle his cabinet as an unwarranted intrusion into the internal affairs of his country.[7] He then launched a press
campaign of his own. In the summer of 1973, a new daily,
Eleftheros Laos ("Free People"), which reflected the ideas
of Makarios, began publication. This newspaper openly advocated the expulsion of Greek officers from the island
and called upon King Constantine (who had been ousted
by the junta) and former premier Karamanlis to set up a
Greek government-in-exile in Nicosia. As a result, the Cypriot capital became a rallying point of Greeks who hated
the junta and wished to reestablish the monarchy. Thus
Makarios had met threat with threat. In December 1973,

6. Revelations made in the Greek and Cypriot press since the
coup of 1974 suggest that a plan under the code name "Hermis" had
been drawn up by key members of the junta according to which Makarios was to be assassinated and the National Guard was to step into the power vacuum thus created under the pretext of having to restore law and order.

7. But the offending ministers, Spyros Kyprianou, the foreign
minister, Tassos Papadopoulos, the minister of labor, and Frixos
Petrides, the minister of education, nonetheless resigned.

when a Greek Cypriot shepherd was murdered by EOKA-B, Makarios for the first time denounced Grivas publicly, calling him "a common criminal and blood-thirsty murderer".[8]

What Makarios did not realize was that he was literally playing with fire and that events were in the making that would unleash a much bigger storm than he had anticipated. In November 1973, the military strongman of Greece, Colonel George Papadopoulos, a comparatively mild dictator who was contemplating a liberalization of his regime, was overthrown by the chief of his military police, General Dimitrios Ioannides, a narrow-minded nationalist fanatic. Ioannides, while serving as a major in the Cyprus National Guard during the 1963-1964 crisis, had befriended Nikos Sampson and had drafted a plan the aim of which had been to massacre the entire Turkish Cypriot population.[9] Disappointed by the rejection of his plan by Makarios and by the latter's political opportunism, he had come to loathe what he was later to characterize as "the treacherous ways of the Red Bishop".[10]

In January 1974, Grivas suddenly died of a heart attack in his hideout. The death of the charismatic guerrilla leader deprived the anti-Makarios forces of their ablest leader and gave the Archbishop the courage to at last take decisive action against EOKA-B. On April 25, he outlawed the organization. On May 4, he ordered all persons illegally possessing arms to surrender them or face prosecution. Some 200 suspected EOKA-B members were then arrested.

By June, Makarios felt strong enough to reassert his authority over the National Guard, hoping to transform it from a center of opposition to his regime and a recruiting ground for future EOKA-B terrorists into a loyal force responsive only to the dictates of his government. To begin with, he decided to enforce a law to the effect that all candidates for officer training in the National Guard had to be

8. Markides, op. cit., p. 170.

9. Interview with Archbishop Makarios in Oriana Fallaci, Interview With History (Boston, 1976), p. 318.

10. Theodoracopulos, op. cit., p. 19.

approved by the Greek Cypriot minister of the interior, and formally requested the Greek junta to comply with it. But the junta, which had deliberately flouted the law for years in order to limit officer training to Greek Cypriots who favored *enosis*, ignored Makarios' request. Thereupon, Makarios, obviously realizing that a showdown with Athens was inevitable, took two extremely drastic steps: on July 1, he reduced the length of military service of Greek Cypriots in the National Guard from two years to 14 months, a measure which would have substantially reduced the size of the force; then, on July 2, he sent to the figurehead president of Greece, General Phaidon Gizikis, and released to the press, a harsh and provocative letter accusing the junta of masterminding the campaign of terror in Cyprus. In this emotionally searing message, he charged that

> the root of the evil is very deep, reaching as far as Athens. It is from there that the tree of evil, the bitter fruits of which the Greek Cypriot people are tasting today, is being fed and maintained and helped to grow and spread. In order to be absolutely clear I say that cadres of the military regime of Greece support and direct the activity of the EOKA-B terrorist organization. . . . It is also known, and an undeniable fact, that the oppositon Cyprus press, which supports the criminal activity of EOKA-B and which has its sources of finance in Athens, receives guidance and line from those in charge of the 2nd General Staff Office and the branch of the Greek Central Intelligence Services in Cyprus. . . . Even the evil spirit which possesses the three defrocked Cypriot Bishops who have caused a major crisis in the Church emanated from Athens.

He then added:

> I have more than once so far felt and in some cases I have almost touched a hand invisibly extending from Athens and seeking to liquidate my human existence.

He reminded the junta that

> I am not an appointed prefect or *locum tenens* of the Greek government in Cyprus, but an elected leader of a large section of Hellenism and I demand an appropriate conduct by the National Center towards me.

Finally, he demanded that all of the 650 Greek officers staffing the National Guard be recalled by the Greek government.[11]

---

11. For a complete text of the letter, see Appendix VIII.

Makarios undoubtedly expected the unpopular Ioannides regime to give in to his demands. Perhaps he even hoped to force it out of office, thereby not only saving his own political neck but also ridding the Greeks of a hated tyranny. But the junta took on the challenge. It ordered the National Guard to seize power and kill Makarios.

At that time, the National Guard consisted of 10,000 officers and men. Among these were thirty-five Air Force officers who supervised the two radar stations on the island and 150 naval officers and sailors who operated one patrol boat, the "Leventis", and five torpedo boats. Although the National Guard had no air force to speak of, it possessed thirty-eight Russian T-34 tanks.

Makarios' forces consisted mostly of the 4,000 *Epikouriki* (auxiliaries of the Tactical Reserve Force). These were provided with Soviet-made AK-47's, Czechoslovakian anti-tank guns and heavy machine guns but had at their disposal only four British-made tanks which had been smuggled into Cyprus in crates marked "refrigerator trucks".

The Greek coup (code-named "Operation President") was planned to start after morning rush hour on Monday, July 15. The primary targets were to be the Archbishopric, the Presidential Palace, the International Airport, the telecommunications center and the headquarters of the Cyprus Broadcasting Corporation. But by far the most important part of the operation was to be the elimination of Makarios. It was assumed by the Greek leaders that once this had been accomplished all resistance would automatically cease.

However, the National Guardsmen blundered badly. Instead of ambushing Makarios early that morning as he made his way to Nicosia from his summer retreat in the Troodos mountains with only a light escort, they waited until he had reached the comparative safety of the Presidential Palace— because that is what the plan called for. Then the storming of the palace itself was bungled. The compound, which was protected by 150 *Epikouriki* and 40 presidential guards, was surrounded by 25 tanks and a large number of commandos and then attacked from several sides simultaneously. But thinking that the palace's defenders were much more numerous than they actually were, the various assault teams advanced cautiously, wasting a lot of time in the process. When the defenders knocked out the lead tank in the main, or frontal, assault with bazooka fire, the other tanks all opened fire on the palace, where Makarios was greeting a delegation of Greek children from Cairo. The barrage reduced much of the palace to rubble, but it also killed many of the commandos who were attacking the compound from the opposite side. The *Epikouriki* and the presidential guards fought on heroically for nearly three hours. However, the attackers remained confident of the success of their mission. They even prematurely announced Makarios' death, prompting the Cyprus Broadcasting Corporation, which had already been captured, to exultantly proclaim: "Makarios is dead. Long live the National Guard! Hellenism lives in Cyprus!"[12] But Makarios was still very much alive. As soon as the shelling had started, he had instructed the visiting children to lie on the floor. Then, divesting himself of his clerical garb, he had taken advantage of the National Guard's poor coordination and the momentary confusion caused by the malfunctioning of the Russian-made tanks (which were not suited to run in high temperatures and had been improperly serviced) and the accidental shelling of the commandos who were attacking the compound from the rear, to exit through a back door with two aides and make good his escape through the National Guard's lines.

Once out of the battle zone, Makarios and his companions hailed a passing car. But it quickly ran out of gas. Luckily, another vehicle soon appeared and was in turn commandeered. Thus, Makarios was able to leave Nicosia unnoticed. That afternoon, he reached Paphos which, except for the naval station, had been entirely occupied by his followers. During this time, the Cyprus Broadcasting Corporation continued to play martial music and to announce the demise of the Archbishop.

---

12. Theodoracopulos, *op. cit.*, p. 46. This work contains the best description of the attack thus far available.

By 1 p.m., most resistance had ceased in Nicosia. Angered at not finding Makarios' body in the Presidential Palace, the National Guard set fire to what was left of the building. Meanwhile, Dr. Lyssarides had fled into the Syrian Embassy and his private army had dispersed into the Troodos mountains.

At 2:50 p.m. Nikos Sampson was sworn in as the new president of Cyprus by the National Guard. This choice of leader was disastrous. Not only was Sampson emotionally unstable (a fact which his first news conference graphically illustrated) but he was also devoid of administrative talent. As Theodoracopulos observed: "Any chance that the coup had of success disappeared when Sampson was made president".[13]

Later that afternoon, the National Guard occupied Kykko monastery and the Greek Cypriot quarter of Limassol, both of which were *Epikouriki* strongholds and had offered stiff resistence. But in Paphos, the supporters of Makarios still retained the upper hand. They attacked the naval station, forcing its defenders to flee. In the commotion, the retreating personnel forgot to destroy the telecommunications equipment. This gave Makarios the opportunity to announce to the world that he was alive and to urge his fellow-Cypriots to reject the new government. By Tuesday afternoon, when the National Guard was at last able to seize Paphos, Makarios had put himself under U.N. protection and had been flown to the British sovereign base at Akrotiri by helicopter.

According to Theodoracopulos, "total casualties resulting from the coup did not exceed 150 dead and 500 wounded".[14] But shortly after the overthrow of Makarios, many of his supporters were killed by the rebels. A Greek Cypriot priest by the name of Papatsestos, who was the superintendent of the Greek Orthodox cemetery in Nicosia, admitted

---

13. *Op. cit.*, p. 48.
14. *Op. cit.*, p. 55.

to having buried 127 bodies during the period immediately following the coup. On July 17 alone, he was forced to bury 77 bodies in mass graves. One of the "bodies" was still alive when buried.[15] There were also massacres outside Kykko monastery and in the vicinities of Paphos and Limassol.[16]

The rise to power of the "Butcher of Omorphita", who was elected to the Greek Cypriot House of Representatives in 1969 with the slogan "Death to the Turks!", was greeted with alarm and dismay by the Turkish Cypriot community. As Rauf Denktaş aptly put it, he was "as unacceptable as Adolf Hitler would be as President of Israel".[17]

On July 15, Prime Minister Bülent Ecevit of Turkey, having received overwhelming evidence of the junta's participation in the coup,[18] formally accused the Greek government of intervention in Cyprus. On the 16th, he sent a note to the British government urging it to cooperate with Turkey in enforcing the Treaty of Guarantee. On the 17th, he flew to London for talks with Prime Minister Harold Wilson and Foreign Secretary James Callaghan. He tried to persuade them to join Turkey in a military operation to preserve the independence of Cyprus. But the British were

---

15. Father Papatsestos' charges were first made public in the Athens daily *Ta Nea* and then reproduced in all the Greek Cypriot newspapers on February 28, 1976.

16. An Irish production director by the name of Derek Reed saw "bodies being buried in a mass grave near Paphos". According to him, "people who were told by Makarios to lay down their guns were shot out of hand by the National Guard" (*The Washington Post*, July 23, 1974, p. 11d). Near Limassol, a university student by the name of Argiris Kyriakides saw the bodies of Makarios supporters "thrown into graves four at a time" (*Ibid.*, p. 11 d & e).

17. Theodoracopulos, *op. cit.*, p. 50.

18. Not only were the 650 Greek officers of the Cypriot National Guard involved, but also the 950 officers and men of the Greek army contingent on the island. Moreover, as *Newsweek* reported (July 29, 1974, p. 48):

> On the night before the coup. . . more than 100 Greek army officers, dressed in civilian clothes, boarded an Olympic Airlines 727 for an unscheduled flight to Nicosia. The men were seen off by Col. Michael Pylikhos, a top aide of Ioannidis. Another flight carrying an additional 100 men followed them 24 hours later.

not willing to jeopardize their economic interests on the island and they were reluctant to endanger the thousands of British servicemen and their dependents who lived in Greek Cypriot towns. They also had their hands full with the I.R.A. insurgency in Northern Ireland and did not want to become quagmired in yet another trouble spot. Hence they favored a cautious approach to the Cyprus problem. In this they were encouraged by Archbishop Makarios, who had been flown to England and in talks with British leaders on July 17 counseled against the use of force.

The Turks were similarly disappointed by the American reaction to the coup. There were no tears for Makarios in Washington. In spite of his political volte-face after the 1963-1964 crisis, he was still widely distrusted, and Secretary of State Kissinger regarded him as a "loser".[19] Kissinger also felt that a conflict within NATO had to be avoided at all costs. In addition, he was apprehensive that the Ioannides regime, if challenged, might be overthrown by a clique of younger, more radical officers with anti-American sentiments, and he did not want to risk losing U.S. air and naval installations in Cyprus by backing the wrong horse. Finally, the crisis in Cyprus occurred at a time when relations between Washington and Ankara were strained because of the opium poppy dispute[20] and at the peak of the Watergate controversy, when Americans were almost wholly absorbed by political events at home and the U.S. presidency was, to

---

19. *Ibid.*

20. In July 1971, the Turkish government, under pressure from the United States, agreed to prohibit the cultivation of the opium poppy in return for $38,800,000 in compensation. But this agreement was ruinous to many of the peasants in Anatolia whose land was too poor to grow anything else. The ban also caused a shortage of opium in world pharmaceutical markets. When the Turkish government learned that the United States was thinking of asking American farmers to grow poppies in order to remedy the shortage, it rescinded the ban, allowing poppy growing to resume, though under strict government controls to prevent illicit traffic. The lifting of the ban, which took place in early 1974, was widely denounced in United States government circles.

all intents and purposes, crippled. As a result, Secretary Kissinger, when confronted with the Cyprus dilemma, followed a policy which was aptly described by a State Department official as one of "constructive ambiguity", limiting himself to sending his deputy, Joseph Sisco, to London, Athens and Ankara to negotiate a peaceful settlement to the conflict—an impossibility in the face of Greece's refusal to withdraw its forces from Cyprus. On the other hand, the Turks had displayed such reluctance to intervene militarily in the Cyprus conflict in the past that there was reason to believe that they were bluffing when they threatened to take unilateral action now. Later, Kissinger was to claim that he opposed making any public proclamation against the Sampson regime for fear of encouraging the Turks to intervene in the crisis. But it was the very fear that the United States was about to recognize the new Cypriot government that convinced the Turkish government to act with haste.[21]

To make matters worse, the United States and Great Britain even prevented the United Nations from condemning the Greek-engineered putsch. The Security Council met in a special session on July 16 to debate the Cyprus issue, but it adjourned without taking action when the representatives of the two powers argued that too little information was available for it to come to any conclusion.

Of the major powers, only the Soviet Union, which had everything to gain by a split in the Western alliance and had lately grown fonder of Makarios owing to his opposition to the junta and his (at least temporary) abandonment of *enosis* as a national goal, strongly backed the Turkish government in its hour of need, going so far as offering to help the Turks reinstate the deposed Archbishop.

On July 18, Ecevit, through the intermediary of Undersecretary of State Sisco, sent the Greek government an ultimatum demanding:

---

21. Stern, *op. cit.*, pp. 113-115.

1) The resignation of Nikos Sampson as President of Cyprus,
2) The withdrawal of the 650 Greek officers of the Cypriot National Guard, and
3) Firm pledges to the effect that the island would remain independent.

However, the junta, convinced that U.S. pressure would, as before, dissuade the Turks from resorting to force, refused to give ground. All it offered by way of compromise was that its officers in Cyprus be rotated. Thereupon, on July 19, Ecevit, exercising his right of intervention according to Article IV of the Treaty of Guarantee, gave the order for Turkish troops to carry out a "peace operation" (*barış harekâtı*)—that is, a military operation to preserve the independence of Cyprus and protect the Turkish Cypriot community.

The operation started at dawn on July 20. Turkish jets bombed and strafed Greek Cypriot strong points in and around the seaport of Kyrenia on Cyprus' north shore. Transport planes also dropped paratroops in the vicinity of the Nicosia International Airport. Then, at 6 a.m. three brigades of Turkish troops, consisting of 6,000 men and 40 tanks, landed at Pentamili beach, five miles west of Kyrenia, under naval and air cover. During the landing, two Greek Cypriot torpedo boats were sunk. As the Turks fought their way inland, commandos were airlifted to the Turkish Cypriot quarter of Nicosia and to various points on the vital Kyrenia-Nicosia highway, where they made contact with TMT irregulars guarding the fortress of St. Hilarion and the 650-man Turkish army contingent which controlled the northern approaches to the capital. Meanwhile, heavy fighting was going on in Nicosia, as the Turkish paratroopers closed in on the airport and as machine gun, mortar and rocket fire was exchanged between the Greek Cypriot and Turkish Cypriot quarters of the city. Turkish fighter-bombers also repeatedly bombed Greek Cypriot strongholds in Nicosia and smashed two motorized columns of the Cypriot National Guard as they attempted to reinforce the Greek Cypriot garrison in Kyrenia. By the end of the first day, the

Turks had established a corridor extending from their beach-
head near Kyrenia to the Turkish Cypriot quarter of Nicosia.
In a recent article, the American military historian, Major
Patrick L. Townsend, highly praised the Turkish strategy.
"By expanding vertical envelopment and amphibious tactics
to include paratroopers", he wrote,

> the Turks gave depth to their area of operations, making it
> possible to have it coincide with their elongated objective. The
> apparent helicopter insertion of the paratroop command group
> was a major factor in executing one of the most organized and
> effective paratroop operations since men first started jumping
> from aircraft.[22]

The Greek Cypriots fought valiantly, especially in Kyrenia and at the Nicosia International Airport. But the Greek
commanders of the National Guard showed incredible shortsightedness in not preparing themselves for an invasion and
in not fortifying the area around Kyrenia, which was the
most likely site of a Turkish amphibious assault. The National Guard also squandered its resources in widely scattered
attacks on Turkish Cypriot enclaves throughout the island.
The primary targets of these attacks were the town of Lefka,
the villages of Kokkina and Limnitis, and the Turkish Cypriot quarters of Paphos, Larnaca, Limassol and Famagousta.
These communities were subjected to a concentrated artillery barrage in which no discrimination was made between
civilian and military targets. In the conquered towns and
villages, the National Guard and EOKA-B indulged in an
orgy of destruction. *The Times*'s correspondent, David
Leigh, wrote:

> Thousands of Turkish Cypriots were taken hostage after the
> invasion of Cyprus, Turkish women were raped, children were
> shot in the street and the Turkish quarter of Limassol was burnt
> out by the National Guard.[23]

In the Turkish quarter of Limassol, which was overrun by
the National Guard on July 20, the inhabitants were especially ill-treated. A fifteen-year old girl reported:

---

22. "Vertical Assault: The Proof is in the Doing", *Proceedings of
the United States Naval Institute*, November 1977, p. 119.

23. *The Times* (of London), July 23, 1974, p. 1b & c.

> I ran through the streets and the soldiers were shooting all the time. I ran into a house and I saw a woman being attacked by soldiers. They were raping her. Then they shot her in front of my eyes.[24]

A British civil servant of Turkish Cypriot origin who was visiting Limassol accused the National Guard of shooting down "many women and children". "I saw myself", he said, "twenty dead children in the street and others crying out who were wounded".[25] The inhabitants of the Turkish Cypriot quarter were all herded into the courtyard of the Limassol hospital. The next day, some of the men were shot. The rest of the men were then taken to a makeshift internment camp.

The ravages in the Famagousta region were also extensive. "The human mind cannot comprehend the Greeks' butchery", a German tourist exclaimed,

> In the villages around Famagousta the Greek National Guard have displayed unsurpassed examples of savagery. Entering Turkish homes, they ruthlessly rained bullets on women and children. They cut the throats of many Turks. Rounding up Turkish women, they raped them all.[26]

Jean Neuvecelle of *France Soir* also witnessed many acts of barbarity in the Famagousta region. "I saw with my own eyes the shameful incidents", he wrote,

> The Greeks burned Turkish mosques and set fire to Turkish homes. . . . Defenseless Turkish villagers, who have no weapons, live in an atmosphere of terror, created by the Greek marauders. . . . The Turks who can save their lives run to the nearby hills and are able to do nothing but watch the callous looting of their homes.[27]

The New York Times describes how, in the village of Alaminos, in the district of Larnaca, fifteen of the defenders were lined up against a stone wall after they had surrendered and were shot by EOKA-B men.[28]

---

24. *The Times* (of London), July 23, 1974, p. 1c.

25. *Ibid.*, p. 5a.

26. Broadcast from "The Voice of Germany", July 30, 1974.

27. Issue of July 24, 1974.

28. Issue of July 29, 1974, p. 3e. For a detailed account of the attacks on Lefka, Paphos, Larnaca, Limassol and Famagousta, see: Vehbi Zeki Serter, *Kıbrıs ve 1974 Barış Harekâtı* (Nicosia, 1976), pp. 144-173; Alper Faik Genç, *The Vampires of Cyprus* (Nicosia, 1974).

A major reason for these attacks was fear that the *müca-bits* in the various Turkish Cypriot enclaves would rise *en masse* and create a multitude of fronts for the already overtaxed National Guard to fight on—a groundless fear inasmuch as the Turkish Cypriots did not even have enough weapons to protect their own homes. The National Guard also wanted to hold the Turkish Cypriots as hostages. As a Greek Cypriot businessman explained to the correspondent of *The Times*, "It was a simple plan. The Greeks decided that as soon as the Turkish invaders got the upper hand they would tell them to stop bombing or the hostages would die".[29] However, the passions of the moment overwhelmed all restraint, with the result that the mass slaughter of the Turkish Cypriots started even before the threat could be made.

As the Turkish "Peace Operation" got underway, Prime Minister Ecevit made an impassioned plea for world support. "The Turkish Armed Forces", he declared,

> have started a peace operation in Cyprus this morning to end decades of strife provoked by exremist and irredentist elements. At the last stage of the Cyprus tragedy, these extremist elements have started massacring even their own people—the Greeks.
>
> It is acknowledged in all the world that the coup which recently took place was manufactured by the dictatorial regime of Athens. In fact it was much more than a coup. It was the forceful and flagrant violation of the independence of the Cyprus Republic and of the international agreements on which this Republic was based.
>
> Turkey is a co-guarantor of the independence and constitutional order of Cyprus. Turkey is fulfilling her legal responsibility by taking this action. The Turkish Government did not resort to armed action before all the other means were tried, but to no avail.
>
> This is not an invasion, but an act against invasion.
> This is not aggression, but an act to end aggression.

· ·

---

29. *The Times* (of London), July 23, 1974, p. 5a.

The operations of peace that started with the breaking of the day, this morning, will bring an end to the darkest period in the history of Cyprus.

The victory of the Turkish Armed Forces will be a victory for justice, for peace, for freedom.

I appeal to all Greeks in Cyprus who have suffered the atrocities of terrorism and dictatorship. Bury with the past dark days the inter-communal enmities and strifes that were the making of those same terrorists. Join hand-in-hand with your Turkish brothers to speed up this victory and together build a new, free and happy Cyprus.

We are there to help you, not to hurt.

We are there with love, not with hate.

We are there not to fight you but to end your plight.[30]

On the same day, the United Nations Security Council held an emergency meeting to discuss the Turkish intervention. After a lengthy debate, it passed the following resolution (Resolution 353):

The Security Council

1) Calls upon all states to respect the sovereignty, independence and territorial integrity of Cyprus,

2) Calls upon all parties to the present fighting as a first step to cease all firing and requests all states to exercise the utmost restraint and to refrain from any action which might further aggravate the situation,

3) Demands an immediate end to foreign military intervention in the Republic of Cyprus that is in contravention of operative paragraph 1.

4) Requests the withdrawal without delay from the Republic of Cyprus of foreign military personnel present otherwise than under the authority of international agreements including those whose withdrawal was requested by the President of the Republic of Cyprus, Archbishop Makarios, in his letter of 2 July 1974,

5) Calls on Greece, Turkey and the United Kingdom of Great Britain and Northern Ireland to enter negotiations without delay for the restoration of peace in the area and constitutional Government in Cyprus and to keep the Secretary General informed,

---

30. *Diş politika* (*Foreign Policy*), Vol. IV, nos. 2-3, pp. 226-227.

    6) Calls on all parties to co-operate fully with UNFICYP to enable it to carry out its mandate,

    7) Decides to keep the situation under constant review and asks the Secretary General to report as appropriate with a view to adopting further measures in order to ensure that peaceful conditions are restored as soon as possible.[31]

But the military situation in Cyprus was still too fluid for the Turkish advance to stop.

On July 21, fighting continued in Nicosia and around the Nicosia International Airport, the defenders of which had been reinforced by 200 members of an elite commando unit flown in from Greece during the previous night. In the north, Turkish troops widened their beachhead and penetrated into Kyrenia. In the afternoon, Turkish air and naval units intercepted a Greek flotilla consisting of six supply vessels loaded with war materiel and several destroyers as it was approaching Paphos. After their warning to the Greek flotilla not to attempt a landing had been ignored, the Turks attacked it, sinking three of the supply vessels and forcing the rest of the convoy to withdraw. But later that day Turkish jets, mistaking the Turkish destroyer "Kocatepe" for a Greek warship, sank it too, along with at least 50 members of its crew.

On July 22, there was more bitter fighting at both ends of the Turkish corridor in Cyprus. At 1 p.m. Kyrenia fell to the Turks. Although the International Airport still remained in Greek Cypriot hands, the Turks had by now established a firm foothold on the island, acquired a major harbor and attained their most immediate political objective—the destabilization of the Sampson regime. Therefore, at 4 p.m., they decided to abide by the Security Council's cease-fire resolution. They also agreed to allow the hotly contested Nicosia International Airport to become a United Nations-protected area.

The Greek leaders who organized the coup of July 15 were as blind in their fanaticism and as politically shortsighted

---

31. *Ibid.*, pp. 218-219.

as the leaders who launched the ill-fated Anatolian campaign some fifty years earlier, and their overblown nationalism brought them nothing but defeat and humiliation. The Turkish intervention which the coup triggered provoked the collapse of the Ioannides regime in Greece and its puppet regime in Cyprus. Ioannides was replaced by Constantine Karamanlis, who was recalled from self-exile in France to form a new civilian government. Nikos Sampson was replaced by Glafkos Klerides, the Speaker of the Greek Cypriot House of Representatives. A lawyer and former RAF pilot, Klerides had a reputation for moderation and had demonstrated a talent for negotiation as his government's representative at the inter-communal talks which were held after the 1967 crisis.[32]

The Turkish "peace operation" (which was later officially called the First Peace Operation) also put an end to the Greek Cypriots' fratricidal struggle. As Father Papatsestos admitted:

> It is a rather hard thing to say, but it is true that the Turkish intervention saved us from a merciless internecine war. They [the Sampson regime] had prepared a list of all Makarios supporters and they would have slaughtered them all.[33]

Finally, the Turkish landings in Cyprus caused an important shift in American foreign policy. When the action started, the United States' representative at the United Nations, John A. Scali, angered the Turks by at once condemning it, although he had previously failed to censure the Greek government for its part in the coup of July 15. But when it became clear that the Turks had every intention of staying on the island until a viable solution to the Cyprus conflict could be worked out, the United States showed a growing inclination to accept the new status quo. The fact was that the United States did not want to risk a confrontation with

---

32. In 1976, he claimed that he had come to a "near agreement" with Denktaş in the talks but that the Greek Cypriot Council of Ministers had rejected it (*The Cyprus Mail*, August 8, 1976, p. 1).

33. *Op. cit.*

Turkey, its principal ally in the eastern Mediterranean, especially when Greece, its other ally in the area, was facing an uncertain political future. Dr. Kissinger now merely sought, by diplomatic means, to limit the scope of the Turkish operation in the hope that the Greeks and the Greek Cypriots would accept it as a *fait accompli*.

The Greek government has never acknowledged the legality of the Turkish military intervention in Cyprus. However, it is interesting to note that the Athens Court of Appeals did so in one of its rulings. In its Decision No. 2658/79, dated March 21, 1979, it stated:

> The Turkish military intervention in Cyprus, which was carried out in accordance with the Zürich and London Accords, was legal. Turkey, as one of the Guarantor Powers, had the right to fulfill her obligations. The real culprits. . . are the Greek officers who engineered and staged a coup and prepared the conditions for this intervention.

CHAPTER IX
THE SECOND PEACE OPERATION

Immediately after the cease-fire of July 22, Foreign Secretary Callaghan of Great Britain, in accordance with Article 5 of Resolution 353, invited Greece and Turkey to participate in a conference to be held at Geneva for the twin purposes of preventing a recurrence of the fighting in Cyprus and laying the groundwork for a permanent settlement which would guarantee the island's independence and territorial integrity. At the conference, which began on July 25, the Turkish representative, Turan Güneş had the advantage of speaking from strength and was determined to impose a solution to the Cyprus crisis which was in keeping with the "new realities" on the island. On the other hand, the Greek foreign minister, George Mavros, had just emerged from a long period of detention on one of the Aegean islands and had the unenviable position of being the representative of what amounted to a defeated nation. Therefore, Foreign Minister Güneş was largely able to impose his will upon the conference.

In the course of a series of heated debates, Foreign Minister Mavros maintained that according to Article 4 of the Security Council resolution the Turks were to withdraw all their troops from the island. He agreed with the other representatives at the conference that a security zone should be established between the Greek and Turkish forces in Cyprus, but he argued that it should be established on the Turkish side of the cease-fire line. Otherwise, he pointed out, 50 Greek Cypriot villages would have to be evacuated. He asserted that the new constitutional order to be set up on the island concerned only the people and government of

Cyprus and was not a problem for an international conference to solve. Anyhow, he added, it made no sense to draft a new constitution inasmuch as the 1960 Constitution was still in force. Finally, he accused the Turks of disregarding the truce and of continuing to advance beyond the ceasefire line.

Foreign Minister Güneş replied that Article 4 of Resolution 353 clearly exempted the Turkish troops from those to be withdrawn because they were in Cyprus "under the authority of international agreements", specifically the Treaty of Guarantee. In any case, he declared, the Turkish troops were in Cyprus to protect the Turkish Cypriot community and they would stay there as long as that community was in danger of attack from the Greek Cypriot community or the National Guard. He pointed out that the Turkish corridor in Cyprus was so narrow that should the safety zone be established on the Turkish side of the cease-fire line, there would not be any Turkish zone left. He claimed that the 1960 Constitution no longer had any validity inasmuch as it was first amended illegally after the expulsion of the Turkish Cypriot members of the House of Representatives in December 1963 and then was overthrown in the coup of July 15, 1974. By the time of the Turkish intervention, the Cypriot state had disintegrated. A new state would now have to be established, taking into account the fact that the Turkish Cypriots had developed their own national and municipal administrations. In other words, only a federated, bi-zonal government could be contemplated. Finally, he maintained that Turkish encroachments along the cease-fire line were merely a reaction to much more serious breaches of the cease-fire agreement on the part of the National Guard and EOKA-B.[1]

---

1. For more details, see Halûk Ulman, "Geneva Conferences", Dış politika, Vol. IV, nos. 2-3, pp. 46-65.

Indeed, for the majority of Turkish Cypriots the cease-fire of July 22 brought no relief from suffering and anxiety. The National Guard continued to attack Kokkina, Limnitis and Louroudjina, in the district of Nicosia. Numerous Turkish Cypriot villages remained under siege by the National Guard and EOKA-B. So did the Turkish Cypriot quarter of Famagousta. The Turkish Cypriot inhabitants of 37 villages, who had been forced to flee their homes, were living in utter destitution as refugees, mostly in Turkish Cypriot enclaves which were themselves under siege.[2] In the Turkish Cypriot quarter of Famagousta, which had been extensively damaged by artillery fire on July 20, 21 and 22, and which suffered from an acute shortage of food, the population had swelled to twice its normal size with the arrival of refugees from Baykal, Sakarya and Karakol, outside of the city walls.[3] In the nearby village of Knodara, the population of 750 had grown to 3,000 as Turkish Cypriots from six surrounding villages had taken refuge there. Some houses now had as many as 60 inhabitants.[4]

In Limassol and Larnaca, where the Turkish Cypriot quarters had surrendered after having been subjected to an intense artillery barrage, the men were herded into makeshift concentration camps while the women and children were left at the mercy of roving gangs of hoodlums. In Limassol, some 1,750 men were detained in the open, in the city's soccer stadium. In Larnaca, 873 men ranging in age from 12 to 90 were confined in a school building built to accommodate 100 students. Since no beds were provided, the prisoners were forced to sleep on the bare concrete floors. There were only two toilets which, by the second

---

2. U. N. Document S/11423.

3. U. N. Document S/11394. For an eyewitness description of Famagousta during its siege, see: J.-C. Pomonti, "Avec les Chypriotes turcs assiégés dans la forteresse de Famagouste", Le Monde, August 3, 1974, p. 2a.

4. The New York Times, August 14, 1974, p. 3b.

day, had become unusable. The prisoners were limited to a diet of five olives, a small piece of cheese and a crust of bread per day. A tin of sardines was shared by six prisoners every other day. There were no doctors and medicines were unavailable. As a result, two of the captives died. On July 26, EOKA-B men kidnapped six of the prisoners, took them to a remote building and beat them up. Only the timely arrival of a U.N. patrol seemingly saved the victims from an even worse fate.[5]

On July 30, the representatives of Great Britain, Greece and Turkey at the Geneva Conference signed an agreement which contained the following provisions:

1) The areas in Cyprus which were controlled by opposing forces on July 30, 1974, at 10 p.m. Geneva time, were not to be extended.

2) All armed forces, including irregular forces, were to desist from all offensive or hostile activities.

3) A security zone, closed to all armed forces except those of UNFICYP, was to be established at the limit of the areas occupied by the Turkish armed forces.

4) All Greek and Greek Cypriot forces were to immediately withdraw from the Turkish Cypriot enclaves which they had occupied.

5) All the Turkish Cypriot enclaves were to be protected by a security zone closed to all armed forces except those of UNFICYP.

6) Military personnel and civilians detained as a result of the recent hostilities were to be exchanged or released under the supervision of the International Committee of the Red Cross within the shortest time possible.

7) Measures were to be elaborated "within the framework of a just and lasting solution acceptable to all parties concerned and as peace, security and mutual confidence are established" which were to lead to the "timely and phased reduction of the number of armed forces and the amounts of armaments, munitions and other war materiel" on the island.

5. Genç, *op. cit.*, pp. 6-18.

8) New talks, to begin on August 8, were to be held "to secure the restoration of peace in the area and the re-establishment of a constitutional government in Cyprus".

9) Representatives of the Greek Cypriot and Turkish Cypriot communities were to be invited to participate in discussions relating to constitutional matters at the projected talks.

10) The three foreign ministers "noted the existence in practice in the Republic of Cyprus of two autonomous administrations, that of the Greek Cypriot community and that of the Turkish Cypriot community" and "problems raised by their existence" were to be considered at the projected talks.[6]

Unquestionably, this agreement represented a diplomatic triumph for Turkey, for it recognized the extensions to the Turkish zone of occupation made after the cease-fire, specified that the planned security-zone was to be established " "at the limit" of the Turkish-controlled area, allowed the continued presence in Cyprus of Turkish troops and paid lip service to the principle of bi-zonalism. The Turks also hoped that it would put an end to attacks on the Turkish Cypriot population by the National Guard and EOKA-B.

However, the Greek Cypriots dragged their feet when it came to complying with the provisions of the agreement. By the time the Second Geneva Conference got underway, on August 8, they had not yet started to withdraw from the Turkish Cypriot enclaves which they had overrun and they still held thousands of political prisoners. Furthermore, they had proven uncooperative when it came to setting up the security zone around the perimeter of the Turkish salient in northern Cyprus. As a result, the Turkish government felt unable to adequately protect either the Turkish

---

6. *Dış politika*, Vol. IV, nos. 2-3, pp. 230-232.

Cypriot population or its own forces on the island. It is, therefore, not astonishing that Foreign Minister Güneş was more determined than ever to impose a bi-zonal solution to the Cyprus problem. In his opinion, it was the only solution which could provide the needed security.

As the Second Geneva Conference opened, the British, Greek and Turkish representatives (at the last named's request) held a series of informal meetings. On August 10, Glafkos Klerides and Rauf Denktaş, the representatives of, respectively, the Greek Cypriot and Turkish Cypriot communities, joined the talks and, in turn, met privately. It is Denktaş's report on his *têtes-à-têtes* with Klerides that formed the basis of the first Turkish proposal. Its full text was as follows:

1) Mr. Glafkos Klerides and Mr. Rauf Dentaş, having met within the framework of the Geneva Declaration of the 30th July from 10-12 August 1974, agreed that a fundamental revision of the Constitutional structure of the Republic of Cyprus is necessary to ensure that the tragic events of the past should not repeat themselves and in order to provide the minimum conditions in which the Greek and Turkish Communities can permanently coexist, together, in the Republic in full confidence so that the security of each is safeguarded.

2) Bearing also in mind the existence in practice in the Republic of Cyprus of two autonomous administrations, they agreed that this revision should result in the establishment of a federal system of government based on the following fundamental elements:

   a) The Republic of Cyprus shall be an independent bi-national state.

   b) The Republic shall be composed of two federated states with full control and autonomy within their respective geographical boundaries;

   c) In determining the competence to be left to the federal government, the bi-national nature of the State shall be taken into account and the federal competence shall be exercised accordingly;

   d) The area of the Turkish Cypriot Federated State shall cover 34 per centum of the territory of the Republic falling north of a general line starting from the Limnitis-Lefka area in the west and running towards the east, passing through the Turkish controlled part of Nicosia, including the Turkish part of Famagusta and ending at the port of Famagusta.

3) Pending an agreement on the final Constitutional structure of the Republic, the two autonomous administrations shall take over the full administrative authority within their respective areas as defined above and shall take steps to normalise and stabilise life in the Republic and refrain from acts of violence, harassment and discrimination against each other.
4) Mr. Klerides and Mr. Denktaş further agreed:
   a) At once to hold discussions between them in Nicosia, with the participation of the representatives of Greece and Turkey in order to elaborate as a matter of immediate urgency the constitutional structure envisaged above, and,
   b) To report to the Foreign Ministers of Greece, Turkey and the United Kingdom of Great Britain and Northern Ireland, at a further meeting to be held in Geneva on 1st September 1974, on the conclusions reached.[7]

But this proposal, in spite of its having been worked out with Acting-President Klerides, was promptly rejected by both him and Foreign Minister Mavros.

Realizing that one of the most controversial features of the proposal was that it would have involved large population shifts, Güneş then offered a cantonal alternative. According to this new proposal:

1) Cyprus would be an independent state with two communities;
2) It would consist of a Turkish Cypriot autonomous region having six districts and an autonomous Greek Cypriot region comprising the remaining areas;
3) The principal district of the autonomous Turkish Cypriot region would cover the Kyrenia-Nicosia-Famagousta triangle;
4) The other districts would cover the regions of Lefka, Polis, Paphos, Larnaca and the Karpas peninsula;
5) The principal district would be evacuated within 48 hours by Greek and Greek Cypriot forces.[8]

But this proposal too was rejected.

---

7. Ülman, *op. cit.*, pp. 60-61.
8. Ülman, *op. cit.*, p. 63.

What was becoming increasingly obvious was that Foreign Secretary Callaghan was encouraging the Greeks in their intransigence. The Secretary, who had had a tendency to favor the Turkish position at the First Geneva Conference (in an apparent effort at placating the Turks, who had just landed in Cyprus), was now favoring the Greek position (in an apparent effort at buttressing the new democratic regime in Athens).[9] As a result, even Klerides who, at the beginning of the talks, seemed ready to accept a solution which would have satisfied the minimum requirements of the Turkish Cypriots, gradually toughened his stand. No wonder then that his report on the Klerides-Denktaş meetings, which constituted the Greek proposal, differed substantially from Denktaş's. As its full text, which follows, indicates, it was also much briefer:

1) Mr. Glafkos Klerides and Mr. Rauf Denktaş, having conferred at Geneva between August 10 and 12, 1974, have agreed that a fundamental revision of the governmental system of the Republic of Cyprus is necessary to provide the conditions in which the Greek Cypriot and Turkish Cypriot communities will be able to coexist in peace in the Republic with an utter and mutual confidence that the security of all will be safeguarded. They have agreed that this revision must result in the establishment of a system based on the existence of two autonomous administrations within suitable boundaries, united under a central government. They have also agreed that these changes will be effected within the framework of a sovereign, independent and united Cyprus Republic.

2) Mr. Klerides and Mr. Denktaş have, moreover, agreed:

a) To hold discussions between them in Nicosia in order to elaborate, as a matter of immediate urgency, the constitutional structure envisaged in the above paragraph.

9. To make things worse, on August 12 Callaghan announced that 600 Gurkha troops were to be flown from Hong Kong to reinforce the garrisons at the sovereign bases of Akrotiri and Dekelia and that the order for the return to England of twelve Phantom jets and 600 marine commandos which had been sent to Cyprus at the height of the Turkish attack had been cancelled, thus giving the impression that Great Britain would forcibly oppose any further Turkish operation on the island.

> b) To report to the Foreign Ministers of Greece,
> Turkey and the United Kingdom of Great
> Britain and Northern Ireland at a further meet-
> ing to be held in Geneva on 1st September
> 1974 on the conclusions reached.[10]

Klerides' report was clearly a watered-down version of Denktaş's. Although it acknowledged the necessity of revising the governmental system of Cyprus and of setting up two autonomous administrations, it was disappointingly vague as to the extent and nature of the geographical separation between the two communities, and merely reiterated the old Greek Cypriot position when it came to the question of constitutional changes—namely that it was a matter for the Cypriots alone to decide, which had proven a dead end in the past. Had the proposal been made several years earlier, it would have been warmly received by the Turkish Cypriot leadership as an important step in the right direction. But now it was too little too late. The Turkish Cypriots had suffered too much and the Turkish government had invested too much effort and money in its military operation in Cyprus to be contented with a proposal that constituted merely a promising start to what could have been lengthy negotiations. As Craig R. Whitney, of *The New York Times*, pointed out:

> In retrospect, it seems that Turkey was determined from the beginning of these talks on Aug. 8 to impose some kind of "permanent" political solutions on the island with its hostile Turkish and Greek communities.
>
> It also seems clear that a new Greek civilian Government in Athens felt itself unable to accept a far-reaching solution now. It would have appeared to Greek public opinion as a capitulation, as yet another acknowledgment of military humiliation by the Turks, following on the harsh cease-fire terms already accepted on July 30.[11]

It is, therefore, not astonishing that the Turks rejected the Greek proposal.

---

10. Ülman, *op. cit.*, pp. 63-64. Author's translation.
11. *The New York Times*, August 15, 1974, p. 14f.

The private meetings having yielded no appreciable results, Foreign Minister Güneş, on August 13, called for a
plenary session, where he formally presented his two proposals for immediate approval or rejection. Although both
proposals had already been rejected by the Greek and Greek
Cypriot representatives, he wanted that rejection to be official. But Foreign Minister Mavros and Acting President
Klerides instead asked for a 48-hour adjournment of the conference, ostensibly to consult their own governments. This,
in turn, was unacceptable to Professor Güneş and, consequently, the conference broke down. At a news conference
at Geneva, on August 14, Denktaş explained that the request
for an adjournment was rejected because the Turks and the
Turkish Cypriots suspected that the Greeks would take advantage of it to bring Makarios back to Cyprus and to reinforce their troops on the island.[12] They had also come to
the conclusion that the Greeks and Greek Cypriots were
simply not yet ready to negotiate realistically and were still
hedging on the key question of bi-zonality. "I think Mr.
Clerides could have averted what happened... by conceding
one principle", Denktaş maintained, "namely, that the
Turks are entitled to full security and [that] this can [only]
be provided by a geographical area".[13]

Perhaps the most insightful comments about the Second
Geneva Conference were made by the anonymous author
of Part I of *Cyprus: Minority Rights Group Report No. 30*:

> Although not participating directly in the talks, the uncom-
> promising spirit of Makarios weighed heavily over the Greek
> Cypriot delegation. Greece itself was in the throes of political
> convulsions following the removal of the junta. There was little
> coordination, little awareness of Turkey's determination and
> the unfortunate overconfidence that somehow, unbelievably,
> the status quo could be restored, mainly with pressure from
> Britain and the United States. The Turks had gone to Geneva
> with definite demands and a firm blueprint which they were
> not about to change. Greek Cypriot demands for "additional
> consultations" were reminiscent of years of political haggling
> during which the Greek side had not yielded an inch.[14]

---

12. *The Times* (of London), August 15, 1974, p. 4a.

13. *Ibid.*

14. *Cyprus: Minority Rights Group Report No. 30* (London,
1976), p. 6.

While the Second Geneva Conference was floundering, the Turks were becoming increasingly irritated by the failure of the Greeks and Greek Cypriots to abide by the Agreement of July 30. During the Conference the latter, as a "gesture of goodwill", started withdrawing from a handful of occupied villages around Limassol and Larnaca. However, this was but a token gesture. Thousands of Turkish Cypriots remained in captivity, some 80 villages remained in Greek Cypriot hands, and some 60 more villages remained cut off from the rest of the island and all hope of relief by the National Guard and EOKA-B. Accordingly, as soon as he learned of the collapse of the talks in Geneva, Premier Ecevit launched a new "peace operation" in Cyprus.

At dawn, on August 14, Turkish Phantom jets attacked strategic targets in Nicosia and Famagousta. With some 200 or 300 tanks, a Turkish division then started moving from the Kyrenia salient towards Famagousta. This force quickly routed the National Guard and occupied, successively, Mia Milea, Kythrea and Khatos. Fighting also broke out between Turkish Cypriot militiamen and elements of the National Guard around the enclaves of Kokkina and Limnitis. On August 15, the Turks continued their eastward push, capturing Lefkoniko, Trikomo and, finally, Famagousta, where the besieged Turkish Cypriot quarter, with its 12,000 inhabitants and refugees, was liberated. Another forced headed westward from the Turkish salient, taking Myrtou and Morphou. On August 16 that force made its way into Lefka. At this point, Premier Ecevit, judging that enough territory had been occupied to substantially improve the bargaining position of Turkey, agreed to a cease-fire and the "Second Peace Operation" came to an end.

The Second Peace Operation had important international repercussions. Most notably, it soured the United States' relations with both Greece and Turkey. During the Second Geneva Conference, Secretary Kissinger had been in frequent contact with Foreign Secretary Callaghan and Premier Ecevit (who had once been a student of his). He had also

sent a representative, Assistant Secretary of State Arthur
Hartman, to the Conference. In an endeavor to convince
the Turks to keep negotiating, Dr. Kissinger had issued the
following statement on August 13:

> The United States position is as follows: we recognize the posi-
> tion of the Turkish community on Cyprus requires considerable
> improvement and protection. We have supported a greater de-
> gree of autonomy for them. The parties are negotiating on one
> or more Turkish autonomous areas. The avenues of diplomacy
> have not been exhausted and therefore the United States would
> consider a resort to military action unjustified. We have made
> this clear to all parties.[15]

Dr. Kissinger obviously believed that his influence with his
former pupil was greater than it actually was and was taken
off-guard by the Turkish action. To complicate matters,
the new crisis in Cyprus took place at a time when Americans were preoccupied by the resignation of President
Nixon and the change of administration that ensued. All
that Dr. Kissinger could do once the Turks had launched
their new offensive was to recommend an immediate resumption of the talks and offer his services as a mediator.

The Greeks also believed that Secretary Kissinger had
more influence in Turkey than he actually had. Consequently, they suspected the United States of complicity in
the Turkish move in Cyprus. They regarded Kissinger's
statement of August 13 as partisan in the extreme. They
were convinced that had he shown the same toughness towards the Turks that President Johnson had in 1964, the
new "peace operation" would never have been launched.
Finally, they were angry that the United States had failed
to come to the help of Greece, a NATO ally, in its hour of
need and found Kissinger's offer of mediation an offensively
mild reaction to what, in their eyes, had been a criminal
action on Turkey's part.

The Greeks gave vent to their ire by withdrawing their
troops from NATO. In Washington, some 20,000 Americans

---

15. Stern, *op. cit.*, p. 132.

of Greek extraction demonstrated in front of the White House. In Athens and Nicosia, there were major anti-American riots. In Nicosia, feelings ran so high that, on August 19, the United States Ambassador, Rodger P. Davis, was shot and killed. Meanwhile, a group of United States congressmen, swayed by the powerful "Greek Lobby" in Washington, began to agitate for an arms embargo against Turkey.

The Foreign Assistance Act of 1961, as well as the bilateral agreements of 1947 and 1960 between the United States and Turkey, all stipulated that the proffered military assistance was to be used strictly for defensive purposes or for the maintenance of internal security. Arguing that Turkey had violated these restrictions, the advocates of an embargo declared that continued military aid to that country was illegal and that President Ford had no choice but to enforce the law. Both President Ford and Secretary Kissinger, keenly aware of Turkey's immense strategic importance, strenuously opposed any sanctions. But the pro-embargo forces finally gained the upper hand, with the result that, as of February 5, 1975, the embargo went into effect, denying Turkey grants, credits and commercial military sales, including the delivery of aircraft that had already been paid for by the Turkish government. The Turkish government retaliated by taking over most of the American bases on its territory and by shutting down secret monitoring facilities at Sinop, Diyarbakır and Karamürsel operated by the National Security Agency, which spied on Soviet ABM launches, military communications, troop movements and advanced research, and acted as an early-warning line in case of a nuclear war with Russia. That the embargo was a purely anti-Turkish measure was confirmed on June 27, 1979, when Israeli F-15 fighters, provided by the United States through a similar bilateral agreement, violated Lebanese air space and proceeded to shoot down six or seven Syrian Mig-21s. Though this constituted a clear violation of the bilateral agreement, there was no move in Congress in favor of an arms embargo against the state of Israel.

The Soviets feared that Turkey's interventionist policy would lead to double *enosis* (the splitting up of Cyprus between Greece and Turkey) and, thereby, the extension of NATO to Cyprus. Therefore, they opposed it and sought to establish better relations with Greece, which was now possible because of the downfall of the military junta and the rising anti-Americanism in that country. The failure of the Second Geneva Conference also prompted the Russians, who all along had hoped to take the Cyprus issue out of the triangular framework of Greece, Turkey and Great Britain (all NATO countries) and drag it into the United Nations, where they might exercise some control over the fate of the island, to propose the convening of an international peace conference which was to include all 15 nations of the Security Council. However, this proposal, which was made on August 24, was at once rejected by Turkey.

In Cyprus itself, the Second Peace Operation caused a major social and political upheaval. At his news conference of August 14, Premier Ecevit asserted that the aim of the operation was "to put an end to the suffering the Turkish Cypriots have had to endure over the years".[16] This was a worthy goal and there was probably no other way of achieving it. But the immediate result of the offensive was to put in jeopardy the lives of the very people the Turks were trying to protect. Indeed, as the Turkish army fought its way towards Famagousta, the National Guard and EOKA-B, in a paroxism of anger and frustration, indulged in wholesale massacres of defenseless Turkish Cypriot villagers, which surpassed in brutality even the mass killings of the previous month.

On the morning of August 14, a group of National Guardsmen and EOKA-B terrorists entered the village of Aloa, northwest of Famagousta, and rounded up all the men, women and children they could find. They then took the 57 villagers in question to a nearby field and shot them

---

16. *The New York Times*, August 15, 1974, p. 15d.

with automatic weapons. Afterwards, they dug a ditch and buried the victims in it by bulldozing earth over them. When the corpses were unearthed a few days later, they were almost beyond recognition, for the bulldozer, while running over the dead villagers, had dismembered them. Arms and heads had been torn off, and the victims had been reduced to a heap of bones and flesh. Only three of the inhabitants of Aloa survived the massacre.

Meanwhile, a few miles away, another group of Greek Cypriot armed men made their way into the village of Maratha and slaughtered its inhabitants. They then took the inhabitants of the nearby village of Sandalaris to Maratha and executed them too. As in Aloa, the victims were buried in a ditch by means of a bulldozer. When the mutilated bodies of the inhabitants of Maratha and Sandalaris were unearthed from their common grave on September 1, as many as 88 corpses were counted.

Also on the same tragic morning, a group of EOKA-B men under the leadership of one Andriko Melani entered the Turkish Cypriot quarter of the mixed village of Tokhni, mid-way between Limassol and Larnaca, and rounded up 69 men between the ages of 13 and 74. On August 15, "Andriko" and his men brought in 15 more Turkish Cypriot men they had picked up in Mari and Zyyi. They then drove 50 of their captives by bus to a spot in the vicinity of Limassol, where a ditch had already been dug, and shot them. One of the victims, though severely wounded, managed to crawl to safety and lived to testify as to the fate of his fellow-villagers. But nothing more was ever heard of the remaining 34 men who had been gathered together by the ferocious "Andriko" in Tokhni. It is by now assumed that they too were shot on August 15.[17]

---

17. This description of the massacres of Aloa, Maratha, Tokhni and Zyyi is based on official Turkish Cypriot documents and personal interviews with the survivors.

In the Turkish Cypriot quarter of Paphos, the National Guard killed five men and a three-year-old boy on August 14. According to a U.N. observer, 30 to 40 bullet holes were found in the body of the child.[18]

In the village of Ayios Ioannis, near Paphos, the National Guard and elements of EOKA-B killed five more men on August 15.[19]

The massacres had the effect of strengthening the resolve of the 42,000 Turkish Cypriots, scattered in southern Cyprus, to move to the Turkish-controlled north. But the Greek Cypriot government strenuously opposed the exodus, fearing that if the entire Turkish Cypriot population would move to the north it might tempt Turkey to establish a permanent protectorate there. Hence, tensions remained at fever pitch during the months following the armistice of August 16.

During this period U.N. Secretary-General Kurt Waldheim undertook repeated efforts to encourage an inter-communal dialogue. These efforts, which finally bore fruit in late August, made it possible for the Greek Cypriots and the Turkish Cypriots to solve at least their most immediate problems without further bloodshed.

The first meeting between Glafkos Klerides and Rauf Denktaş, who represented their respective communities, took place in Nicosia on August 26. It was also attended by Secretary-General Waldheim, the United Nations High Commissioner for Refugees, and Waldheim's Special Representative. The two communal representatives decided to meet at least once a week, starting on September 6, for the purpose of addressing themselves to the most pressing humanitarian needs of the moment. As these meetings got under way, Klerides and Denktaş quickly agreed on a scheme for the mutual release of prisoners and detainees, for assisting the aged and infirm left behind in isolated villages and for allowing sick persons and pregnant women to cross the

18. U. N. Document S/11458.
19. U. N. Document S/11466.

boundary between the two zones for medical treatment. The two leaders also agreed:

1) To allow Greek Cypriot college students in the Turkish Cypriot zone and Turkish Cypriot college students in the Greek Cypriot zone to resume their studies abroad,

2) To allow teachers with their families to take up posts to which they had been appointed by their government,

3) To permit foreigners cut off by hostilities, including nationals of Greece and Turkey, to return to their homes, and likewise to allow stranded Greek Cypriots and Turkish Cypriots to rejoin their families,

4) To facilitate the work of ICRC (International Committee of the Red Cross) in the search for missing persons,

5) To allow children to accompany mothers being evacuated,

6) To cooperate with an adviser, to be appointed by UNESCO, for the preservation and restoration of cultural monuments, and

7) To make tentative arrangements for the sale of the tobacco crop of the Greek Cypriot and Turkish Cypriot growers on the Karpas peninsula.[20]

The exchange of prisoners and detainees was completed on October 31. The Greek Cypriots released 3,308 Turkish Cypriot and 12 Turkish prisoners; the Turkish Cypriots released 2,487 Greek Cypriot and 9 Greek prisoners. As regards university students who wished to study abroad, a suitable exchange was also carried out: 106 Greek Cypriot students from the north and 325 Turkish Cypriot students from the south were able to leave the island to pursue their studies. Finally, by means of a special agreement between Klerides and Denktaş, 313 Turkish Cypriot inhabitants of the village of Tokhni, with their livestock and personal belongings, were evacuated to the Turkish zone on November

---

20. U.N. Document S/11568, paragraphs 64-66.

24 and 25. Klerides approved of this population transfer on "compassionate grounds" to atone for the massacre of August 15.[21]

As time passed, Acting-President Klerides appeared increasingly willing to settle for a bi-zonal solution to the Cyprus problem. In a speech in Nicosia, on November 6, he admitted that Greek Cypriot thinking before the Turkish intervention had been based on "false assumptions, terrible mistakes and illusions". The main illusion, he pointed out, had been "that we could treat the Turkish Cypriot community as a simple minority, without taking into account it was backed by Turkey with a population of 33 million". He observed that he saw "no prospect of the Turks accepting any settlement that does not include federation and some geographic basis for it". He then concluded that "accepting federation with Turkish Cypriots was the only realistic way of settling the island's political crisis".[22] But many Greek Cypriots still tenaciously clung to the illusions mentioned by Klerides. They believed that all that was needed to reestablish the island's pre-1974 status was Archbishop Makarios' special brand of political magic. Accordingly, Klerides was under growing popular pressure to step aside and let Makarios resume the presidency. Already on September 29, upwards to 30,000 Greek Cypriots had staged a pro-Makarios rally in Limassol. When Makarios finally returned to Cyprus on December 7, he was given an even more triumphant welcome than he had received in 1959, when he had been released from exile by the British, and he was at once installed in the newly rebuilt Presidential Palace at Nicosia. Upon supplanting Klerides, he remarked that his predecessor had "demonstrated an overenthusiasm for making concessions" and declared that he would "never accept a settlement involving transfer of population and amounting to the partition of the island".[23]

21. *Ibid.*, paragraphs 51-53.
22. *The New York Times*, November 7, 1974, p. 18a.
23. *Newsweek*, December 16, 1974, p. 46.

Constitutionally, Makarios' assumption of the presidency without having been re-elected to that office was illegal, for he had been absent from the country for a period in excess of 75 days. Outraged by this new violation of the Constitution, the Turkish Cypriots decided to form their own separate, federated state in the Turkish-controlled sector of the island. The resulting "Turkish Federated State of Cyprus" (*Kıbrıs Türk Federe Devleti*) officially came into being on February 13, 1975. It was to last until a suitable arrangement could be worked out with the Greek Cypriot government which would satisfy the minimum requirements of the Turkish Cypriot community (i.e. the establishment of a bi-zonal, federated republic). According to its constitution, executive power was vested in a President, to be elected by universal suffrage for a period of five years, and a Prime Minister, to be appointed by the President from among the deputies. Legislative power was vested in an Assembly composed of 40 deputies elected for a period of five years.[24] Rauf Denktaş, who had succeeded Dr. Fazıl Küçük as President of the Executive Committee of the Provisional Turkish Cypriot Administration in February 1973, continued to serve as head of state. He was formally elected as President of the Turkish Federated State of Cyprus on June 20, 1976.

Although President Denktaş insisted that it was by no means a unilateral declaration of independence, the proclamation of the Turkish Federated State of Cyprus nonetheless had the effect of a bombshell in Nicosia and Athens. Both Makarios and Karamanlis bitterly denounced the action and blamed the United States for not preventing it. There was a large demonstration in the Cypriot capital and there was even talk of launching a guerrilla campaign against the Turkish-controlled zone.[25] But this new crisis only momentarily interrupted the process of negotiation initiated

24. For details, see Zaim Nedjati and Geraint Leathes, "A Study of the Constitution of the Turkish Federated State of Cyprus", *Anglo-American Law Review*, Vol. V, No. 1 (January-March 1976), pp. 1-27.

25. EOKA-B terrorists had been training in the Troodos mountains. See: *Newsweek*, September 9, 1974, p. 36.

by Secretary-General Waldheim. The Sub-Committee on Humanitarian Matters set up by Klerides and Denktaş resumed its weekly meetings on April 4, after a suspension of barely two months. Secretary-General Waldheim also organized a series of meetings in Vienna for the purpose of discussing the future status of the island. These meetings, which began on April 28, 1975, were attended by representatives of the Greek Cypriot and Turkish Cypriot governments, as well as by the Secretary-General himself. According to the latter:

> The discussions concentrated in particular on the powers and functions of the future central Government of a federal State of Cyprus, the structure of that State, the territorial extent of the zones which constitute it and the pressing problem of the return of the refugees to their homes.[26]

Heated debates soon arose over the thorny question of priority: the Greek Cypriot representative wished first to establish the powers and functions of the central government-to-be, whereas the Turkish Cypriot representative felt it was more urgent to clarify the territorial aspects of a future settlement. The reason for the Turkish Cypriot stand was that Denktaş wanted to know for certain where he could settle the refugees from the south. He dreaded their having to be dispossessed once more as a result of future negotiations.

Indeed, the question of refugees had become the most important single emotional issue in Cyprus. Most of the Greek Cypriot population of the north moved to the south during and immediately after the Second Peace Operation. Most fled either because they had been taught to believe in the legend of the "terrible Turk" or because they were fearful of possible Turkish Cypriot retribution for past wrongs. But some were also pushed out by the Turkish Cypriots, most of whom were now firmly convinced that their safety could be guaranteed only by consolidating the widely scattered Turkish Cypriot enclaves into one all-Turkish Cypriot zone. According to Greek Cypriot statistics, by June 9, 1975 as many as 182,000 Greek Cypriots had crossed the

---

26. U. N. Document S/11717, paragraph 66.

so-called "Attila Line", which separated the Turkish-occupied area from the rest of the island.[27] Whereas 36,000 of these were self-supporting, the remaining 146,000 had to be fully supported with food and allowances by the Greek Cypriot government. Only 10,500 Greek Cypriots were left in the north.[28] Thus, for the first time, the Greek Cypriots had to endure the heartache of leaving behind them their homes, fields, orchards, shops and businesses.

Meanwhile, the Turkish Cypriots in the south were all desperately trying to reach a safe haven in the north. Many succeeded in purchasing their freedom from corrupt Greek Cypriot government officials or leaders of EOKA-B.[29] Others were spirited out by Turkish Cypriot guides like Yakub Cemal (see Introduction). In January 1975, the British transported some 9,000 Turkish Cypriot refugees who had sought shelter at the sovereign base of Akrotiri to the Turkish-controlled zone.[30] But in early June 1975 approximately 10,700 Turkish Cypriots were still stranded in the south.[31]

The Denktaş regime's concern for the safety of the latter, which was very great to start with, increased sharply when a group of Turkish Cypriot refugees, while crossing the Troodos mountains, was intercepted by the Greek Cypriot police on June 25, 1975. The refugees, comprising 48 men, women and children, were brutally assaulted and then forced to mop up their own blood, after which they were simply

27. Whether or not this figure is inflated is debatable. All we know for certain is that, at the time of the 1960 census, a total of 138,823 Greek Cypriots lived in towns and villages which today form part of the Turkish Federated State of Cyprus.

28. U. N. Document S/11717, paragraphs 34 & 36.

29. For example, 860 persons from Mari purchased their freedom at the rate of 100 Cyprus pounds per head and 20 additional pounds per bag of clothes.

30. This humanitarian action provoked a rash of demonstrations in southern Cyprus as well as attacks by Greek Cypriots on the offices of the British High Commission, the British Council and, inevitably, the United States Embassy in Nicosia.

31. U.N. Document S/11717, paragraph 35.

dropped in a Paphos street to fend for themselves. So angry was President Denktaş when he learned of this incident that he promptly expelled some 800 Greek Cypriots from the north, including the entire population of the village of Davlos, on the Karpas peninsula. At the same time, he warned that

> the Turkish side would have no alternative but to transfer all the Greeks in northern Cyprus to the Greek part of the island, if the ill-treatment of Turks in the south continued and if the Greek authorities continued to prevent these Turks from crossing to the Turkish-controlled part of the island.[32]

In an attempt to defuse the new crisis, the Makarios government suspended the 13 policemen involved in the incident of June 25 and allowed the 48 refugees to leave the south. Then, to avoid any further incident, it agreed to a comprehensive population exchange. The terms of the agreement, which was signed in Vienna on August 2, 1975, were as follows:

> 1) The Turkish Cypriots at present in the south of the island will be allowed, if they want to do so, to proceed north with their belongings under an organized programme and with the assistance of the United Nations Peace-keeping Force in Cyprus.
>
> 2) Mr. Denktaş reaffirmed, and it was agreed, that the Greek Cypriots at present in the north of the island are free to stay and that they will be given every help to lead a normal life, including facilities for education and for the practice of their religion, as well as medical care by their own doctors and freedom of movement in the north.
>
> 3) The Greek Cypriots at present in the north who, at their own request and without having been subjected to any kind of pressure, wish to move to the south, will be permitted to do so.
>
> 4) The United Nations will have free and normal access to Greek Cypriot villages and habitations in the north.
>
> 5) In connexion with the implementation of the above agreement, priority will be given to the reunification of families, which may also involve the tranfer of a number of Greek Cypriots, at present in the south, to the north.[33]

---

32. *The Times* (of London), July 1, 1975, p. 7b.

33. U. N. Document S/11789.

As a result of the agreement, 8,033 Turkish Cypriots left the south during the months of August and September 1975. By September 7, only 130 Turkish Cypriots, scattered in 22 localities, remained behind.[34]

As regards the Greek Cypriot inhabitants of northern Cyprus, they too declined in number after the agreement of August 2, 1975. As they came to realize that the stalemate in Cyprus might be long-lasting, that the Turkish Federated State of Cyprus was probably here to stay and that they constituted a very small Christian minority in a Muslim nation, most of them decided to leave. 3,582 of them moved south during 1975, 5,828 during 1976 and 910 during the first nine and one-half months of 1977.[35] By November 30, 1981, only 1,076 of them remained, scattered in several villages.[36]

The establishment in Cyprus of two ethnically separate zones was the final result of the Second Peace Operation. Through the population exchanges all Turkish Cypriots were, for the first time, free from fear. In their view, this alone justified the enormous cost in human suffering of all the changes that had taken place since the rise of the murderous and fanatical Nikos Sampson. The Turkish Cypriot exodus to the north also deprived the Greek Cypriot government of the only weapon it had left with which to impose a bargain favorable to itself in future negotiations with the Turkish Cypriot government, namely the presence of thousands of Turkish Cypriot hostages in the south.

---

34. U. N. Document S/11900, paragraphs 10, 31 & 36.
35. U. N. Document A/32/282, paragraph 21.
36. U.N. Document S/14778, paragraph 25.

CHAPTER X
STALEMATE

In the years since the traumatic events of 1974, the search for a formula to end the Cyprus conflict has continued. But both sides have been unwilling to make major concessions. The Turkish Cypriots, determined never again to expose themselves to Greek Cypriot tyranny, have opposed any solution which would reverse the population exchanges or create a strong, Greek Cypriot-dominated government. They have also been reluctant to give up a substantial amount of territory. Having been forced to survive on their own meager resources ever since Makarios established his economic blockade during the 1963-1964 crisis, they want an area which is economically viable. Although they occupy 35.6 % of the island, which is more than their ratio of the total Cypriot population, this area is largely arid and mountainous, and contains only 17.30 % of the water resources, 28.66 % of the agricultural productivity, 2 % of the minerals and 2.17 % of the forests of Cyprus.[1] Should they surrender a significant amount of land, they would clearly not be able to survive.

On the other hand, the Greek Cypriots firmly believe that the whole island belongs to them by right. Therefore, they have opposed any solution which would dilute the powers of the central government or perpetuate the population exchanges.

Inasmuch as they already occupy the area being contested and have the full military and political backing of Turkey, the Turkish Cypriots have been in the enviable

---

1. Necati Münir Ertekün, *Inter-Communal Talks and the Cyprus Problem* (Nicosia, 1977), p. 26; also U.N. Document S/12723, Annex I.

position of arguing from strength. Most of the Greek Cypriot leaders, however, have not let that factor discourage them. With remarkable optimism, they have pinned their hopes on their abilities to strangulate the Turkish Cypriot economy by means of a trade embargo and to elicit big power support to force the Turks to withdraw their troops from the island. In the latter, they were encouraged by the United States' arms embargo against Turkey and by the passage, on November 1, 1974, of United Nations Resolution 3212, which urged "the speedy withdrawal of all foreign armed forces and foreign military presence and personnel from the Republic of Cyprus" and requested that "all the refugees should return to their homes in safety", the parties concerned being called upon to "undertake urgent measures to that end".[2]

It should be added that the Greek Cypriots have had little economic incentive to come to terms with the Turkish Cypriots. As Martin Woollacott points out in his incisive article "Cyprus: Dealing for Dollars":

> Greek Cyprus must rank as one of the most subsidized nations in the world. With a population of only half a million people, it receives something like $54 million annually in grant aid from the United States, Greece, the United Nations, Britain, Germany and other countries, as well as an average $12 million a year in soft loans. In addition, it benefits massively from the UN military presence—costs estimated at $29 million a year, of which Canada pays a hefty share—and from the British bases.

> Foreign aid and loans approach a fifth of all government revenues, and the over-all contribution to the economy, including the military spending, may be of the same order. This provides a solid, if rarely acknowledged, base for the dynamic Greek Cypriot economy. But since much of the money directly derives from the division of the island, it also creates, as one diplomat put it, 'a vested interest in keeping things as they are'. The booming Greek Cypriot economy, partly fueled by such foreign injections, gives the Greek Cypriots no economic incentive for a settlement and tends to reinforce those hard-liners who prefer the strategy of the 'long struggle', which is really a strategy for the economic defeat of the Turkish zone.[3]

2. U.N. Document A/RES/3212 (XXIX).
3. *Maclean's Magazine*, June 25, 1979, p. 29.

Thus, as the negotiations proceeded, no dramatic shift in position could be expected from either side, and every new proposal tended to elicit a sense of *déja vu*.

Glafkos Klerides, who had resumed his former position as Speaker of the Greek Cypriot House of Representatives, and President Denktaş represented their respective governments at the talks until April 1976. But from the very start, Klerides' position was exceedingly precarious. He was appointed as his government's chief negotiator, or "interlocutor", largely at the insistence of Premier Karamanlis of Greece and Secretary-General Waldheim, who respected his ability as a diplomat and regarded him as the most likely Greek Cypriot leader to reach an agreement with the Turkish Cypriot government. But Archbishop Makarios still clung too tenaciously to his dream of bringing back to life the Cyprus of 1964 to trust a man who was willing to negotiate a settlement on the basis of the new demographic and political realities. As a result, he repeatedly sabotaged Klerides' peacemaking efforts. Klerides also had to contend with the virulent opposition of most of the Greek Cypriot press, which advocated the adoption of a hard line in the talks.

The first three rounds of the inter-communal talks were held in Vienna between April 28 and May 3, June 5 and June 7, and July 31 and August 2, 1975. Because of the disagreement over the question of priorities described in Chapter IX, the first two rounds were generally unproductive.[4] In the third round, there was a momentary glimmer of hope that a real breakthrough in the negotiations was about to take place: not only was a comprehensive population exchange agreement signed, but Denktaş and Klerides seemed close to an understanding as regards bi-zonality and the establishment of a loose federation. They also agreed to hold private talks on the territorial aspects of the projected settlement before the fourth round of talks and to

---

4. One of the few concrete achievements was an agreement to reopen the Nicosia International Airport (although it has yet to be implemented).

exchange maps indicating the extent of the proposed zones. But after the meeting Klerides was so savagely attacked by the Greek Cypriot press that he felt compelled to declare that, contrary to what had been bruited about, no agreement, in principle or otherwise, had been reached and that he had no territorial map to submit. Rebuked, in turn, by his own government, he did not even bother to meet with President Denktaş, as promised, before the next round of talks.

The failure of the very promising third round of talks doomed the fourth, which was held in New York between September 8 and 10, to unproductivity. "Despite strenuous efforts", Secretary-General Waldheim reported, "it did not prove possible to make further progress".[5]

On January 14, 1976, Klerides submitted his resignation as his government's interlocutor at the inter-communal talks. As the promoter of a moderate negotiating policy, he had long been out of step with the Makarios regime. But Premier Karamanlis and Secretary-General Waldheim, as well as the members of his Unified Party and many of his parliamentary colleagues, urged him to change his mind. As a result of these appeals, he finally withdrew his resignation on January 17.

A fresh impetus was given to the negotiations by the so-called "Brussels Accord" of December 12, 1975, between the Greek and Turkish foreign ministers. In the first article of this accord, the ministers stated their intention

> To ask the Secretary-General of the United Nations to appeal to the representatives of the two communities to continue their talks without prior conditions with a view of arriving at a package deal on an agenda containing the following subjects: territorial issues, federal structure, powers of the central government.[6]

It was also agreed that

> 1) Details of these subjects would be examined by two sub-committees to the extent that would be required.

---

5. U.N. Document S/11789/ADD. 2, paragraph 7.

6. Ertekün, *op. cit.*, p. 104.

2) The two Ministers would encourage the representatives of
   the two communities to respond positively to the appeal of
   the Secretary-General and accept the earliest possible date
   for the first meeting under him.

3) Until the talks were completed all the parties concerned
   would avoid revealing the content of the points on which
   there might be provisional agreement since that would be
   contrary to the principle of a package agreement. The parties would also abstain from statements which could jeopardize the progress already made. Therefore, each party
   would reserve the right to deny statements of leakages
   which would be contrary to the present agreement.[7]

Secretary-General Waldheim responded by calling the representatives of the two Cypriot communities to Vienna for
a fifth round of talks. At this meeting, which lasted from
the 17th to the 21st of February 1976, Klerides and Denktaş agreed to abide by the provisions of the Brussels Accord.
More specifically, they offered:

1) To exchange, within a period of six weeks, written
   proposals covering all aspects of the Cyprus problem,
   and

2) To establish special committees to consider the constitutional, as well as the territorial, aspects of the case.

But Klerides also made a secret and highly controversial
agreement with Denktaş to submit the Greek Cypriot proposals to him ten days before the deadline so as to give him
time to draft a set of counter-proposals. Later, he claimed
that he had done so in order "to deprive the Turkish side
of any pretext for not submitting comprehensive and concrete proposals".[8] However, he failed to inform Archbishop
Makarios of the arrangement.

   When Klerides' secret agreement became known, it
caused a major political storm. Temporarily disgraced, he
had to resign his post as chief negotiator for the Greek Cypriot government on April 7. The Unified Party, which he
headed, broke up into squabbling fragments and, to avoid

7. *Ibid.*
8. *News Bulletin*, March 31, 1977, p. 3.

certain defeat, he refused to seek re-election as Speaker of the Greek Cypriot House of Representatives when his third five-year term expired in July. Tassos Papadopoulos, the deputy-leader of the Unified Party, replaced him as interlocutor at the inter-communal talks and, later, succeeded him as Speaker of the House of Representatives as well. But President Denktaş strongly objected to the nomination of a former EOKA leader as chief negotiator for the Greek Cypriot government. At first, he refused to proceed with the talks. However, on April 12, he relented and announced his government's acceptance of Papadopoulos. On April 15, he appointed Umit Süleyman Onan, a distinguished banker and lawyer, as his government's interlocutor at the talks.

Both the Greek Cypriot and Turkish Cypriot governments issued a set of proposals by the agreed deadline, April 21. The principal provisions of the Greek Cypriot proposals were:

1) The solution of the Cyprus problem should ensure the well-being of the people of Cyprus as a whole and should preserve the sovereignty, independence, territorial integrity and non-alignment of the Republic of Cyprus.

2) All foreign armed forces and foreign military presence and personnel should be withdrawn without further delay from the Republic of Cyprus and all foreign interference in its affairs should cease.

3) Urgent measures should be undertaken for the voluntary return of all refugees to their homes in safety and the settlement of all other aspects of the refugee problem.

4) Unilateral actions in contravention of the United Nations resolutions, including the colonization of Cyprus and changes in its demographic structure should cease.

5) Any situation already created, which is inconsistent with any of the above, should be rectified.

6) The Constitution of the Republic of Cyprus shall provide for the establishment of a federal State, the Federal Republic of Cyprus which shall be a federation, and not a confederation.

7) There shall be a right of free movement through the territory of the Republic and freedom of residence in any place in which [one] may choose to reside.

8) The participation of the two communities in the federal or-
gans should be proportionate to the ratio of the population.

9) [The] Turkish Cypriot administration . . . shall, within the
framework of the Federal Republic of Cyprus, extend to
20 per cent of the territory of the Republic.[9]

It was also stipulated that the new federal government would
exercise extensive powers over foreign affairs, defense, security, the administration of justice, immigration, trade,
commerce, industry, shipping, navigation (including aerial
navigation), transport, public utilities, mines, forests, fish-
eries, antiquities, currency, postal and telecommunication
services, customs, industrial property, finance, labor, social
welfare, professional associations, movable and immovable
property, prisons, public health and agriculture.

In other words, although *enosis* was again officially abandoned as a national goal and the Turkish Cypriots were to
enjoy limited local autonomy, the population exchanges
were to be reversed (leading once more to the isolation of
the Turkish Cypriot enclaves), the Turkish Cypriot population was again to rely upon the Greek Cypriot armed forces
and police for protection, a strong, Greek Cypriot-dominated
central government was to be established and a constitution
was to be approved giving the Turkish Cypriots even fewer
rights and privileges than they had gotten through the 1960
Constitution.

The principal provisions of the Turkish Cypriot proposals
were:

1) Cyprus shall be a Federal Republic composed of two Federated States, one in the north for the Turkish national community and one in the south for the Greek national community.

2) The Federal Republic shall be independent, sovereign and
territorially integral.

3) The sovereignty shall continue to be shared equally by the
two national communities as co-founders of the Republic.

4) The Federal Republic shall be secular. Religion shall be kept
strictly out of politics in federal and federated affairs.

---

9. U. N. Document S/12093, Annex I.

5) Equality of power and status of and non-discrimination between the two Federated States shall be ensured. Either of the States can in no way overpower, dominate, overrun or interfere with the other in political, judicial, military, economic,or other fields.

6) Each Federated State shall be free to maintain and regulate its own constitutional structure and take all such measures relating to its administration as may be necessary.

7) Under no circumstances shall Cyprus, in whole or in part, be united with any other State. Unilateral declaration of independence by either of the Federated States shall be prohibited.

8) Laws and all other measures, such as administrative, ecomomic, social, etc., of the Federal Government shall not discriminate against either of the two Federated States or of the two national communities.[10]

In short, these proposals advocated the setting up of a loose federation with two geographically separate, ethnically homogeneous states participating as equal partners in a weak central government. On the question of boundaries between the two zones, the Turkish Cypriots maintained that "It was agreed in Brussels and confirmed in the fifth round of Vienna talks that the proposals on the territorial aspect of the problem, which is part of the problems to be taken up on the basis of a 'package deal', were to be presented by the Greek side first and that these proposals would be reasonable".[11] The Turkish Cypriots also renewed a proposal (originally made on July 18, 1975) for the establishment of a "transitional joint government" with the aim of "preventing any further alienation and separation of the two communities".[12]

Secretary-General Waldheim had hoped that if both sides issued detailed proposals a piecemeal agreement might be reached. But the proposals issued on April 21 only emphasized the enormous gap which still separated the views of the two governments.

---

10. U. N. Document S/12093, Annex II.

11. *Ibid*.

12. *Ibid*.

The Greek Cypriot parliamentary elections of September 5, 1976, had a further dampening effect on the negotiations. As the elections approached, Klerides decided to make a last stand for moderation in the talks. On July 5, he founded a new political party, the Democratic Rally (DISY). On the assumption that only the Western powers could persuade the Turks to withdraw their forces from Cyprus, it espoused a pro-Western policy. It also advocated making substantial concessions to the Turkish Cypriots on the grounds that any delay in reaching an agreement with them would encourage them to settle down permanently in the occupied territories. However, the Democratic Rally, by becoming the principal vehicle of opposition to Makarios' policies, attracted not only pro-Western moderates but also anti-Makarios nationalists, sympathizers of EOKA-B, diehard enosists and followers of Nikos Sampson.[13] These unsavory elements did much to discredit the new party in the eyes of the Greek Cypriot electorate.

Opposing Klerides was a coalition of pro-Makarios parties which included Spyros Kyprianou's middle-of-the-road Democratic Front (DIKO), Vassos Lyssarides' socialist EDEK party and Ezekias Papaioannou's communist AKEL party. The leaders of these parties favored a tough negotiating policy in the inter-communal talks. They maintained that because of Turkey's strategic importance to the Western democracies no help could be expected from these nations in getting the Turks out of Cyprus, and that, consequently, the Greek Cypriots should turn to the United Nations, the Third World countries and the Socialist camp for support. They asserted that inasmuch as the realization of their aims would probably require a long-term struggle it was necessary to secure "the cooperation of all political

---

13. The latter were especially miffed at Makarios for having had their hero arrested and tried for his part in the coup of July 15, 1974. In August 1976, Sampson was given a 20-year jail sentence. But two years later, he was allowed to go to Europe for "health reasons" and has remained in Paris ever since.

parties through a national front, headed by the non-party
figure of President Makarios as the undisputed Greek Cypriot
leader".[14] Finally, they denounced the Democratic Rally
for harboring what they regarded as treasonable elements.
"A vote for Clerides", they claimed, "is justification of the
1974 fascist coup".[15]

The elections were a stunning defeat for Klerides. Although DISY received 24.1 % of the votes cast, it did not
even get a single seat in the 35-seat Greek Cypriot House
of Representatives, owing to the simple majority system
used in counting the ballots. According to a pre-election
agreement, 21 seats were allocated to DIKO, 9 seats to
AKEL and 4 to EDEK. Tassos Papadopoulos, who ran as a
coalition-backed independent, was also elected. Thus, in a
few months, the moderate Klerides had been replaced as
his country's most powerful politician by the intransigent
Kyprianou, who now became Makarios' heir apparent as
chief of state.

For several months after the Greek Cypriot election, no
new initiatives were taken to resume the inter-communal
talks. Then, on January 9, 1977, President Denktaş wrote
to Archbishop Makarios, expressing his willingness to meet
with him with a view to agreeing on a basic approach to
future negotiations. The letter, in part, stated:

> This is to put on record that I am ready to meet you in the
> presence of the Representative of the Secretary-General in
> order to give you my views on these and all other matters relat-
> ing to the Cyprus problem in the hope that we may thus reach
> some understanding on our respective positions. I feel that with-
> out such a meeting where we can settle the basic approach to
> the problem, our represenatives will be unable to make progress
> even if they agree to meet.
>
> Needless to say I am also ready to discuss with Your Beatitude
> the establishment of a transitional bi-communal administration
> as a first step in the right direction as I feel that the prolongation
> of the present situation will make it harder for us to re-establish

14. *The Times* (of London), September 4, 1976, p. 4h.
15. *Ibid.*, p. 4f.

bi-communal federalism in the future. Generations of Greeks and Turks are growing who regard each other as enemies. A bi-communal political show in which the actors will be these "enemies" does not seem to be a just and fair inheritance which we can leave to our own people.

Any positive step which can be taken in this direction will, I am sure, contribute to a peaceful settlement of the Cyprus problem and consequently to the alleviation of much of the hardship which is at present being suffered by members of both communities, the alleviation of which is contingent upon a political settlement.[16]

Archbishop Makarios having accepted the invitation, the two leaders met twice at the U.N. Headquarters in Nicosia. The first meeting took place on January 27 and was attended by Secretary-General Waldheim's Special Representative, Javier Pérez de Cuéller. The second meeting took place on February 12 and was attended by the Secretary-General in person. The meetings were unexpectedly cordial considering the fact that the two heads of state had been bitter enemies for many years. At the second meeting, Denktaş and Makarios agreed to reconvene the inter-communal talks in Vienna by the end of March and issued the following communiqué:

1) We are seeking an independent, non-aligned, bi-communal Federal Republic.

2) The territory under the administration of each community should be discussed in the light of economic viability or productivity and land ownership.

3) Questions of principles, like freedom of movement, freedom of settlement, the right of property and other specific matters, are open for discussion, taking into consideration the fundamental basis of a bi-communal federal system and certain practical difficulties which may arise for the Turkish Cypriot community.

4) The powers and functions of the Central Federal Government will be such as to safeguard the unity of the country, having regard to the bi-communal character of the State.[17]

This agreement represented a major concession on the part of Archbishop Makarios, for it recognized that the territory to be placed under the administration of each community was to be economically viable. But later Makarios seems to

---

16. Ertekün, *op. cit.*, p. 110.
17. U.N. Document S/12323, paragraph 5.

have had second thoughts about the question, for he assured
a Greek Cypriot newspaper correspondent that his signature
would "never be put under an agreement that will give even
a stone to the Turks".[18]

At the sixth round of the inter-communal talks, which
was held in Vienna between March 31 and April 7, the
Greek Cypriot side for the first time submitted a specific
territorial proposal, together with a map indicating two
separate zones, one to be under Turkish Cyrpiot administration and the other to be under Greek Cypriot administration. Thus, the Greek Cypriot government at last con-
ceded that the proposed bi-communal Federal Republic
should be bi-zonal—although it preferred to use the term
"bi-regional", which it viewed as having less of a separatist
implication. Up to that time, the Greek Cypriots had been
thinking in terms of setting up several small Turkish Cypriot enclaves in the north. But the "region" to be placed
under Turkish Cypriot administration according to the
new proposal would have deprived the Turkish Cypriots of
the water resources of the Kythrea area, the agricultural resources of the Morphou area and all mineral resources.
Therefore, the scheme was rejected on the grounds that it
failed to take account of the requirements of economic
viability and productivity mentioned in Paragraph 2 of the
communiqué of February 12.

Both sides also submitted constitutional proposals. But,
as these were mere elaborations of the proposals of April
1976, they were mutually unacceptable. Tassos Papadopoulos, the Greek Cypriot interlocutor, argued that the Turkish
Cypriot plan "would be in effect a treaty between independent entities, providing not for a federal government
but for a confederal system without powers, which could
only evolve, if at all, in the direction of complete separation".[19] On the other hand, Ümit Süleyman Onan, the Turkish Cypriot interlocutor, asserted that the Greek Cypriot
plan "would create a unitary rather than federal state, and
was therefore unacceptable".[20]

18. *Phileleptheros*, August 6, 1977, p. 1.
19. U. N. Document S/12323, paragraph 12.
20. *Ibid.*, paragraph 13.

During the succeeding months, Secretary-General Waldheim and his Special Representative in Cyprus tried to lay
the groundwork for a seventh round of inter-communal
talks. However, on August 3, Archbishop Makarios died
suddenly of a heart attack.

Makarios was a romantic dreamer who steadfastly refused to face reality, and the *International Herald Tribune*
portrayed him accurately in its obituary:

> He seemed to share the widespread Greek view that Turks
> were inferior barbarians, and he never tried very hard to make
> them feel part of a Cypriot nation. He acted, said an obser-
> ver, 'as if Cyprus were 40 miles from Greece instead of 40
> miles from Turkey'.[21]

But towards the end of his life he appeared to have realized
that he had made some serious mistakes. In an interview
with the Danish correspondent Arvid Bryne, in March
1977, he admitted the following:

> I must say that I am not happy, looking back, on how I acted
> in some cases. . . . It is in the name of *enosis* that Cyprus has
> been destroyed. . . . I regret many things and most of all *enosis*
> on my part.[22]

Makarios was succeeded as head of state by Spyros
Kyprianou, who served as Acting-President until elected
for a full five-year term as President in February 1978.
He was succeeded as Ethnarch by Khrysostomos, the
Metropolitan of Paphos.

Kyprianou's presidency has thus far been marked by
turbulence and controversy.

On December 15, 1977, Kyprianou's son, Akhilleas, was
kidnapped by EOKA-B terrorists, who demanded the release of fellow-guerrillas who had been imprisoned for
plotting against the Makarios regime. On December 18,
after Kyprianou had promised that the kidnappers would
not be punished, the young man was set free.

On February 18, 1978, Yusuf as-Sabai, the Chief Editor
of the prestigious Egyptian newspaper *Al Ahram*, was

---

21. Issue of August 4, 1977, p. 1h.
22. *Dagbladet*, March 12, 1977.

assassinated in the Hilton Hotel, in the Greek Cypriot quarter of Nicosia, by two Palestinian terrorists while attending a meeting of the Afro-Asian People's Solidarity Organization, of which he was Secretary-General. In an attempt to effect a getaway, the gunmen seized a number of hostages, forcing the Greek Cypriot government to provide a DC-8 at Larnaca Airport. The DC-8, with the gunmen and some hostages on board, took off, but it was not allowed to land anywhere else. It finally returned to Larnaca Airport, where the gunmen began negotiating with Greek Cypriot officials. However, the untimely arrival of an Egyptian military transport full of commandos transformed this tense but otherwise peaceful scene into a bloodbath. The Egyptians were under the impression that the Greek Cypriot authorities had consented to a commando operation to seize the DC-8 and liberate the hostages. But the Greek Cypriots apparently expected only the arrival of a team of Egyptian negotiators. In any case, the Egyptian commandos burst upon the scene, firing indiscriminately. Whereupon, the Greek Cypriot National Guard, as well as armed elements of Dr. Lyssarides' EDEK party, who were guarding the airport, opened fire on the Egyptians. In the resulting fusillade, 15 of the 60 Egyptian commandos were killed. This incident caused a major diplomatic crisis between Egypt and the Greek Cypriot community. It also severely undermined Kyprianou's efforts to garner the support of the Arab nations for his stand on the Cyprus problem. Both the Egyptian and Greek Cypriot governments recalled their ambassadors, President Sadat called Kyprianou a "political pigmy", and the latter was caught in a no-win position: if he had the terrorists punished, he would antagonize the Arab radicals; if he set them free, he would antagonize Egypt even more.[23]

In May 1978, the Kyprianou administration was accused by the opposition newspaper *Simerini* of selling foodstuffs being sent as aid by the World Food and Agricultural Organization for distribution to school children.[24]

---

23. For a detailed account of the incident, see *Newsweek*, March 6, 1978, pp. 33-34.
24. *Simerini*, May 14, 1978, p. 1.

In July 1978, Kyprianou announced that he had crushed a conspiracy, inspired from abroad, to overthrow him. He dismissed Tassos Papadopoulos as chief negotiator in the peace talks, arrested Kikis Konstantinou, the co-leader of EOKA-B, and expelled Paul Kurbjuhn, a former counsellor at the West German Embassy in Nicosia, and Eli Fuchs, the Israeli coach of a Nicosia football team from the island. When pressed for details of the plot, Kyprianou remained deliberately vague, asserting that reasons of "internal security and public interest" prevented him from divulging further information. But it was rumored that Franz-Josef Strauss, the leader of the West German right-wing Christian Social Union (CSU), was suspected of being the mastermind behind the conspiracy. Kyprianou handed his files on the alleged plot to the Attorney-General for action. But the latter found the evidence inconclusive and refused to press charges. This episode caused widespread anger and consternation in Greek Cypriot political circles. Kyprianou was accused of having dreamed up the whole affair. Some even expressed doubt as to his sanity.[25]

In September 1978, it was revealed that Akhilleas Kyprianou was the leader of a new terrorist organization. In a court of law, he was accused of having been responsible for a bombing incident at the British sovereign base of Dekelia in November 1977 and of having arranged his own kidnapping with Vassos "Yiatros" Pavlides, the other co-leader of EOKA-B, who was later tried for seditious conspiracy.

In January 1979, the Kyprianou administration was rocked by a major scandal when the Greek construction firm XEKTE, which had outbid all the competing Greek Cypriot companies for a contract to build the new Nicosia-Limassol highway, demanded and received from the government permission to raise its prices.

On December 15, 1979, two important officials of the Palestinian Liberation Organization were shot and killed in Nicosia by unknown assailants.

25. See *The Times* (of London), July 18, 1978, p. 5e; July 19, 1978, p. 8h; July 20, 1978, p. 8a; also *Special News Bulletin*, February 15. 1979, p. 3.

In 1980, there was another scandal. Andreas Azinas, the Co-operatives Commissioner and one of the closest associates of President Kyprianou, was accused of misappropriating £ 168,000 belonging to the mutual assistance fund of co-operative employees.

On August 5 of that year, gunmen fired on the home of the Socialist leader Vassos Lyssarides.

Through all these trials Kyprianou has managed to preserve his reputation for probity. But he has often given the impression of being a weak, unstable leader who is not firmly in charge of his government. This has reduced his effectiveness as a negotiator, for the Turkish Cypriots are doubtful he would be able to live up to an agreement with them in the face of determined opposition by nationalists within his own administration. On the other hand, he has taken such a hard line in the talks that there has thus far been very little movement at the bargaining table.

When he succeeded Archbishop Makarios, Kyprianou said: "I will faithfully follow the policies of our late great leader and president in all fields".[26] But in his policy towards the Turkish Cypriots he has proved even more uncompromising. An ardent advocate of the "long-term struggle" approach to solving the Cyprus problem, he has assured the Greek Cypriot refugees in the south that he will never "sell them down the river" to achieve a quick settlement with the Turkish Cypriots. Accordingly, he has been pursuing what he calls an "aggressive diplomacy" which has consisted mostly of a vigorous campaign to convince the governments of other nations to put pressure on Turkey to withdraw its troops from northern Cyprus and to isolate the Turkish Federated State of Cyprus commercially. He has shown little interest in the inter-communal talks, and during the early months of his presidency he refused to meet President Denktaş on the grounds that it would imply recognition of his status as head of state. Whereas Klerides was probably more willing to make concessions to the Turkish

---

26. *The New York Times*, September 1, 1977, p. 10c.

Cypriots than most Greek Cypriots were willing to tolerate, Kyprianou has dismayed most of his fellow-countrymen by the rigidity of his views and his utter unwillingness to make any compromise.

In January 1978, the Greek Cypriot government agreed to resume negotiations if the Turkish Cypriot side would produce a set of proposals which Secretary-General Waldheim would judge to be "concrete and substantial". On April 13, the Turkish Cypriot government issued a document outlining its negotiating position. After having studied the document, Secretary-General Waldheim declared that "the Turkish Cypriot proposals deal with the constitutional and territorial aspects of the Cyprus problem in a concrete and substantial way".[27] He then personally transmitted the document to President Kyprianou. However, the latter found the proposals "not acceptable as a basis for the resumption of the inter-communal talks"[28] and, in spite of his promise, refused to resume negotiations with the Turkish Cypriots.

Both Presidents Denktaş and Kyprianou attended the tenth special session of the United Nations General Assembly during the months of May and June, 1978. In an address to the General Assembly, on May 24, Kyprianou proposed "the total demilitarization and disarmament of Cyprus" and the "establishment of a mixed police force of Greek Cypriots and Turkish Cypriots, in accordance with the proportions of the population and under the permanent guidance and control of an international United Nations police force".[29] But he refused President Denktaş's offer to meet and discuss this proposal, or any other aspect of the Cyprus problem, with or without an agenda. He even refused to meet him socially when Secretary-General Waldheim invited the two leaders to attend a cocktail party at the United Nations. This negative attitude was also reflected

27. U. N. Document S/12723, paragraph 52.
28. *Ibid.*, paragraph 53.
29. *Ibid.*, paragraph 57.

in Kyprianou's talks with members of the United States Congress and created a generally unfavorable impression in Washington.

By July, Kyprianou's intransigence had become the talk of Nicosia and there was mounting criticism of his American tour. Even Tassos Papadopoulos expressed disappointment, publicly castigating Kyprianou for deviating from the Makarios-Denktaş guidelines of February 12,1977—an action which probably led to his being linked with the "plot" against Kyprianou.

On the other hand, Denktaş was determined to impress U. N. and U. S. government officials by a display of reasonableness. He met with Secretary of State Vance, who found his ideas "positive and encouraging",[30] he offered to make geographical readjustments that would allow "a considerable number of Greek Cypriots to resettle"[31] in territories controlled by Turkish forces since 1974, he proposed that even before an agreement is reached 30,000 or 35,000 former Greek Cypriot residents of Varosha (the Greek Cypriot quarter of Famagousta) be permitted to return to their homes, and he called for a resumption of the inter-communal talks, pledging to negotiate "with an open mind and in a spirit of conciliation and flexibility".[32] Finally, during the summer of 1978 he offered a comprehensive resettlement plan for Varosha, which proposed the setting up of an interim administration under the aegis of the United Nations to supervise the restoration of municipal services. This plan was to be implemented simultaneously with the start of meaningful negotiations for a solution to the Cyprus problem as a whole.

On September 26, President Carter, having found that Turkey was "acting in good faith to achieve a just and peaceful settlement of the Cyprus problem", lifted the embargo

---

30. *The New York Times*, May 25, 1978, p. 15a.

31. *Ibid.*

32. *Ibid.*

on arms transfers to Turkey. The Senate had voted for the measure on July 25; the House had followed suit on August 1. This represented a major diplomatic triumph for Premier Ecevit and President Denktaş. It also dealt a crippling blow to the Greek Cypriots' ambition of using big power pressure to force the Turks to withdraw their troops from northern Cyprus and strengthened Kyprianou's determination to seek the support of the Third World and Iron Curtain countries.

On November 7, the United States offered a plan of its own to end the deadlock in the negotiations. According to *The New York Times*, the plan, which was not released officially, contained the following twelve points:

1) Cyprus would be a bicommunal federal state with two constituent regions, one populated mostly by Greeks and the other by Turks. The incorporation of either of the two parts into any other state would be 'expressly prohibited'.

2) The new constitutional structure of Cyprus would be based on the US plan, and the negotiators would hold their talks on the basis of previous agreements, including the 1960 Constitution and relevant UN resolutions.

3) The federal constitution would provide for all fundamental rights, including those of movement and property.

4) The federal government would have responsibility for foreign affairs, defence, currency and central banking, interregional and foreign trade, communications, federal finance, customs, immigration and emigration, and civil aviation. Other functions would rest with the two regions.

5) The federal government's legislative authority would be vested in a bicameral legislature, with the upper house evenly divided between Greeks and Turks, and the lower house based on population. Legislation would need the approval of both houses, but rejection of a bill by the upper house could be overridden by a two-thirds majority of the lower house, provided that 38 per cent of each community's representatives were present and voting. The president and vice-president, one of whom must be Greek and the other Turkish, would jointly select the council of ministers, of which neither community could have less than 30 per cent of the membership. The president and vice-president would have a joint power of veto over any federal legislation, although this could be overridden by two-thirds majorities in both houses. There would be a federal supreme court, comprising one member from each community with a non-Cypriot as president.

6) Regional governments would be established with responsibility for the powers not assigned to the federal government.

7) An agency would be set up to develop practical co-operation between the two regions.

8) The territory under the administration of each region would be negotiated, taking into account economic productivity and viability, land ownership, security, population patterns and historical factors. The Turkish Cypriot side would agree to significant geographical changes in favour of the Greek Cypriots.

9) Provision should be made for the return of displaced persons to their properties and for the settlement of claims from those unable or unwilling to return.

10) All non-Cypriot military units, except for agreed contingents, should be withdrawn.

11) A special fund, financed by the federal government and administered jointly by the two regions, would be used for development in areas most in need of financial and social assistance.

12) To create good will and solve humanitarian problems the Varosha area, the Greek Cypriot part of Famagusta, should be resettled under UN auspices, in accordance with 'specific arrangements'.[33]

The Turkish Cypriot leaders thought that there were several points in this proposal that were worthy of consideration. However, the Greek Cypriot government rejected it outright.

In late 1978 and early 1979, Secretary-General Waldheim made renewed efforts to get the talks moving again. By May 1979 he had finally convinced President Kyprianou to return to the bargaining table, although the latter continued to express skepticism about the value of a high-level meeting.[34] On May 18 and 19, Presidents Denktaş and Kyprianou met in Nicosia under the chairmanship of the Secretary-General to set the stage for a seventh round of inter-communal talks to be held in the Cypriot capital during the following month. After two days of intense bargaining, a 10-point agreement

33. *The New York Times*, November 29, 1978, p. 2d.

34. See Glen D. Camp, "Greek-Turkish Conflict Over Cyprus", *Political Science Quarterly*, Vol. XCV, No. 1 (spring 1980), p. 66.

was reached concerning the resumption of the talks. According to this agreement, "the basis for the talks [would] be the Makarios-Denktaş guidelines of 12 February 1977 and United Nations resolutions relevant to the Cyprus question" (Point 2) and "priority [would] be given to reaching agreement on the resettlement of Varosha under United Nations auspices simultaneously with the beginning of the consideration by the negotiators of the constitutional and territorial aspects of a comprehensive settlement" (Point 5). Furthermore, it was agreed that both sides would "abstain from any action which might jeopardize the outcome of the talks", and that special importance would be given to "initial practical measures by both sides to promote goodwill, mutual confidence and the return to normal conditions" (Point 6).[35] Point 6 quickly became a subject of controversy. The Turkish Cypriots maintained that it implied an obligation on the part of the Greek Cypriot government to abandon its "aggressive diplomacy" against the Turkish Federated State of Cyprus. But the Greek Cypriots, being unwilling to sheathe their diplomatic swords without major concessions by the Turkish Cypriots at the bargaining table, denied that any such assurance was given, even tacitly.

The seventh round of talks lasted from June 15 to June 22. Ümit Süleyman Onan represented the Turkish Cypriot government; George Ioannides, the Minister to the President, represented the Greek Cypriot government; Pérez de Cuéllar, then United Nations Undersecretary-General, presided. In spite of the elaborate preparations which preceded it, however, the meeting never really got started. Because Point 5 of the agreement of May 19 indicated that the talks would give priority to the question of Varosha, Ioannides insisted that that point should be discussed first. But Onan maintained that the agreement was in effect an agenda for the talks and that, accordingly, Point 2 was to take precedence. He also demanded that Ioannides acknowledge that "the agreement on the 1977 guidelines, in addition to their

---

35. U. N. Document S/133/69.

published text, comprised also the concepts of 'bi-zonality' and of the 'security of the Turkish Cypriot community'".[36] Inasmuch as the two points of view could not be reconciled, no negotiations took place and the meeting was adjourned.

In the hope of reviving the stalemated talks, President Denktaş, on July 30, proposed the creation of four committees which would simultaneously consider the four major aspects of a Cyprus settlement:

1) The resettlement of Varosha,
2) Practical measures to promote good will, mutual confidence and a return to normal conditions,
3) Constitutional matters, and
4) Territorial adjustments.[37]

However, the proposal proved unacceptable to the Greek Cypriot government, which still insisted upon discussing the future of Varosha first.

On August 2, Ioannides issued an aide-mémoire indicating his government's acceptance of bi-zonality "in the sense of a federation of the two constituent parts, but not in the sense of accepting the Turkish Cypriot position concerning the relationship between those parts".[38]

In October, the Turkish Cypriot government approved a new set of suggestions put to the two sides by Secretary-General Waldheim as a basis for the resumption of negotiations. But the Greek Cypriot government let Waldheim's initiative go unanswered.

As 1980 dawned, Secretary-General Waldheim, Under-Secretary-General Pérez de Cuéllar and the United Nations Special Representative in Cyprus, Hugo Gobbi, continued to search for a new formula that would enable the talks to resume. On August 9, Sr. Gobbi announced that both sides had at last agreed to hold a new round of talks on the basis of an understanding in which they had "reaffirmed their support for a federal solution of the constitutional aspect and

---

36. U. N. Document S/13672, paragraph 44.
37. *Ibid.*, paragraph 46.
38. *Ibid.*, paragraph 47.

a bizonal solution of the territorial aspect of the Cyprus problem".[39] But at a hastily convened news conference a few hours later, President Kyprianou pointed out that "the only interpretation that can be given to 'bizonal' when referring to the territorial aspect is that it means two regions".[40] And Archbishop Khrysostomos threw more water on the fire by asserting that the inter-communal talks were an "opiate" to lull the Greek Cypriots to sleep and by calling for a popular struggle to liberate northern Cyprus.[41]

Since then, the two interlocutors, Ioannides and Onan, have met numerous times in Nicosia and, in Secretary-General Waldheim's words, have indulged in a "frank exchange of views".[42] In August 1981, the Turkish Cypriot government issued yet another comprehensive peace proposal. For the first time, the Turkish Cypriots offered specific territorial concessions. These included six regions and the entire U.N. Buffer Zone—an area covering nearly 6 % of the total land surface of Cyprus.[43] In exchange, they demanded the establishment of a bi-communal, bi-zonal federal republic in which the "equal co-founder partnership status of the Turkish Cypriot community would be protected".[44] The new central government would not be given

---

39. *Keesing's Contemporary Archives*, November 14, 1980. p. 30570.

40. *Ibid.*, p. 30571.

41. *The Washington Post*, August 24, 1980, p. 26c.

42. U. N. Document S/14275. See also S/14490.

43. The six regions in question are: the Kokkina salient; the Limnitis region, west of Lefka (including the villages of Amadies, Ambelikou, Ayios Ioannis-Selemani, Galini, Limnitis, Loutros, Varosha and Xerovouno); the village of Avlona and vicinity, half-way between Nicosia and Lefka; the Louroudjina salient (including the villages of Louroudjina and Pyroi, as well as the segment of the Nicosia-Larnaca highway which passes through the salient); a large, crescent-shaped area north of the British sovereign base of Dekelia (including the villages of Akhna, Akhyritou, Kalopsida, Kondea, Kouklia, Lysi, Makrasyka, Pergamos and Türkiyeli); a major part of the Varosha region, south of Famagousta (including Varosha and Derinia).

44. *Cumhuriyet*, August 8, 1981. This would entail the establishment of a presidency alternating between the two communities.

powers "incompatible with the powers of the units forming the federal state" and restrictions would be imposed upon freedom of movement between the two zones which would be "adjusted in accordance with the principles indicated in the third paragraph of the Makarios-Denktaş agreement of 1977".[45]

Meanwhile, Kyprianou has been pursuing his "aggressive diplomacy" with sustained vigor. At the summit conference of non-aligned countries at Havana, in September 1979, his efforts were rewarded with the passage of a resolution which was strongly supportive of his policies and views, and at the United Nations, in November 1979, he succeeded in getting the General Assembly to pass Resolution 34/30 which requested "the immediate withdrawal of all foreign armed forces and foreign military presence from the Republic of Cyprus" and called for "the instituting of urgent measures for the voluntary return of the refugees to their homes in safety".[46] He has also done his best to ingratiate himself with the Soviet bloc and with the Arab countries. In keeping with this policy, in January 1980 he refused to vote for the United Nations resolution deploring the Russian invasion of Afghanistan. He has also allowed the P.L.O. to use his country as a training ground for its guerrillas. There is even evidence to the effect that Kyprianou has been encouraging Armenian terrorists in their activities against the Turkish state.[47]

The victory of Andreas Papandreou's Panhellenic Socialist Movement in the Greek general elections of October 18, 1981, brought to power in Athens a man who shares Kyprianou's tough-mindedness towards the Turks and the Turkish Cypriots. During the election campaign, Papandreou attacked Turkey almost daily, and because he believes that the United States is too pro-Turkish he has threatened to withdraw from NATO. But there are indications that this policy

45. *Ibid.*

46. UNFICYP Press Release No. CYP/79/17, Nicosia, November 21, 1979.

47. See Mümtaz Soysal, "The Trigger and the Finger", *Turkish News*, London, Vol. VIII, No. 8 (April 1980), pp. 20-22.

is backfiring. The United States, convinced now that Turkey is its only reliable ally in the eastern Mediterranean, is more inclined than ever before to support its government and has stepped up efforts to strengthen its armed forces.

CHAPTER XI
THE OUTLOOK

By now (1982), the refugees from the north have all been fully integrated into the Greek Cypriot economy, and south Cyprus is enjoying a period of comparative affluence. But in recent months there has been a rapidly rising inflation and a growing trade deficit, owing to the expansionary policies followed since 1974 and to increases in the cost of energy. Another economic handicap has been that no long-range planning can take place until an agreement is reached with the Turkish Cypriots.

Politically, the Greek Cypriots have been suffering from weak, uncertain leadership. Their two charismatic nation-founders, Makarios and Grivas, have both died and lesser men have taken their place. The present Greek Cypriot leadership is so divided by political squabbles, personal feuds and conflicting ideologies that it is incapable of speaking with one voice, even on the vital issue of negotiations with the Turkish Cypriots. Kyprianou is widely regarded as inept, even by members of his own party. In 1980, the grand coalition which had buttressed the regime since the days of Makarios disintegrated, as did Kyprianou's own Democratic Front, putting an end to consensus politics in south Cyprus. On May 25, AKEL (the Communist Party) withdrew its support from the coalition. Its leader, Ezekias Papaioannou, accused Kyprianou of having bungled the negotiations with the Turkish Cypriots and warned him that intransigence is a two-edged sword which is likely to encourage Turkish chauvinism which, in turn, might well exacerbate Greek chauvinism. He also faulted Kyprianou for not having made any effort to establish a dialogue with the opponents of President Denktaş in the north.[1] On September 24, 1980,

---

1. *The Economist*, May 31, 1980, p. 58; also Liliane Princet, "Chypre dans l'attente", *Le Monde*, February 27, 1980, p. 7.

Minister of Education Khrysostomos Sophianos, who had
been championning a new Cypriot nationalism, resigned
from the Democratic Front and formed his own party, the
Pan Cyprian Reformist Front.[2] On October 14, Alekos
Mikaelides, one of the founders of the Democratic Front
and Speaker of the Greek Cypriot House of Representatives, in turn resigned from the party and founded the New
Democratic Front. In an interview with a correspondent of
the Turkish daily *Hürriyet* earlier in the year, he had asserted
that no settlement of the Cyprus problem was possible as
long as Kyprianou was in power.[3] On November 12, Tassos
Papadopoulos, who had been a coalition-backed independent in the Greek Cypriot House of Representatives, formed
a party of his own, the Union of the Center. At a press conference, he accused the Kyprianou regime of being too auto-
cratic and of not having a precise policy in the negotiations.[4]

All these defections greatly weakened the Democratic
Front as the general election of May 24, 1981, approached.
This was clearly reflected in the election results. Although
none of the three new parties won any seats in the Greek
Cypriot House of Representatives, the Democratic Front
ended up with only 8 seats. On the other hand, AKEL and
Klerides' Democratic Rally got 12 seats each. EDEK (the
Socialist Party) garnered the remaining 3 seats.

As a consequence of the election, President Kyprianou's
authority has been further eroded. But the political resur-
rection of the moderate, statesmanlike Klerides is an encouraging sign and suggests that there is a growing number
of Greek Cypriots who favor a fresh approach to the negotiations.

---

2. In a speech in the Greek Cypriot House of Representatives he
had summarized his views thus:
> We are proud of our origins and of our national tradition, but
> we will not allow the ideology-mongers to sow the seeds of
> confusion and doubt amongst the younger generation. . . we
> do not forget that it is the exploitation of ideology and intoler-
> ance which has covered our island with tombs and crosses. . . .
> As a result, our education remains faithful to our traditions,
> but it must also strengthen our identity as a state.

(Princet, *op. cit.* Author's translation).

3. Interview with Orhan Turel, *Hürriyet*, March 5, 1980, p. 1.

4. *The Cyprus Mail*, November 13, 1980, p. 1.

Of course, whether or not Kyprianou has a political future will ultimately depend upon the success or failure of his "long-term struggle" policy—the one policy which he has consistently maintained and with which he has become universally identified. What are its chances of success? It appears to this observer that they are slim, for the policy is flawed both in its ends and in its means.

The goal of the policy is to reestablish the pre-1974 status quo on the island, or something close to it. But it is an unrealistic goal for the following reasons:

1) The Turkish Cypriot refugees who have moved to the north have already lost their homes, lands and businesses at least once before. They would not tolerate losing them again.

2) Since moving to the north, the Turkish Cypriot refugees have, for the first time in their lives, enjoyed a feeling of security. They would be as reluctant to return to the south as German Jewish refugees would have been to return to the Third Reich.

3) By now the two communities hate each other so much that they could not possibly live together in peace. A recent editorial in the Greek Cypriot newspaper *Makhi* reads as follows:

> Let us not forget that all dogs are of the same species. . . . Despite differences in breeds, dogs cannot escape being dogs. No matter how you wash them, no matter how well you take care of them, they are still dogs! Turks are the same. Because you can wash them and scrub them and yet they still smell like dogs. Turkish Cypriots are the same.[5]

In his book, *Peace Without Honour*, H. Scott Gibbons illustrates this hatred by a discussion he had with a Cyprus Airways hostess. He writes that when talking about Turkish Cypriots "she lapsed into glumness" and declared: "They should all be killed!" "What about the women and children?" inquired the Englishman. "The

---

5. Issue of February 7, 1979.

children must be killed too!" she replied. "In ten years they will marry and breed again, and we will have to kill them once more!"[6] Needless to say, the Turkish Cypriots have by now learned to respond to this hatred with a hatred of their own no less intense than that of the Greek Cypriots. To them, the massacres of 1974 constituted the ultimate outrage which they can neither forgive nor forget. As a Turkish Cypriot shopkeeper explained to Nicholas Gage, of *The New York Times*, "Our relationship with the Greeks was always like a cracked glass. It was shattered in 1974 and it cannot be glued back together again".[7]

4) The Greek Cypriot leaders still proclaim it as their intention to create a "Hellenic" state, EOKA-B still exists and Nikos Sampson has been released. This shows that the Greek Cypriots have learned little from their nation's tragic history and that there is still no room for a Muslim Turkish people in the state which they hope to establish.

5) Should a unified Cypriot state be established, at least 20 % of the Greek Cypriot bureaucrats and administrators would have to resign to be replaced by Turkish Cypriots. It is highly unlikely that they would tolerate such a procedure.

The means which Kyprianou has chosen to force the Turkish Cypriots to bow to his will is that of economic strangulation. He has tried to isolate North Cyprus by subjecting it to a trade boycott and by exploiting the fact that his government is recognized as the only legitimate government in Cyprus by all nations except Turkey. As Zaim M. Nedjatigil recently wrote:

The fact of the continued recognition of the Greek Cypriot administration as the formal Government of Cyprus is seriously prejudicing the Turkish Cypriot position in the political as well as economic fields. Turkish Cypriots are not allowed direct access to the General Assembly of the United Nations Organization, so that only the Greek Cypriot point of view is being heard

6. *Op. cit.*, p. 117.
7. Issue of April 29, 1978, p. 2.

there; the Central Bank of Cyprus is in the Greek Sector, so
that no benefits from foreign currency loans or grants reach
the Turkish side; the new airport built by the Turkish Cypriots
at Ercan is not accepted by I.C.A.O. as an international airport,
because it is not approved by the "Government of Cyprus";
Famagusta is declared an "illegal" port by the "Government of
Cyprus" and foreign skippers who use it are imprisoned and
fined if they subsequently enter a port in the Greek Cypriot
zone. The Greek Cypriot authorities, with the aim of damaging
the economy of the North have taken steps to hinder communications and trade with the North through the air and seaports
and pressure has been brought to bear on those who intend to
call at these ports or who intend to trade with the northern
part of Cyprus.[8]

Because of this kind of pressure and also because many nations have heeded Kyprianou's appeal for an international
boycott of the Turkish Federated State of Cyprus, the
Turkish Cypriots have had difficulty selling their products
abroad. As a result:

1) They have been accumulating sizable trade deficits
   (in 1980 in the amount of TL 3,743,600,000 or
   $46,795,000).
2) They have been suffering from a shortage of foreign
   currency.
3) They have been forced to depend upon Turkish largesse
   for survival (the Turkish subsidy in 1980 reaching TL
   811,500,000 or $10,143,750).
4) They have been compelled to integrate their economy
   with Turkey's, which is itself already in very bad
   shape.

Will these hardships bring the Turkish Cypriots to their
knees? There is no doubt that the Turkish Cypriots are facing major social, economic and political problems, and that
these are exacerbated by the trade boycott. Sectoral unem-
ployment and a high rate of inflation are causing widespread

8. "Setting the Record Straight on Cyprus", *Special News Bulletin*, August 8, 1979, p. 2. A case in point was the elimination by the
Syrian government of the ferry service from Famagousta to Latakia,
in January 1979, under pressure from the Kyprianou regime.

discontent. The emigration of skilled labor to Turkey and abroad is impeding economic growth. There are tensions between the Turkish Cypriots and settlers from Turkey brought about by cultural differences and by suspicions on the part of the Turkish Cypriots that the newcomers are being given better jobs and housing than they are. Political instability is increasing as students, who have been educated in Turkey and have been radicalized by involvement in the political struggles there, return home. Another unsettling factor has been that political parties, as in south Cyprus, generally reflect the personal ambitions of their leaders rather than well-defined ideologies. Thus they have a tendency to fragment along the fault lines of personal feuds and rivalries. Especially vulnerable to this fissiparous process has been the ruling National Unity Party, because it is a loose alliance of strong-willed individuals most of whom rose to prominence in the years of strife that preceded the Turkish intervention of 1974. In the general election of June 20, 1976, this conservative party headed by President Denktaş won 29 seats in the 40-member Assembly. The main opposition party, the left-leaning Communal Liberation Party of Alpay Durduran, ended up with only 6 seats. As for the extreme-leftist Republican Turkish Party, headed by Özker Özgür, it got a mere 2 seats.[9] But the National Unity Party's ability to govern effectively was undermined from the very start by powerful personality clashes. As a result there have been several cabinet clashes,[10] and in 1978 and 1979 a total of eleven deputies resigned from the party, destroying its majority in the Assembly. By the general election of June 28, 1981, the party's popular support had

9. The centrist Populist Party of Alper Orhon also got 2 seats. The remaining seat was won by an independent candidate.

10. Nejat Konuk served as Prime Minister until April 1978. He was replaced by the Speaker of the Assembly, Osman Örek. In December of the same year, Örek was, in turn, replaced by Labor Minister Mustafa Çağatay.

eroded to such an extent that not even Denktaş's charisma could save it from receiving a severe drubbing from the electorate. It retained only 18 seats in the Assembly, whereas the Communal Liberation Party garnered 13 seats and the Republican Turkish Party 6 seats.[11]

However, in the same election President Denktaş was re-elected to a second five-year term. The fact that this remarkable man remains at the helm of the Turkish Federated State of Cyprus is a great source of strength for the Turkish Cypriots and will, no doubt, make it easier for them to shoulder the burdens imposed upon them by Kyprianou's "long-term struggle" policy.

Other signs of strength abound: the Turkish Cypriots are determined to maintain their status as a free, self-governing community, and many of them display a genuine pioneer spirit about creating a new nation out of the rubble of war. It should also be pointed out that by living long years in isolated villages surrounded by hostile Greek Cypriots, most Turkish Cypriots have become experts at survival. If they managed to survive in isolation, then certainly they can survive as a group. Finally, it is an incontrovertible fact that the Turkish Cypriot government is gradually becoming better organized to cope with the continuing emergency and establishing more links with the outside world. Slowly but surely, the Turkish Federated State of Cyprus is being accepted at international conferences and by the world at large as a separate entity. In 1978, the Turkish Cypriot Chamber of Commerce was admitted as a full member to the Union of Islamic Chambers of Commerce. In 1980, the Eighth World Muslim Congress met in north Cyprus. Parliamentary delegations of many nations have visited the Turkish Federated State of Cyprus. Tourism has become a major industry. In spite of the economic blockade, foreign trade is steadily growing in volume. For example:

11. The Democratic People's Party, composed mostly of dissidents from the National Unity Party and headed by the erstwhile premier, Nejat Konuk, won 2 seats. A new ultra-rightist party, the Turkish Unity Party, headed by Ismail Tezer, won the remaining seat. Before the election, Alper Orhon's Populist Party merged with the Democratic People's Party.

1) Exports of the Turkish Federated State of Cyprus increased from TL 1,248,300,000 or $16,212,000 in 1979 to TL 3,340,524,000 or $41,756,550 in 1980, an increase of 257.56 %.
2) Whereas in 1976 29.4 % of exports went to Turkey, in 1980 only 13.8 % of exports went to that country.

Kyprianou's economic blockade, by putting a premium on self-sufficiency, has also strengthened the determination of the Turkish Cypriots to keep most of the territory seized during the Second Peace Operation of 1974. The need for increased agricultural productivity has, in turn, precipitated further demographic changes which would be difficult to reverse, namely the influx of impoverished farmers from mainland Turkey.

Then, there is the language problem. With every passing year the Greek Cypriots forget more of their Turkish and the Turkish Cypriots forget more of their Greek. Soon neither will speak the language of the other.

Thus, it is clear that in spite of Kyprianou's frequent assertions that time works to the advantage of his cause, the reverse is true. Already in 1976, the distinguished Greek Cypriot journalist, C. G. Lordos, writing in the daily *Alithia*, warned that to wait even three more years before reaching an agreement with the Turkish Cypriots would prove disastrous. He warned that, in the absence of an agreement, a "specific development" would be "the complete bedding down and consolidation of the present situation and the division of the island into two separate states".[12] He explained:

> It would be naive to expect the Turks to yield us any authority over their own affairs after leading an independent life for five years. The only trump card we have got is the recognition of our State and the non-recognition of the 'Turkish Cypriot Administration'. But East Germany did not receive any recognition for years. Did it matter?... I believe that many a Muslim state that can influence the world because of its petrol resources is going to recognize the 'Turkish Cypriot State'. And, with the help and support of Turkey, in a few years' time either the 'Turkish Cypriot State' or a completely independent state within the confederation of Cyprus will be recognized. As for us, we shall probably draw the wrath of the world upon us for not having recognized this state.

---

12. *Alithia*, December 6, 1976.

We allege that Turkish Cypriots are an economic burden to Turkey and that she will not be able to bear it. This argument is illogical. It is like saying that Turkey, whose population is 40 million, will collapse if its population increases by another 120-150 thousand. But what will become of us in the meantime? The refugee problem will have been largely settled. Our children will grow up, make new friends and settle down away from their ancestral homes. As a result of this, the number of people wishing to return home, after a thirty-year struggle that has been going on since 1950, will be greatly reduced. International help will slow down and the de facto situation will become the status quo.[13]

But if the "long-term struggle" policy is doomed to failure, what is the best bargain which the Greek Cypriots could strike with the Turkish Cypriots in the immediate future? They would have to accept the basic conditions of the Turkish Cypriots, namely the creation of a bi-zonal and loosely-federated state. In exchange for freedom of trade and whatever benefits they might derive from a permanent settlement of the Cyprus problem, the Turkish Cypriots would surrender Varosha and probably from 10 to 15 per cent of the area which they now occupy.

Would such an agreement be fair to the Greek Cypriots? Yes, if one takes into account the facts that

1) It is the Greek Cypriots themselves who, during the 1963-1964 and 1967 crises, forced the Turkish Cypriots to live in their own separate enclaves and to form their own administration,

2) It is the Greek junta which, in its attempt to annex Cyprus, overthrew the Makarios regime, forcing the Turks to intervene in the conflict, and

3) It is the massacres carried out by the Greek Cypriot National Guard and EOKA-B which forced the Turkish Cypriots in south Cyprus to flee to the north.

Inasmuch as it is the Greeks and the Greek Cypriots who were solely responsible for bringing about the present state of affairs, the Turkish Cypriots are justified in insisting that an agreement be negotiated on the basis of present realities

---

13. *Ibid.*

rather than in terms of past realities. Assuming this to be the case, the Turkish Cypriots have offered much more generous terms for a settlement than have the Greek Cypriots. The Turkish Cypriots have offered significant territorial concessions. The Greek Cypriots have made only demands— demands which could not be met without depriving many Turkish Cypriots of their homes and means of livelihood and jeopardizing the security of all the Turkish Cypriots.

Should the stalemate continue much longer, the Turkish Cypriots will probably issue a unilateral declaration of independence, thus confirming officially their actual status. This would enable them to acquire international recognition and facilitate trade with the world at large. If they have not yet issued such a declaration it is because they still hope to reach an agreement with the Greek Cypriots and because Turkey is worried that the Greek Cypriots would retaliate by proclaiming *enosis* or, at least, by allowing Greece to establish a large military base on the island. But in the years to come, Turkey might well outgrow its fear of encirclement by a power which is, after all, of vastly inferior military might. Or yet, it might be willing to tolerate this threat if it means that it won't have to continue its onerous yearly subsidy to the Turkish Federated State of Cyprus.

EPILOGUE

The village of Bellapais clings to the northern slope of the craggy Kyrenia range like a flock of white migratory birds resting after a long and perilous journey. Nesting in its midst is the delicate-looking, but nonetheless imposing, thirteenth century Abbey of Peace, the most noteworthy Gothic structure to be found in Cyprus. Once so important a place of worship that it rated a mitred abbot who had the privilege of carrying a gilded sword and wearing golden spurs, it has miraculously survived centuries of neglect, despoliation, earth tremors, invasion and civil war. Its atmosphere is one of contemplative calm, and it imposes its ambiance upon the surrounding community as a kindly parent radiates benevolence upon his children.

The distinguished British novelist, Lawrence Durrell, who lived in Bellapais in the 1950's, has given us a rhapsodic description of the village's many charms in his volume of reminiscences entitled *Bitter Lemons*. In the shade of a magnificent plane tree spread Dimitri's Café, the social nucleus of the community. There, Durrell would converse with the habitués of the place, "mostly grandfathers wearing the traditional baggy trousers and white cotton shirts. . . a splendid group, grey-bearded, shaggy-haired, gentle of voice and manner".[1] Today, the visitor to Bellapais encounters a similarly peaceful scene. While the young are busy tilling the fields, a group of aged but surprisingly clear-eyed men sit on Van Gogh chairs sipping coffee or brandy in the shade of the same plane tree and, like their predecessors, punctuate

---

1. Lawrence Durrell, *Bitter Lemons* (London, 1973), p. 76.

[231]

long sentences of silence with an occasional terse comment about the weather or the latest political controversy. But nowadays the coffee house is called Ulusoğlu Kahvehanesi and the only language spoken there is Turkish. As a recent visitor described it, the experience of returning to the village after an absence of several years is "like seeing a familiar film only to realize belatedly that it has been reshot with a different cast".[2]

But beneath Bellapais' placid surface there is an undercurrent of sadness and even tragedy, for its new inhabitants have all been deeply scarred by the Cyprus conflict. In this way, Bellapais is a microcosm of the north as a whole and the fears and anxieties of its inhabitants are those of all Turkish Cypriots. Therefore, a visit to the village can be highly instructive. While there, I met Hüseyin Salih Tuğyay, a man who looks crushed with despair, and his wife, a woman who appears as though she had been drained of tears. In 1958, Hüseyin Salih's brother, Kâzim Salih, who lived in Omorphita and was an icecream vendor, was shot and killed, apparently at random, by EOKA terrorists. In August 1974, three of the Tuğyays' four sons, Mehmet, Taner and Erol, were slaughtered in the Tokhni-Zyyi massacre. I also met Yusuf Hüseyin Kaderoğlu, an old man who looks like a wounded bird. His four sons, Turgut, Cuma, Salih and Hüseyin, as well as his son-in-law, Hüda Veleddin, like the Tuğyay boys, perished in the Tokhni-Zyyi massacre.[3]

Inasmuch as all but ten of the present-day inhabitants of Bellapais are from the village of Mari (Tatlısu), near Limassol, I was able to get a good idea of what life was like in a village in South Cyprus before the population exchanges took place. According to Özkan Emirali, the Mayor of Bellapais, the first time that the village was affected by the growing inter-communal conflict was during the latter

---

2. Loren Jenkins, "A Town of Peace and Sorrow", *The Washington Post*, August 31, 1980, p. C1.

3. A fellow villager in Tokhni, Sultan Hanım Kâşif, lost her husband, her four sons and a brother in the same massacre. She now lives in Vouno (Taşkent), a village near Bellapais.

stages of the 1955-59 civil war. It became increasingly dangerous for the men in Mari who were bus or truck drivers to ply their trade. Students who attended the Turkish high school in Limassol, as well as workers who were employed at a nearby Greek Cypriot mine or at the British sovereign base of Akrotiri, had to be escorted to their destination by British military units. On several occasions there were rumors of an impending Greek Cypriot attack. As a result, the villagers had to organize a local militia.

The years 1960 to 1963 were relatively pleasant, but the 1963-64 crisis brought about a new reign of terror. The inhabitants of Mari were forced to remain in the village for two months and could not even go out to graze their flocks. Hayri Ahmet Küçük, who was 13 at the time, ventured out with his flock one day and was promptly arrested. He was taken to Kalavasos and then to Khirokitia, where he was savagely beaten in an endeavor to make him reveal how many *mücahits* there were in his village.

From 1963 to 1974, the Turkish Cypriots were treated like social outcasts by the Greek Cypriots. The inhabitants of Mari were deliberately humiliated at the many check points which had been set up on the roads, the women especially being subjected to lengthy body searches; they were insulted, and always served last, when shopping in Limassol or Nicosia; they were denied access to the beaches in summer. During the 1967 crisis, the village was surrounded and then shelled. Luckily, no one was injured, but several houses and a car were destroyed.

On July 21, 1974, Greek Cypriot National Guardsmen once more surrounded the village. The Turkish Cypriot leaders were urged to surrender, but they refused to do so because they had just heard that at nearby Alaminos the Guardsmen had shot fifteen of its defenders after they had surrendered. The Guardsmen attacked at 9:30 a.m. on the 22nd. They pounded large parts of the village into rubble with field artillery, wounding many of the inhabitants. By 1:30, the defenders had run out of ammunition and were forced to lay down their arms. A Greek major entered the village with two Greek Cypriot soldiers. He ordered the villagers to gather in the schoolyard. A number of Guardsmen then moved in. They were accompanied by a U. N. detachment, which confiscated the defenders' weapons and gave them to the Greek Cypriots. When this had been accomplished, the National Guardsmen withdrew from the village and were replaced by a team of EOKA-B terrorists under the leadership of the notorious "Andriko". The EOKA-B men at once started to beat the villagers, claiming that they were hiding weapons. More than thirty of the inhabitants were brutally assaulted. Özkan Emirali was so savagely pummeled and kicked that he developed a hernia.

On July 24, Refet Tahir, the owner of the coffee house in Mari, was taken to the police station at Kalavasos with three other men from his village. For three days and nights, the prisoners were repeatedly beaten. On the third day, an EOKA-B man pointed to some sparrows and jeered: "There are your Turkish planes and they have come to save you!" Later that day, the prisoners were released. But at noon the following day they were rearrested. As they were being driven out of the village in a jeep, the police sergeant who had made the arrest ordered the driver to stop in front of the village mosque. He and his men ransacked the building under the pretext of looking for weapons, breaking most of the furniture. Then they grabbed all the Korans, which the sergeant proceeded to tear to shreds as they were speeding away to Kalavasos. The prisoners were once more subjected to physical abuse. On the seventh day, Refet Tahir was taken out and ordered to walk towards a pear tree up the side of a nearby hill. But to do so he had to climb over a barbed wire fence. After he had overcome that obstacle and was starting to climb the hill, he heard shots. He suddenly realized that the EOKA-B men, who had been guarding him, expected him to run up the hill in a panic, whereupon they could shoot him for having "attempted to escape". However, instead of running he turned around and faced his would-be executioners. This unexpected turn of events apparently unsettled the EOKA-B men, who then seemingly changed their minds and took the prisoner back inside the building. In early August, Refet Tahir and his friends were finally set free.

At 6:30 a.m., on August 14, a police jeep came to Refet Tahir's café. An EOKA-B leader got out and ordered all the villagers to stay home that day. Then he drove all over the village, shooting in the air as he repeated the order. Later, more EOKA-B men arrived. They collected 91 of the men and took them to Limassol, where they locked them up with 1,100 other Turkish Cypriots in an empty school building. There, the men were kept for 68 days with nothing but the concrete floor to sleep on. Soon after that, Andriko and his men murdered a 75-year-old man in the village.

The prisoners in Limassol were finally released and taken to the north in October 1974 as a result of the exchange of prisoners agreement. They were then able to purchase their relatives' freedom. 860 persons from Mari thus made their way to safety. In August 1975, the remaining 130 inhabitants from the village were allowed to immigrate to the Turkish Cypriot zone.

For all these individuals, survivors of a long and ghastly nightmare, Bellapais is the end of the road. They have seen all they ever care to see of man's inhumanity to man. All they want to do is to make new, terror-free lives for themselves and their children in this gentle village, clustered around the aptly-named "Abbey of Peace"—and within sight of the Turkish shore.

APPENDICES

APPENDIX I

A) *Villages Evacuated by Turkish Cypriot Population During 1955-1959 Civil War*

In parentheses: Turkish Cypriot population according to 1946 census.
Asterisk indicates villages in which only Turkish Cypriots lived.

Nicosia District
   Büyük Kaymaklı (56)
   Analiondas & Kataliondas (35)
   Kato Lakatamia (88)
Famagousta District
   Asha (Paşa Köy) (136)
   Kondea (13)
   Melanagra (54)
   Peristerona (186)
   Spathariko (25)
   Styllos (24)
   Vassili (50)
Paphos District
   Amargeti (86)
   Anarita (30)
   Moronero (36)*
   Myrmikoph (13)

Total Population Evacuated: 832

B) *Villages Partly Evacuated by Turkish Cypriot Population During 1955-1959 Civil War*

Nicosia District

   Kato Deftera (21 out of 58 Turkish inhabitants left the village)
   Morphou (56 out of 179)
   Psomolophou (20 out of 21)

Kyrenia District
  Ayios Epiktitos (52 out of 61)

Famagousta District
  Ayios Seryios (81 out of 82)
  Ayios Theodoros (47 out of 70)
  Kilanemos (5 out of 17)
  Lefkoniko (123 out of 126)
  Lythrangomi (5 out of 110)

Paphos District
  Kritou Marottou (22 out of 25)

Limassol District
  Pissouri (11 out of 30)

Larnaca District
  Alethriko (32 out of 57)
  Anglisides (28 out of 152)

Total Population Evacuated: 502

APPENDIX II

Villages Evacuated by Turkish Cypriot Population in December, 1963
In parentheses: Turkish Cypriot population according to 1960 census.
Asterisk indicates villages in which only Turkish Cypriots lived.

Nicosia District
  Ayios Vasilios (117)
  Dali (206)
  Eylendja (316)
  Karavostasi (333)
  Mathiati (208)
  Nisou (Dizdar Köy) (108)
  Omorphita (Küçük Kaymaklı) (5,126)
  Skylloura (289)
  Trakhonas (921)

Kyrenia District
  Ayios Ermolaos (20)

Famagousta District
  Aloa (Aloda) (41)*
  Arnadi (100)
  Ayios Theodoros (23)
  Kilanemos (12)
  Lythrangomi (105)
  Trikomo (7)

Paphos District
  Ayios Isidoros (28)
  Loukrounou (35)*

Larnaca District
  Alethriko (25)
  Anaphotia (94)
  Anglisdes (124)
  Aplanda (55)*

Total Population Evacuated: 8,293

APPENDIX III

Villages Evacuated by Turkish Cypriot Population in January 1964
In parentheses: Turkish Cypriot population according to 1960 census.
Asterisk indicates villages in which only Turkish Cypriots lived.

Nicosia District
Akaki (156)
Arediou (90)
Argaki (72)
Ayia Marina Skyllouras (65)
Ayios Epiphanios (66)*
Ayios Yeoryios Lefkas (143)
Denia (128)
Dyo Potami (40)*
Eliphotes (91)*
Kalokhorio Lefkas (Çaml ı Köy) (307)
Kato Deftera (37)
Korakou (13)
Linou (18)
Morphou (123)
Neokhorio (Minareli Köy) (230)
Orounda (39)
Pano Koutraphas (50)*
Palekythro (251)
Peristerona (476)
Peristeronari (61)
Petra (63)
Phlasou (97)
Pyroi (86)
Vroisha (235)*

Kyrenia District
Ayios Epiktitos (9)
Ayios Yeoryios (203)
Diorios (156)
Klepini (27)
Lapithos (370)
Liveras (12)
Trapeza (79)*
Vasilia (213)

Paphos District
  Kithasi (Ciyas) (162)*
  Lemba (162)
  Pano Archimandrita (72)
  Prastio (83)*

Limassol District
  Anoyira (93)
  Cherkez (13)
  Kato Kovides (117)
  Kilani (35)
  Kolossi (108)
  Moniatis (90)
  Phasoula (18)
  Pissouri (19)
  Silikou (166)
  Trakhoni (117)
  Yerovasa (83)

Larnaca District
  Ayia Anna (102)
  Kalavasos (243)
  Maroni (103)
  Meneou (22)
  Pano Lefkara (361)
  Perivolia (45)
  Pyrga (108)
  Sophtades (117)*

Total Population Evacuated: 6,445

APPENDIX IV

*Villages Evacuated by Turkish Cypriot Population from February 2
to February 14, 1964*

In parentheses: Turkish Cypriot population according to 1960 census.
Asterisk indicates villages in which only Turkish Cypriots lived.

Nicosia District
    Ayios Sozomenos (172)
    Potamia (319)

Famagousta District
    Vitsada (136)

Paphos District
    Asproyia (101)
    Galataria (58)
    Khoulou (119)
    Kourtaka (38)*
    Kritou Terra (156)
    Mamoundali (121)*
    Pano Arodes (101)
    Phasli (76)*
    Pitargou (192)*
    Prodromi (129)
    Yeroskipos (170)

Limassol District
    Asomatos (177)

Larnaca District
    Petrophani (120)*

Total Population Evacuated: 2,185

APPENDIX V

Villages Evacuated by Turkish Cypriot Population in March, 1964

In parentheses: Turkish Cypriot population according to 1960 census. Asterisk indicates villages in which only Turkish Cypriots lived.

Kyrenia District
   Kazaphani (598)

Paphos District
   Lapithiou (156)*

Total Population Evacuated: 754

APPENDIX VI

Villages Evacuated by Turkish Cypriot Population in May, 1964
In parentheses: Turkish Cypriot population according to 1960 census.

Famagousta District
  Monarga (57)
  Syngrassis (102)

Total Population Evacuated: 159

APPENDIX VII

Villages Evacuated by Turkish Cypriot Population in August, 1964

In parentheses: Turkish Cypriot population according to 1960 census. Asterisk indicates villages in which only Turkish Cypriots lived.

Nicosia District
  Alevga (123)*
  Amadies (141)*
  Ayios Ioannis (Selemani) (142)*
  Ayios Theodoros Tillyrias (232)*
  Mansoura (127)
  Selain t'Api (66)*

Total Population Evacuated: 831

APPENDIX VIII

ARCHBISHOP MAKARIOS' LETTER TO
PRESIDENT GIZIKIS OF GREECE, DATED JULY 2, 1974*

Mr. President,

It is with profound grief that I have to set out to you certain inadmissible situations and events in Cyprus for which I regard the Greek Government responsible.

Since the clandestine arrival of General Grivas in Cyprus in September, 1971, rumours have been circulating and there have been reliable indications that he came to Cyprus at the urge and with the encouragement of certain circles in Athens. In any case, it is certain that from the first days of his arrival here Grivas came in touch with officers from Greece serving the National Guard from whom he received help and support in his effort to set up an unlawful organisation and allegedly to fight for Enosis. And he established the criminal EOKA-B organisation, which has become the cause and source of many sufferings for Cyprus. The activity of this organisation, which has committed political murders and many other crimes under a patriotic mantle advancing Enosis slogans, is well known. The National Guard, which is staffed and controlled by Greek officers, has been from the outset the main supplier of men and material to EOKA-B, the members and supporters of which gave themselves the nice ringing titles of "Enosists" and "Enosis camp".

I have many times asked myself why an unlawful and nationally harmful organisation which is creating divisions and discords, cleaving rifts in our internal front and leading the Greek Cypriot people to civil strife, is supported by Greek officers. And I have also many times wondered whether such support has the approval of the Greek Government. I have done a great deal of thinking and made many hypothetical assumptions in order to find a logical reply to my questions. No reply, under any prerequisites and assumptions, could be based on logic. However, the Greek officers' support for EOKA-B constitutes an undeniable reality. The National Guard camps in various areas of the island and nearby sites are smeared with slogans in favour of Grivas and EOKA-B and also with slogans against the Cyprus Government and particularly myself. In the National Guard

---

* A Public Information Office press release, Nicosia, July 6, 1974.

camps propaganda by Greek officers in favour of EOKA-B is often undisguised. It is also known, and an undeniable fact, that the opposition Cyprus press, which supports the criminal activity of EOKA-B and which has its sources of finance in Athens, receives guidance and line from those in charge of the 2nd General Staff Office and the branch of the Greek Central Intelligence Service in Cyprus.

It is true that whenever complaints were conveyed by me to the Greek Government about the attitude and conduct of certain officers, I received the reply that I ought not to hesitate to report them by name and state the specific charges against them so that they would be recalled from Cyprus. I did this only in one instance. This is an unpleasant task for me. Moreover, this evil cannot be remedied by being faced in this way. What is important is the uprooting and preventing of the evil and not merely the facing of its consequences.

I am sorry to say, Mr. President, that the root of the evil is very deep, reaching as far as Athens. It is from there that the tree of evil, the bitter fruits of which the Greek Cypriot people are tasting to-day, is being fed and maintained and helped to grow and spread. In order to be absolutely clear I say that cadres of the military regime of Greece support and direct the activity of the EOKA-B terrorist organisation. This explains also the involvement of Greek officers of the National Guard in illegal activities, the conspiracy and other inadmissible situations. The guilt of circles of the military regime is proved by documents which were found recently in the possession of leading cadres of EOKA-B. Plenty of money was sent from the National Centre for the maintenance of the organisation and directives were given concerning the leadership after the death of Grivas and the recall of Major Karousos, who had come to Cyprus with him, and generally everything was directed from Athens. The genuineness of the documents cannot be called in question because those of them which are typewritten have corrections made by hand and the handwriting of the writer is known. I indicatively attach one such document.

I have always adhered to the principle and I have on many occasions stated that my co-operation with the Greek Government for the time being is for me a national duty. The national interest dictates harmonious and close co-operation between Athens and Nicosia. No matter which Government of Greece was in power it was to me the government of the mother country and I had to co-operate with it. I cannot say that I have a special liking for military regimes, particularly in Greece, the birth-place and cradle of democracy. But even in this case I have not departed from my principle about co-operation. You realise, Mr. President, the sad thoughts which have been preoccupying and tormenting me following the ascertainment that men of the Government of Greece are incessantly preparing conspiracies against me and, what is worse, are dividing the Greek Cypriot people and pushing them to catastrophy through civil strife. I have more than once so far felt and in some cases I have almost touched a hand invisibly extending from Athens and seeking to liquidate my human existtence. For the sake of national expediency, however, I kept silent. Even the evil spirit which possessed the three defrocked Cypriot bishops who have caused a major crisis in the Church emanated from Athens. However, I said nothing in this connection. I am wondering what the object of all this is. I would have continued to keep silent about the responsibility and role of the Greek Government in the present drama of Cyprus if I had been the only one to suffer on the scene of the drama. But covering things up and keeping things silent is not permissible when the entire Greek Cypriot people are suffering, when Greek officers of the National Guard, at the urge of Athens, support EOKA-B in its criminal activity, including political murders and generally aiming at the dissolution of the state.

Great is the responsibility of the Greek Government in the effort to abolish the state status of Cyprus. The Cyprus state should be dissolved only in event of Enosis. However, as long as Enosis is not feasible it is imperative that the state status of Cyprus should be strengthened. By its whole attitude towards the National Guard issue, the Greek Government has been following a policy calculated to abolish the Cyprus state.

A few months ago the National Guard General Staff consisting of Greek officers submitted to the Cyprus Government for approval a list of candidates for cadet reserve officers who would attend a special school and then serve as officers during their military service. Fifty-seven of the candidates on the list submitted were not approved by the Council of Ministers. The General Staff was informed of this in writing. Despite this, following instructions from Athens, the General Staff did not take at all into account the decision of the Council of Ministers, which under the law has the absolute right to appoint National Guard officers. Acting arbitrarily, the General Staff trampled upon laws, showed contempt for the decisions of the Cyprus Government and enrolled the candidates who had not been approved in the Officers Training School. I regard this attitude of the National Guard

General Staff, which is controlled by the Greek Government, as absolutely inadmissible. The National Guard is an organ of the Cyprus state and should be controlled by it and not from Athens. The theory about a common area of defence between Greece and Cyprus has its emotional aspects. In reality, however, the position is different. The National Guard, with its present composition and staffing, has deviated from its aim and has become a hatching place of illegality, a centre of conspiracies against the state and a source of supply of EOKA-B. It suffices to say that during the recently stepped up terrorist activity of EOKA-B, National Guard vehicles transported arms and moved to safety members of the organisation who were about to be arrested. The absolute responsibility for this improper conduct of the National Guard rests with Greek officers, some of whom are involved heads over ears and participants in the activity of EOKA-B. And the National Centre is not free from responsibility in this connection. The Greek Government could by a mere beckon put an end to this regrettable situation. The National Centre could order the termination of violence and terrorism by EOKA-B because it is from Athens that the organisation derives the means for its maintenance and its strength, as confirmed by written evidence and proof. The Greek Government, however, has failed to do so. As an indication of an inadmissible situation I note here in passing that in Athens also slogans were recently written against me and in favour of EOKA-B on the walls of churches and other buildings, including the building of the Cyprus Embassy. The Greek Government, even though it knew the culprits, did not seek to arrest and punish anybody, thus tolerating propaganda in favour of EOKA-B.

I have a lot to say, Mr. President, but I do not think that I should say any more. In conclusion I convey that the Greek officered National Guard, the plight of which has shaken the Cypriot people's confidence in it, will be restructured on a new basis. I have reduced military service so that the National Guard ceiling may be reduced and the extent of the evil may be limited. It may be observed that the reduction of the strength of the National Guard due to the shortening of the military service does not render it capable of carrying out its mission in case of national danger. For reasons which I do not wish to set out here I do not share this view. And I would ask that the officers from Greece staffing the National Guard be recalled. Their remaining in the National Guard and commanding the force would be harmful to relations between Athens and Nicosia. I would, however, be happy if you were to send to Cyprus about one hundred officers as instructors and military advisers to help in the reorganisation and restructuring of the armed forces of Cyprus. I hope, in the meantime, that instructions have been given to EOKA-B to end its activities, even though, as long as this organisation is not definitely dissolved, a new wave of violence and murders cannot be ruled out.

I am sorry, Mr. President, that I have found it necessary to say many unpleasant things in order to give a broad outline with the language of open frankness of the long-existing deplorable situation in Cyprus. This is, however, necessitated by the national interest which has always guided all my actions. I do not desire interruption of my co-operation with the Greek Government. But it should be borne in mind that I am not an appointed prefect or *locum tenens* of the Greek Government in Cyprus, but an elected leader of a large section of Hellenism and I demand an appropriate conduct by the National Centre towards me.

The content of this letter is not confidential.

With cordial wishes,

INDEX

'Abbasid Caliphate, 1
Abdülhamit II, Turkish sultan, 48-49
Acheson, Dean, 116-117
Akçura, Yusuf, 49
AKEL, or Greek Communist Party, see Progressive Party of the Working People
Akritas Plan, 81-84, 97, 121
Alasya, Halil Fikret, 54
Alexander I, King of Greece, 24
Alexander IV, Pope, 2
Arms Embargo (against Turkey), 183, 212-213
As-Sabai, Yusuf, 207-208
Atatürk, Mustafa Kemal, 24-26, 50-53, 88
Autonomous Turkish Cypriot Administration (*Otonom Kıbrıs Türk Yönetimi*), 145n
Averoff-Tossizza, Evangelos, 73
Azinas, Andreas, 210

Ball, George W., 106
Bellapais, 231-235
Beyazit II, Turkish sultan, 4n
Bridel, Professor Marcel, 63
Brosio, Manlio, 143
Brussels Accord, 198-199, 202
Bulla Cypria, 2

Cahun, Léon, 49
Cairo Conference, 124
Callaghan, James, 160,171, 178, 181

Carter, President Jimmy, 212-213
Carver, Major General R.M.P., 111
Clark, Sir Arthur, 99
Communal Chambers: Greek Cypriot, 64-65, 79, 83; Turkish Cypriot, 64-65, 75, 79, 84-85, 109, 144-145
Communal Liberation Party (*Toplumcu Kurtuluş Partisi*), or TKP, 226-227
Congress of Berlin, 14
Constantine: as Crown Prince of Greece, 13; as King Constantine I, 17, 24-25, 27
Constantine II, King of Greece, 154
Constantinople, see İstanbul
Constantinople Conference, 13
Constitution of 1960, 63-67, 71ff, 87-88, 102-103, 143, 172, 201, 213
Council of Ephesus, 18
CTP, see Republican Turkish Party
Cyprus Broadcasting Corporation, 68-69, 78, 88, 96, 157-158
Cyril II, Archbishop, 19
Cyril III, Archbishop, 33

Çağatay, Mustafa, 226n
Çağlayangil, İhsan Sabri, 141
Çelik, Vedat A.
Çoşkun, Kemal, 134

[251]

BROOKLYN COLLEGE STUDIES ON SOCIETY IN CHANGE

Distributed by Columbia University Press (Except No. 5)

Editor-in-Chief Béla K. Király

No. 1

Tolerance and Movement of Religious Dissent in Eastern Europe
Edited by Béla K. Király, 1975. Second Printing, 1977.

No. 2

The Habsburg Empire in World War I. Edited by R. A. Kann, B. K. Király,
P. S. Fichtner, 1976. Second Printing, 1978.

No. 3

*The Mutual Effects of the Islamic and the Judeo-Christian Worlds: The
East European Pattern.* Edited by A. Ascher, T. Halasi-Kun, B. K. Király,
1979.

No. 4

Before Watergate: Problems of Corruption in American Society.
Edited by A. S. Eisenstadt, A. Hoogenboom, H. L. Trefousse, 1979.

No. 5

East Central European Perceptions of Early America. Edited by B. K.
Király and G. Barány Lisse, The Netherlands: Peter de Ridder Press, 1977.

No. 6

The Hungarian Revolution of 1956 in Retrospect. Edited by B. K. Király
and Paul Jónás. Second Printing, 1980.

No. 7

Rita S. Miller. *Brooklyn U.S.A.: Fourth Largest City in America*, 1979.

No. 8

János Décsy. *Prime Minister Gyula Andrassy's Influence on Habsburg
Foreign Policy.* 1979.

No. 9

Robert F. Horowitz. *The Great Impeacher: A Political Biography of
James M. Ashley.* 1979.

War and Society in East Central Europe
Subseries